Penguin Special
Civil Liberty: The N C C L Guide

Anna Coote is 24. She studied Modern History and
Politics at Edinburgh University. On graduation she
worked for the *Observer* for two years as a feature-writer,
when she began to compile this book. She has since
worked as a staff writer on *Ink* newspaper and as a
freelance journalist.

Lawrence Grant graduated with a law degree from Leeds
University in 1963. As a solicitor in private practice he
has worked in Bradford and in north-west London.
In July 1970 he joined the N C C L as its full-time legal
officer.

This hardcover edition

has been specially bound and supplied

by

Cedric Chivers Ltd.

Portway Bath

in association with

Penguin Books

A Chivers-Penguin
Library Edition

Civil Liberty:
The NCCL Guide

Anna Coote (editor)

and Lawrence Grant (legal editor)

Penguin Books

Penguin Books Ltd, Harmondsworth,
Middlesex, England
Penguin Books Inc., 7110 Ambassador Road
Baltimore, Maryland 21207, U.S.A.
Penguin Books Australia Ltd, Ringwood,
Victoria, Australia

First published 1972
Copyright © NCCL, 1971
Made and printed in Great Britain by
Hazell, Watson & Viney Ltd, Aylesbury, Bucks
Set in Monotype Times

Contents

v

Introduction

This Guide has three major objectives: to explain in simple terms the legal rights of British citizens; to suggest ways of putting these rights into practice; and to highlight aspects of British law which adversely affect civil liberties.

There are few positive rights under British law. We have no written constitution and – unlike the United States and Canada – we have no Bill of Rights. Consequently rights in Britain are based on the negative concept that anything is lawful unless it is expressly forbidden by Act of Parliament or common law. We have had to devote much of the text to telling the reader what he may *not* lawfully do, leaving him to discover his rights by process of elimination.

We have tried to present as much straightforward and practical information as possible, avoiding legal complexities and theoretical discussion. The Guide is aimed at people who need help in the areas it deals with. It is also designed to be of use to social workers, teachers, and others who act as advisers in these fields. We cannot hope to provide a complete description of every subject, nor a complete answer to every problem, but where appropriate we have named specialist organizations which can give further help and advice. The NCCL is one of these and can help directly or indirectly on a wide range of matters.

Many of the chapters indicate that there is a wide gap between principle and practice, which seriously inhibits the rights of individuals. It is a well-established principle, for instance, that a person has the right to be presumed innocent until proved guilty –

yet the defects of the judicial system provide formidable obstacles for the accused. The Judges' Rules do not have the force of law and they are not always obeyed. Prisoners often have to wait so long for their appeals to be heard that they have nearly completed their sentences before they have had a chance to assert their innocence. In theory, everyone who is tried on a criminal charge should have the right to legal representation, yet far too many defendants face the courts without it because they cannot afford to pay a solicitor or because magistrates are reluctant to grant Legal Aid. A large number of problems are dealt with by administrative tribunals which perform the same basic function as ordinary courts – but Legal Aid is not available for them.

An increased awareness of rights is essential if we are to combat injustice. There are no grounds for complacency while thousands are locked away in Victorian prisons, East African Asians with British passports are helplessly shuttlecocked from one continent to another, black people suffer discrimination in housing, employment and education, students are denied the right to participate in decisions that affect their own future, sexual minorities meet with bigotry and suspicion and young people are arbitrarily searched for drugs.

We hope that this Guide will help to prevent such injustices, by informing individuals of their rights and by provoking thought, discussion and action to protect and promote civil liberty.

Rights are quite distinct from privileges or concessions. People should know their rights and understand the principles upon which they are based. Essentially a citizen's relationship with society involves cooperation. Power can be abused, but the proper functioning of public service does not in itself imply abuse. Police officers and other public servants have a right to public understanding as well as a duty to observe the rights of individuals.

This is a successor to the NCCL's *Handbook of Citizens' Rights* which it has published for many years to provide a practical guide to the law in areas where civil liberties might be denied. But the scope of this book is wider and includes subjects with which the NCCL has not traditionally been involved: the rights of tenants, motorists and consumers. Contributions and advice have been given by many people, who are acknowledged at the end of the Introduction. Without their help this book could never have been produced.

By attempting to explain the law in normal everyday language we have sometimes risked oversimplification; and we have occasionally resorted to imprecise terms such as 'generally', 'usually', 'normally' and 'reasonably', in order to avoid minor inaccuracies or the inclusion of endless detail. The NCCL will be grateful for any comments and criticisms, which are essential if the Guide is to be revised and improved. Any suggestions for additional material will be welcomed.

It is almost impossible to be completely up to date. At the time of writing this Introduction (but not the chapter itself) the Industrial Relations Act came into force. The Immigration Bill has not yet been completed but it almost certainly will be by the date of publication. The Consumer Protection Act, the Unsolicited Goods Act and the Criminal Damage Act were all enacted while the text was being written, and are now in force. Similarly the Courts Act and the Misuse of Drugs Act have been passed but have not yet come into force. Except where we have stated to the contrary the law referred to in the Guide was in force on 1 August 1971.

Anna Coote
August 1971   Lawrence Grant

Contributors

Rodney Austin; Grace Berger; Geoffrey Bindman;
Ben Birnberg; Richard Blake; Ian Brownlie; Ray Budden;
David Christie; Geoffrey de N. Clark; Peter Coleman;
Melvin and Jennifer Colman; Stephen Cooper; Annie Davies;
Francis Deutsch; Bruce Douglas-Mann; Martin Ennals;
Richard Freeman; Edward Garraty; Jack Gaster;
Yvette Gibson; Cyril Glasser; James Goudie; Paul Hampton;

Introduction

Audrey Harvey; Henry Hodge; John Hostettler;
Malcolm Hurwitt; Keith Latimer; Mary Leslie;
Beryl McAlhone; Ian MacDonald; Alan Paterson;
Michael Schofield; Oliver Sells; Bernard Simons;
Tony Smythe; Jack Straw; David Tribe; John Walters;
Tony Waters; David Williams; Ann Windsor; James Wright.

We also wish to express our gratitude to Gill Bacon for her help in typing the manuscript and to Carol Marshall for her work on the index.

1. Arrest, Bail, and Questioning

If a person is to be charged with a criminal offence, there are three ways in which he can be brought before a court: summons, arrest with a warrant, and arrest without a warrant.

Summons

By this procedure, the accused person is sent a summons, signed by a magistrate, which tells him what the offence is and orders him to appear before a magistrate's court on a certain day, to answer the charge. If he ignores the summons, the magistrate will probably issue a warrant for his arrest. For minor traffic and similar offences, it is more usual to issue a summons than a warrant, unless there is a reasonable suspicion that the accused may fail to turn up at court.

Arrest

This is the formal procedure whereby a person is taken into custody in order to answer a charge. In some cases, the accused may only be arrested by a police officer with a warrant; in others, he may be arrested without a warrant, and not only by a policeman but also by a private citizen.

Arrest with a Warrant

A warrant is a written document, signed by a magistrate, which directs a policeman to arrest a suspected offender. It cannot be issued to a private citizen. To obtain a warrant, a policeman must first give the magistrate details of the case in a written and sworn statement; it is then up to the magistrate to decide whether or not to issue a warrant.

The warrant must include the name of the accused person and a description of the offence in simple language. If the offence was created by a written law, there should be a reference to the section of the relevant Statute or Regulation. The warrant may contain a direction which allows the prisoner bail. ($\Diamond$ p. 4)

A warrant may be put into operation anywhere in England or Wales by anyone to whom it is directed or by any constable within his own police area. The directions of the warrant must be strictly observed.

If a policeman says he has a warrant to arrest you, ask to see it. If the warrant concerns a particular offence, the policeman can arrest you without having it with him, but it must be shown to you as soon as possible. Check that your name is on the warrant and see whether it says that you are to be released on bail. Even if you are doubtful about its validity, do not resist arrest, as this may lead to further charges.

Arrest without a Warrant

There are many offences for which a person may be arrested without a warrant. They include:

(a) 'Arrestable offences', i.e. those carrying a maximum penalty of 5 years or more, including theft, blackmail, criminal deception, most serious offences against the person, and unlawful possession of drugs. A person may be arrested without a warrant if he is suspected of committing or being about to commit any of these offences (Criminal Law Act 1967).

(b) Breach of the peace. ($\Diamond$ pp. 53–4)

(c) Possessing an offensive weapon (Prevention of Crime Act 1953). This has been interpreted in different circumstances as possessing anything from a knife to a penny. This power is restricted to possession at the time of arrest.

(d) Suspected possession of a loaded gun, in a public place or in a building which the accused person was not allowed to enter. Anyone suspected of possessing a firearm can be arrested without a warrant if he has already served 3 years' imprisonment (Firearms Act 1968).

(e) Suspected possession of an article for use in connection with theft or cheating (Theft Act 1968).

(f) Refusal or failure to take or pass a breath test under the Road Safety Act 1967. (⟡ p. 231)

Where (a) and (b) are concerned, private citizens also have powers of arrest, but these are limited by the fact that they can be sued for damages if they arrest the wrong person, or if the offence has not in fact been committed. If necessary, anyone may use force to prevent crime or to help arrest a suspected person. There is an increasing tendency to encourage people to give more help to the police, but if a person is injured while doing so, there are difficulties in obtaining adequate compensation. Nevertheless a claim can be made to the Criminal Injuries Compensation Board. (⟡ note, p. 13)

If troops are called in to help keep order, they have the same powers and obligations to keep the peace as any other citizen, *but no more*. Only if the Government uses the Emergency Powers Acts 1920 and 1964 are they given special powers.

If you are arrested without a warrant and not told why, you should ask: the policeman is duty bound to tell you. The only time when this is not so is when the accused makes explanation impossible by resisting arrest, or when he is caught red-handed and makes an explanation unnecessary. Even then, the policeman must give the reason for the arrest at the first possible opportunity.

If the policeman does not say that he is arresting you, but just wants you to go with him to the police station, you do not have to go. However, if you refuse, he may arrest you. If he tells you that he is arresting you, it is advisable not to resist, as resisting may involve further offences. But if you object to the way he has treated you, you should make a complaint at the earliest opportunity to a senior police officer at the police station, preferably an Inspector or Superintendent. If you are arrested wrongly, you may be able to sue the police for false imprisonment. (◇ p. 92)

Bail

After arrest, you are entitled to ask for bail, for Legal Aid, and to see a solicitor. (◇ pp. 18 ff.)

The police may release you on bail before a magistrate's hearing, and they must do so if you cannot be brought before a magistrate within 24 hours (48 hours at a weekend), unless the offence appears to be serious. Prisoners under 17 must be given bail unless there is a strong reason for not doing so.

If you have been arrested with a warrant which does not say that you should have bail, the police cannot grant bail; but you may be granted it later by the magistrate. If you were arrested without a warrant, a senior police officer may grant bail.

Bail does not mean handing over cash. You will be asked to enter into a *recognizance*, i.e. that you promise to appear at court on a fixed date and undertake to pay a certain sum if you fail to do so. The police or the court must be satisfied that you have property to the value of that amount, or at least that you have a steady job. You may also be asked for one or more *sureties*, i.e. guarantees made by other people that they will pay certain sums if you do not turn up in court. A householder is usually accepted as a surety, if the court is satisfied that he has sufficient assets.

If you are asked to stand bail for someone, it is important to remember that if he does not appear in court at the right time, you may be made to pay all or part of the agreed sum, whether or not he turns up later; and if you do not pay, you will almost certainly go to prison. If a surety feels that this could happen, he may protect himself by telling the police and asking to be released from his obligation. This should be done in writing. A note posted or handed into a police station will be sufficient. The accused will then be arrested, but he will be able to make a fresh application for bail.

If the hearing cannot be completed in one sitting, the magistrate may remand the accused in custody for up to 8 days; or he may release him on bail. Bail is granted at the magistrate's discretion, and for certain minor offences he is more or less obliged to grant it. If you are over 16 and you are charged with a 'summary' offence (one that can only be tried by a magistrate, not by a higher court), carrying a maximum penalty of 6 months or less, you must be remanded on bail, except under any of the circumstances listed below. Magistrates can be asked by your solicitor to give reasons for not granting bail. If you are not represented, the magistrate must give reasons whether you ask him or not (Criminal Justice Act 1967). This may be of help to you when appealing. (◊ pp. 34 ff.)

Reasons for Refusing Bail

(a) You have already been imprisoned or sentenced to Borstal training.

(b) You have been released on bail on another occasion and failed to turn up.

(c) You are charged with an offence which you are alleged to have committed while on bail; or it appears likely that you will commit another offence if granted bail.

(d) It is necessary to detain you to find out your name and address; or you have no fixed address or are resident outside the UK.

(e) You are charged with an offence of violence, or having a weapon, or indecent assault.

(f) It appears necessary to detain you for your own safety.

If one or more of these factors applies, the magistrate may refuse bail at his discretion, but this is not a hard and fast rule – the prisoner may still be released on bail.

Where more serious offences are concerned, the court has discretion to grant or refuse bail; the above circumstances will be taken into consideration, as well as questions such as the nature of the offence, the weight of the evidence against the prisoner, and the likelihood of the prisoner interfering with prosecution witnesses or disposing of stolen goods. If bail is granted, these factors will determine how large the sum is to be (i.e. how much money must be paid if the accused fails to reappear in court). There is a tendency for magistrates to accept police objections to bail uncritically.

If you are not represented and you wish to apply for bail you can ask the police officer questions on any point where you think he is wrong or mistaken, or where his emphasis of the facts may be misleading. After you have questioned the officer you can then address your remarks to the court to explain why bail should be granted.

Application to Reverse the Magistrate's Decision

If you are refused bail or, if the amount is unreasonably high, you may apply to a 'judge in chambers', i.e. a single High Court judge. Unfortunately Legal Aid is not available; the Official Solicitor will act on your behalf. Forms of application are available at prisons, but the procedure is slow and inadequate. The Official Solicitor does not argue the case but merely presents information and documents to the judge. You will not be allowed to attend. Success is more likely if a prisoner or his relatives can manage to instruct a lawyer to apply.

Magistrates sometimes refuse bail to people accused of minor offences, particularly those concerned with drugs or demonstrations, where there are almost certainly no grounds for refusing bail. When this happens, refusal to grant bail is being used – quite wrongly – as a form of punishment, and any application should include a complaint on this ground.

It is not unlikely that the police will say, before the magistrate's hearing, that they object to the sureties you offer – this means that they will inform the magistrate that they are not acceptable. At this stage, it may be better to try to find alternative sureties. If the police eventually accept them, the magistrate is more likely to grant bail. But remember that if the police object, that is not the end of the matter: if they keep refusing sureties, it is better to wait and apply directly to the magistrate when you appear in court.

Contacting Your Family and Solicitor

If you are arrested, it is advisable to see a solicitor. You have the right to receive legal advice in private. If you do not know a solicitor, ask your relatives or friends to find one and insist on using the telephone to contact them. Individual police stations have different practices concerning the use of telephones but generally speaking you have the right to make at least one telephone call. It may be in your own interests not to answer any questions or sign any documents until you have consulted a lawyer.

The police may refuse to let you see your family or friends, but if you apply to the magistrate, he may, at his discretion, allow you to see them. This will not be in private, and nothing will be allowed to change hands between you.

If you maintain that you are innocent of the charge, you should write down an account of the incident which led to your arrest as soon as possible after it happens (preferably while at the police station). When the case comes to court you will be allowed to refer to your 'contemporaneous note'. Police officers nearly always write statements into their notebooks at the time and refer to them in court: so this should be of some advantage when you are presenting your evidence.

Identification

If the police want to identify someone connected with a crime, they are allowed to show photographs to anyone who might be able to identify the criminal but they should not allow witnesses to study a photograph of the accused person before being called to identify him. If a witness has already identified the accused person, the police should not corroborate this evidence by showing the witness a photograph of the person he has identified.

The police may ask the accused person to take part in an identification parade, but they cannot force him to do so. The accused can ask to be put on an identification parade to establish his innocence, but he should not do so without legal advice, and it is advisable for a solicitor to be present.

Following a number of cases where people claimed to have been wrongly identified, the NCCL conducted an investigation into identification and came to these conclusions:

(a) Once a suspect has been identified, even in unsatisfactory circumstances and even where he has an unbroken alibi, it is almost impossible for him to avoid conviction unless someone else comes forward and admits to the crime.

(b) Although it is obvious that identification parades can be unreliable, an identification is taken far too seriously by judge and jury, while contrary evidence such as an alibi or forensic evidence is given much less weight.

Fingerprints and Photographing

You may refuse to let the police take your fingerprints. If you do refuse, the police may then apply to a magistrate to make an order that your fingerprints be taken without your consent. (They can do this to anyone who is over 13 and has been charged with an offence before a court.)

Fingerprints will sometimes help the police to investigate a crime, but more often they are a means of finding out from the Central Fingerprint Registry whether you have been accused and convicted before. Request to fingerprint must be made by an officer of the rank of Inspector or above. If you refuse to have your prints taken the police may decide to hold you in custody and apply to a magistrate for an order when you appear in court. Your refusal may affect the police attitude towards bail. If your fingerprints are taken with a court order and you are later acquitted, the fingerprints and all copies and records must be destroyed.

There is no authority in English law for taking photographs without his consent of a person who has not been charged with an offence. If you have been charged and are awaiting trial in prison, your photograph (and measurements) can be taken only with the consent of a magistrate on application from a senior police officer. The application must show that there is some reason for suspecting that you have been involved in a previous offence. If you are acquitted, all photographs (negatives and copies) must be destroyed or handed over to you.

Questioning

You do not have to answer police questions, whether they are informal or part of an official inquiry (questions about motoring offences are an exception, ⟡ p. 233). It might be better to say something like 'I do not want to say anything until I have seen my solicitor,' than to remain completely silent, although it should not be counted against you if you say nothing at all. It could be dangerous to attempt any further explanation.

When the police question a suspect, their conduct is governed by the Judges' Rules and the Administrative Directions. These are not legally binding. Any statement that the accused person makes voluntarily can be used, at the judge's discretion, as evidence against him, even when the rules have not been obeyed. The main provisions of these rules are as follows:

(a) A police officer can question anyone, whether suspected or not, if he thinks he can obtain useful information from him. He can do this without arresting the person, provided that he has not been charged with an offence or informed that he may be prosecuted for it.

(b) As soon as a police officer has reasonable grounds for

suspecting that the person has committed the offence, he must caution him as follows: 'You are not obliged to say anything unless you wish to do so but what you say may be put in writing and used as evidence.'

(c) Another caution is given when the person is charged, or informed that he may be prosecuted for an offence. He should be asked if he wishes to say anything and told that he need say nothing, but that whatever he does say may be taken down in writing and used as evidence. As a general rule, no questions should be put at this stage unless their purpose is to prevent harm being done to other people, or to clarify the meaning of answers or statements already made. If such questions are to be asked, a further caution must be given.

(d) If the accused is questioned, or decides to make a statement after he has been cautioned, a record should be kept of the time and place of the questioning; of who was present; and of what refreshments were given. Alcohol must never be served.

(e) Prisoners should be told what rights and facilities are available to them. Notices saying what these are should be displayed in conspicuous places in police stations and drawn to the attention of the prisoners.

(f) Reasonable arrangements should be made for the comfort and refreshment of people being questioned. Whenever possible, the prisoner and the interrogator should both be seated.

(g) Questions and answers should be recorded in full. The record must be signed by the prisoner or, if he refuses, by the interrogating officer. Answers can be used as evidence whether or not the prisoner signs the record – there is no such thing as an off-the-record statement.

(h) Statements made by a person under caution should be written on the forms provided for that purpose. Policemen's notebooks should be used only when there are no forms available.

(i) If the prisoner makes a written statement, he must do so without prompting and in his own words; or he can dictate it to a policeman and will then be asked to sign it. If he refuses, a policeman must do so. Foreigners should make statements in their own language.

(j) When a policeman writes down a statement, the words should not be translated into 'official vocabulary'.

(k) The prisoner must not be led to believe that any statement he makes can only be used against him: this may prevent an innocent person from making a statement which might help clear him of the charge.

(l) *Interrogation of children:* As far as possible, children under 17 – whether they are suspected of a crime or are merely being questioned as witnesses – should only be interviewed in the presence of a parent or guardian, or if these are not available, in the presence of someone who is not a police officer and is of the same sex as the child. A child should not be arrested or questioned at school if this can possibly be avoided; but if it is essential to do so, it should be done only in the presence of the headmaster or his nominee, and with his consent. (◊ p. 154)

If the police question you at your place of work, you should consult the local representative of your trade union or professional organization at once. If the offence has nothing to do with your place of work, it is advisable to refuse to discuss it in the presence of your employer. Even if the offence is concerned with your place of work, you are not obliged to say anything.

Statements out of Court

Statements made by the accused person should not be used in evidence unless the court is convinced that they were made voluntarily. The prosecution must prove that this is so. If inducements or threats are made to the accused during the course of questioning, his statement will not be considered voluntary.

If the accused person makes a confession to someone who is not in authority over him (i.e. someone who is not a policeman, magistrate, parent, or employer), this may be used as evidence, even if made as the result of an inducement. The exception to this is if the accused was intimidated by the fact that a person of authority was there but did not actually ask the questions.

Statements in Court

If the accused makes a confession in court, it should be accepted only with reluctance and subject to certain conditions: it must have been preceded by a warning that the accused need not say anything in answer to the charge unless he wants to; that he has nothing to hope for or fear as an inducement to speak; and that anything he says will be taken down in writing and may be given as evidence at his trial.

If he makes a statement after this caution, his words are taken down in writing and must be read over to him and signed by the magistrate. The accused may sign them if he wants to. The statement is then sent to the court which is to try him.

If the accused has made a statement under oath at any other judicial proceedings, such as a tribunal or a coroner's inquest, it may be used as evidence at his trial. However, it cannot be used if he was forced to make the statement after he had objected on the grounds that it might tend to incriminate him.

Pleading Guilty or Not Guilty

It is usually unwise to plead guilty unless advised to do so by a lawyer. Although a plea of guilty may result in a lighter sentence, the court should never treat a plea of not guilty as a reason for imposing a heavier penalty.

If you plead not guilty, the charge will be fully investigated. If you plead guilty, the magistrate will hear the facts of the case and mitigating statements (reasons for making the penalty lighter); he will then convict and sentence, or commit you for trial at a higher court. (◊ p. 23)

Even if you plead guilty before the magistrate, you are still free to plead not guilty if you are sent to a higher court for trial. If you plead guilty and are sentenced, you cannot later appeal on the grounds that you did not commit the offence, but you can, of course, appeal against sentence. (◊ p. 34)

Note

Criminal Injuries Compensation Board

The Board was set up to deal with applications by victims of crimes of violence for payment of compensation. A claim can be made if you sustain personal injury under any of the following circumstances:

(a) If the injury is directly attributable to a crime of violence.
(b) When trying to prevent someone from committing a crime.
(c) When trying to arrest a suspected offender.
(d) When helping the police to do either of these things.

The Board will consider your claim; any payment will be in the form of a lump sum and should be assessed on the basis used by the courts to award damages, although in practice the awards are often less than might be expected.

You will not be able to obtain compensation unless the Board is satisfied of a number of factors including:

(a) That your injury is one for which at least £50 will be awarded.
(b) That the assailant was prosecuted or the police were notified without delay (the Board has a discretion to waive this requirement).

Compensation will not be awarded for traffic offences, and the award can be reduced if the Board thinks that you should not receive the full award because of your conduct, both before and after the offence which led to your injury, and because of your character and way of life.

The address of the Criminal Injuries Compensation Board is Russell Square House, London wc 1.

2. Legal Aid and Advice

Legal Advice

This is oral advice, given by a solicitor about your legal rights and obligations.

It is available for civil and criminal matters. In each area there is a panel of solicitors who will give legal advice and aid. Their names can be obtained from Citizens' Advice Bureaux and Public Libraries.

(a) If your capital is £125 or under and your net income does not exceed £9·50 a week (small allowances being made for wife and children), you will only have to pay 12½p for legal advice and if you are receiving supplementary benefit you will not have to pay anything. This applies to everyone over 16, whether or not he is a British citizen (Legal Aid and Advice Act 1949).

(b) If you do not qualify for this, you can ask for advice from a solicitor who is a member of a voluntary scheme run by the Law Society. The charge will be £1 for 30 minutes. If the solicitor agrees to advise you at this rate, he cannot charge more, but he may refuse to give his advice and he does not have to justify this.

It is always worth applying for legal advice, if you need it. In practice, however, the schemes work badly, since most solicitors find the form-filling and other formalities more trouble than they are worth.

Alternatives

A Citizens' Advice Bureau may be able to deal with the problem. In a few cities there are 'Poor Man's Lawyers' and other voluntary agencies giving free legal assistance (e.g. Toynbee Hall, Cambridge House, the Mary Ward Settlement in London; specialist organizations such as Release and Advise; Britain's first Neighbourhood Law Centre, recently opened in North Kensington). Unfortunately, these are isolated exceptions and there is clearly a need for legal advice to be provided as a social service.

Legal Aid

Legal aid is assistance from a lawyer in court proceedings.

Civil Legal Aid

A 'civil' case is where one party is involved in legal action against another. The Legal Aid scheme is administered by the Law Society on behalf of the Government. Legal Aid can be obtained for:

(a) *Claims:* legal negotiations leading up to but not including the preparation of a case for court. Here, anyone is eligible whose 'disposable capital' does not exceed £125 and whose 'disposable income' does not exceed £300 per annum. (▷ p. 16) But in practice, Legal Aid is seldom used for claims.

(b) *Court Proceedings*: Legal Aid is commonly used for High Court and for County Court cases such as divorce, breach of contract, unlawful arrest, damages for personal injuries, etc.; and in magistrates' courts for affiliation proceedings, maintenance claims by a wife, etc. It is *not* available for libel, slander, or for proceedings before tribunals.

How to Apply

If possible, you should first get legal advice to find out whether there are reasonable grounds for proceeding.

You can get the application form from a Citizens' Advice Bureau, a Court Office, or a Law Society Legal Aid Office. Your solicitor, if you are already dealing with one, may have a form and help you fill it in. The completed form should be submitted as soon as possible, as the whole procedure is lengthy.

You can choose any solicitor, provided his name is on the right panel and he is willing to act. There are usually a number of solicitors' offices next to magistrates' and county courts: most of these solicitors will be on Legal Aid panels and willing to take up the case and help fill in the forms. If none of them is willing to take up your case, contact your Citizens' Advice Bureau or ask the Law Society or its local society to suggest the name and address of a solicitor in your area.

The application must be considered and approved by the local committee of the Law Society, which decides whether you have reasonable grounds and whether your means fall within the limits for the granting of Legal Aid. Usually you will have to be interviewed by the Supplementary Benefits Commission, and you will be asked for documentation about your income and expenditure. If Legal Aid is refused you can usually appeal to the area committee of the Law Society. You may do so by letter or ask for an oral hearing.

There is an emergency procedure for urgent cases with special forms available.

Who Is Eligible?

If your 'disposable income' does not exceed £300 a year and your 'disposable capital' does not exceed £125, you are eligible for *free* Legal Aid. Above this level, you will have to pay a contribution towards the cost. If your 'disposable income' is above £950 or your 'disposable capital' is above £500, you will not be eligible.

'Disposable income' is a person's income during one year

after allowances have been made for rent, rates, income tax, maintenance of dependants, and other necessary expenditure. 'Disposable capital' is calculated by subtracting from a person's gross capital certain allowances which may include debts. Standard personal and household effects are not included in capital, but owner-occupied property with an unencumbered value exceeding £5,000 (after deducting any mortgage) may be taken into account.

If your application is accepted, you will be informed of:

(a) The probable cost of the action and your contribution towards it.

(b) The maximum contribution you may have to pay if the cost is higher.

(c) The terms on which the Legal Aid certificate is issued. You will have 28 days in which to accept the terms.

The following table gives an indication of the practical effects of the Legal Aid scheme in certain typical cases:

Type of application	Maximum income permitting free certificate	Minimum income making applica- tion ineligible
1. Single man	£604 p.a. (£11·65 p.w.)	£1,615 p.a. (£31·05 p.w.)
2. Married couple, plus 1 child	£955 p.a. (£18·37 p.w.)	£1,944 p.a. (£37·37 p.w.)
3. Married couple, plus 2 children	£1,052 p.a. (£20·22 p.w.)	£2,037 p.a. (£39·17 p.w.)
4. Married couple, plus 3 children	£1,178 p.a. (£22·65 p.w.)	£2,161 p.a. (£41·55 p.w.)
5. Man – married/apart – paying court order £390 wife, £260 2 children	£1,292 p.a. (£24·85 p.w.)	£2,265 p.a. (£43·55 p.w.)

6. Separated wife with 2 children receiving court order, £650 (£390 self; £260 children), plus family allowance (90p). Disposable income £151.

Criminal Legal Aid
(For Defence against Police Prosecution)

Every person who is accused of a criminal offence needs a lawyer – except in the most trivial cases. The technicalities of court procedure and rules of evidence are so complicated that the ordinary man has little chance of defending himself successfully against knowledgeable prosecutors.

Unless you can afford to pay a lawyer's fees, you should apply for Legal Aid.

If you intend to plead 'not guilty', you would be quite wrong to assume that your innocence will protect you. It is always possible that evidence against you might – deliberately or accidentally – be false. If you intend to plead 'guilty', you will need a lawyer to present mitigating factors to the court, so that you have a chance of getting a reduced sentence.

Who Is Eligible?

Officially, Legal Aid should be granted to anyone whose means are 'insufficient to pay for his own defence' and when 'it is in the interests of justice that he should have Legal Aid'.

Everyone who applies for Legal Aid has to fill in a questionnaire on means. If you are receiving supplementary benefit or allowance, or if your net income is not above £250 and your capital does not exceed £25, you should receive Legal Aid entirely free.

If your income or assets are above this level, you will probably have to pay a contribution towards the cost of your defence (Criminal Justice Act 1967). You may even have to make a down payment before you are granted Legal Aid: this does not usually exceed £10 in cases heard before magistrates, or £25 in cases heard before higher courts. In practice, this system varies enormously from one court to another. Most courts rarely order down payments, but some do so whenever the accused person has appreciable means.

When the case has been concluded, the magistrate or judge may order you to pay a contribution which is assessed on your answers to the means questionnaire. Alternatively, the matter may be referred to the Supplementary Benefits Commission to investigate or report.

You may be ordered to contribute even if you have been acquitted. In contrast, if you are found guilty, and either fined or imprisoned, any contribution order may take the effect of the sentence into consideration (for example, you may be asked to pay less if you have been fined). It seems illogical that a defendant should suffer financially from being acquitted, and the state's financial savings from the whole contributions scheme have proved to be minimal.

How to Apply

Apply as soon as possible. Do not wait until the day of trial. If you are in custody, you should be given the necessary forms to fill in, whether you ask for them or not. If you are not in custody, you should go to the court office, where you can obtain the forms and fill them in.

If you find yourself in court before you have been able to fill in the forms, you should apply directly to the magistrate at the earliest opportunity; the magistrate will either deal with the matter on the spot or adjourn the hearing to enable you to complete your application. If you want to deal with a particular solicitor, you can name him on the application form.

In practice, it is up to the accused person to apply for Legal Aid. If he is too confused or slow to apply, there is no legal obligation on the court to offer it.

When the case is sufficiently serious to be tried in a higher court (Quarter Sessions, Assizes, Crown Courts or Central Criminal Court), Legal Aid is granted fairly regularly. In magistrates' courts, the decision is left to the discretion of the magistrate. Where there is doubt, the decision must be in favour of the applicant. There is no appeal if the magistrate refuses, but the application can be repeated if there is an adjourned hearing.

A Legal Aid order for a magistrates' court usually only covers representation by a solicitor; but a barrister may be instructed and reimbursed by the solicitor. If the case is complex, however, your solicitor can make an application for the Legal Aid order to cover both solicitor and barrister. In the higher courts the Legal Aid order will provide for both a solicitor and barrister because solicitors do not have a right of audience in such courts.

You can obtain Legal Aid to appeal but you must apply separately. Criminal Legal Aid in higher courts includes advice on appeal. (▷ p. 25)

Legal Aid should be a basic right of every person accused of a criminal offence. In law, however, it is merely discretionary. In practice, the system is unsatisfactory because the granting of Legal Aid is arbitrary and varies widely between the different courts.

As a result of a large-scale survey into aspects of representation in London area criminal courts, it was found that: 'In a very large proportion of cases before magistrates, the defendant was unrepresented and these included a high proportion of cases ending in prison and other custodial sentences.' (*Legal Aid as a Social Service*, a report by the Cobden Trust)

Further Information and Advice

Citizens' Advice Bureaux
Law Society

3. Court Procedure

Magistrates' Courts

Scope and Organization

Magistrates' courts deal with nearly all minor offences; the vast majority of criminal matters including traffic offences and juvenile cases; maintenance claims and other matrimonial matters; claims to enforce payment of rates; and the granting of various licences. Many offences *must* be dealt with in a magistrates' court and neither the defendant nor the prosecution has a right to ask for trial by jury in a higher court. They include most petty offences, such as drunkenness, and many offences under the Highways, Road Traffic and Vagrancy Acts. There are some offences, including assault of a police officer in the execution of his duty, where the choice of court lies entirely with the prosecution, who can insist on the case being dealt with by the magistrates. There are other offences, e.g., dangerous driving and many theft offences, where the defendant has a right to choose in which court he wants his case to be heard. Finally, most serious offences, such as murder, robbery and rape, must be tried before a jury and cannot in any circumstances be dealt with by the magistrates.

Outside London, magistrates' courts usually consist of a bench of part-time lay J.P.s, with a legally qualified clerk to advise them on points of law. In London and some cities, the busier courts are staffed by full-time salaried magistrates (called stipendiaries) who are legally qualified.

What to Expect

A person on trial before a magistrate will find himself faced with a number of decisions. Should he plead guilty and 'get it over'? Should he try to defend himself? Should he ask to have a lawyer, either privately or on Legal Aid? Should he ask for remand (i.e. for the case to be put off to another day to give him time to prepare his case and contact witnesses)? If the charge against him is one which can either be tried before a magistrate or sent to a higher court before a jury, which course should he choose?

One of the most difficult decisions is whether or not to opt for trial by jury. It is often felt that a jury will be more sympathetic than a magistrate, but much depends on the type of offence. Trial by jury inevitably leads to long delays and if the accused is found guilty, there is a possibility that he may be given a heavier sentence.

The amount of guidance that the accused can expect varies from one court to another. In some courts, the magistrates' clerk will explain these points carefully, but in many others he may do so only briefly, and some points (such as Legal Aid) may not be mentioned at all, unless the accused makes a specific query. (◇ p. 19)

Each case must be considered on its merits, so the only general advice that can be given here is that the accused should get legal advice and representation.

Committal for Trial by Jury

If it is decided to refer the case to a higher court, the magistrate still hears the preliminary proceedings to decide whether the prosecution has sufficient evidence to justify this.

Most committal cases are now dealt with on the basis of written statements of prosecution witnesses submitted by the police, which are given to the defence beforehand. Verbal evidence is not given unless the accused's lawyer asks for it.

If the accused is not legally represented, all evidence is given verbally, with opportunities for cross-examination.

If the magistrates are not satisfied that the prosecution has a case, they will dismiss the charges and discharge the defendant. They may award the defence costs, which will usually be paid out of public funds. Normally it is very difficult for a successful defendant to get costs. If they are satisfied, they will commit the case for trial, and then deal with applications for bail and Legal Aid.

Higher Criminal Courts

Organization

A case committed for trial by jury may be tried at the Old Bailey (Central Criminal Court) in London and at Assizes in county towns, Crown Courts in Liverpool and Manchester, or Quarter Sessions. The system is being reorganized (⟡ p. 27), but one important factor remains: the defendant will face someone who acts as a judge by presiding over the court, instructing the jury, deciding questions of law, and pronouncing the sentence.

The question of guilt or innocence must be decided by a jury of 12 whose verdict must be unanimous or by a majority of not less than 10 to 2. If they cannot reach a decision, there will be a re-trial before a new jury, unless the prosecution decides to drop the case.

Before the trial, the prosecution must set out the charges in a formal document called an 'indictment'. At this stage, further charges may be added, provided they are connected with the original ones and depend on the same evidence. Additional charges and evidence may be put in at any time, as long as the defence is not taken by surprise. Defendants often regard this as unfair practice, but the only remedy is to try to persuade the court to exclude the new charges and evidence, or grant an adjournment.

What to Expect

The basic procedure is as follows: charges are read out; the defendant pleads 'guilty' or 'not guilty'; if the plea is 'not guilty' the jury is sworn in; the prosecution counsel makes an opening speech and calls his witnesses; the defending counsel cross-examines them and puts forward the case for the defence; his witnesses are cross-examined; final speeches are made; the judge sums up; the jury retires, and then gives its verdict.

There are numerous variations on this pattern, which are too detailed to explain in full. One of the most important is 'plea bargaining'. This often happens in contested cases involving several charges and possibly a long hearing: the prosecution agrees to withdraw the most serious charges and the defence agrees to plead 'guilty' to one or more of the less serious. The practice is open to abuse and has been criticized by the Court of Appeal.

The choice should always lie with the defendant: no matter how strongly his lawyer feels that a deal would be in the interests of his client, he should never bring pressure to bear if the defendant wishes to fight on and assert his innocence.

Where most vital decisions are concerned, the defendant has to rely almost totally on his counsel and solicitor. Unlike the 'Perry Mason' set-up where the defendant sits with his lawyers, the defendant in British courts nearly always has to sit in an old-fashioned dock, cut off from the rest of the court. He can only communicate with his lawyers by passing notes or by attracting their attention.

A legally aided defendant who is found guilty is entitled to proper advice from his counsel and/or solicitor about the possible grounds for appeal; he should not let himself be fobbed off with a few hurried words in the cells corridor after the verdict has been given. (▷ p. 34)

County Courts

Scope and Organization

County Courts deal with civil disputes and claims where the amount is not more than £750; bankruptcy matters in some courts outside London; 'equitable' matters such as the administration of estates, trusts and mortgages where the amount does not exceed £5,000; landlord and tenant cases and other actions concerning title to and possession of land where the rateable value is not more than £400; and undefended divorce cases.

County Courts are presided over by a single judge. Usually there is a second court where the registrar deals with rent summonses and claims, hire purchase debt cases, etc., where the amount of the claim is under £100, or above that amount if both parties consent.

What to Expect

Most County Court judges and registrars will take a debtor's means and commitments fully into consideration, provided that he turns up at court and explains his position. County Court officials are usually helpful to those who ask for advice.

Few people will be able to contest a case successfully without legal advice and representation. Legal Aid is available, to those who qualify, for all major matters but not for 'small or trivial claims' – usually considered as those under £30.

Higher Civil Courts

Scope and Organization

The High Court of Justice is in the Strand. Traditionally, there are three Divisions: Chancery (trusts, estates, guardianship, etc.); Queen's Bench (civil claims and disputes, particularly accident claims); Probate, Divorce and Admiralty. These are being

25

reorganized to include a new Family Division, dealing with all matrimonial, guardianship and other matters affecting the family. Outside London the Assize Courts also deal with civil cases.

Most cases are tried by a judge sitting alone. In the appeal court (criminal and civil) there are normally three judges and the verdict is by majority.

What to Expect

The atmosphere in these courts is overwhelmingly formal. The procedure is technical: it is similar to that of criminal trials, but more than in other courts there will tend to be legal argument, points of procedure and references to previous court judgments ('precedents'), often read out at length. Contested cases frequently take several years to come to trial, although many are settled out of court.

Ordinary citizens who have to take or defend proceedings in the High Court should try to obtain Legal Aid. If not, they could risk financial ruin as a result of heavy legal fees.

Witnesses

Witnesses called to give evidence at any court case are normally entitled to allowances and expenses, and they should not hesitate to claim them from the solicitor who summoned them. This also applies to the plaintiff or defendant and his wife if she is called to give evidence.

In order to make sure that a witness turns up, the solicitor conducting the case will often issue him with a document called a 'subpoena' (witness summons). This is an official direction by the court to attend and give evidence, and it should not be ignored. Sufficient cash should be handed over with the subpoena to cover the witness's travelling expenses.

Representation in Court

Any person, whether he is professionally qualified or not, can attend a trial as a friend for the defendant. He can take notes, and may quietly make suggestions and give advice. This right was recently confirmed by the Court of Appeal (McKenzie *v.* McKenzie, 1970), and applies to all courts, civil and criminal. The friend will not be allowed to speak on the defendant's behalf – he may only give advice.

The Courts Act 1971

The present courts structure is far from satisfactory. Growing delays in civil and criminal cases, inefficiencies arising from overlapping jurisdictions and location of courts and the lack of a unified court system led to the Courts Act 1971, which is expected to come into operation on 1 January 1972. Criminal and civil work will be completely separate – the High Court will deal with civil work only and a new Crown Court will deal entirely with criminal work. All criminal proceedings not dealt with by the magistrates' courts will be brought before the Crown Court. Either court can sit anywhere in England and Wales and the courts of Assizes and Quarter Sessions will be abolished.

4. Sentencing, Appeals, and Prisoners' Rights

Sentencing

Where a person has committed a criminal offence, he is usually sentenced immediately after he has pleaded or been found guilty. If the matter is more serious he may be:

(1) Sent to a higher court for sentencing if the lower magistrates' court believes that a heavier sentence is required.

(2) Remanded in custody while reports – psychiatric, medical, social, or probation – are obtained, in order to assist the court in reaching a decision. A person may be remanded for a fortnight or more while these reports are being obtained.

(3) Remanded on bail for these reports.

Legal Aid should always be granted if a person is likely to receive a custodial (prison or Borstal) sentence. Even if Legal Aid has not been obtained for the original hearing an application can always be made for the hearing which decides sentence. If the defendant has a lawyer at this stage, he can make a plea of 'mitigation', which explains the circumstances of the offence and the person's own circumstances, with a view to obtaining the lightest sentence possible.

Bail can be applied for if there is to be a remand for reports. It is not likely to be granted if bail has been refused before the trial, and bail is often objected to at this stage even if it has been granted previously.

Types of Sentence

Absolute Discharge

This means that a person is found guilty but no restrictions are placed on him. Although a conviction, it is usually an indication by the court that the charge should not have been brought or the circumstances are such that any form of punishment would be unjust:

A reporter was sentenced to 9 months' imprisonment for possession of cannabis. On appeal he was given an absolute discharge because it was established that he had the cannabis only for the purpose of writing an article about the ease with which drugs could be obtained.

Conditional Discharge

This is a similar method of convicting a person without punishing him. It is used where any other form of punishment would be unfair but where the court wishes to have some method of keeping a check on the person. The discharge can be made conditional for up to 3 years. If the person is found guilty of any other offence within that period he can then be sentenced for the original offence. The court must explain this to him when giving the conditional discharge.

Binding Over

(The term 'binding over' is used elsewhere to mean the procedure by which a person is required to pay a sum of money if he fails to keep the peace and be of good behaviour. This can be done even where there has been no conviction.) (◊ p. 54)

Binding over as a form of sentencing has a different meaning. A person may be bound over 'to come up for judgment', usually subject to some specific condition. It is similar to a conditional discharge although there is no limit to the period for which it can apply and conditions may be attached to a binding over order which may not be a conditional discharge, e.g. residence in a hostel.

Fine

A fine may be imposed for almost all offences in addition to, or instead of, any other sentence (except discharge and probation). There is no limit to the amount of the fine unless a maximum fine has been fixed by law, which is so for most offences.

The main principle governing the use of fines is that the offence must be one for which a sentence of imprisonment would be wrong. The ability of a person to pay may reduce the amount of the fine but should not affect the type of punishment, i.e. it would be wrong for the court to imprison someone because he cannot afford a fine. The court must make an order fixing a period of imprisonment up to 12 months to be served in default of payment. But no person can be sent to prison for not paying a fine unless one of the following four conditions is satisfied:

(1) The person appears to have enough funds to pay immediately.

(2) He is unlikely to remain in the country and to obtain the money by any other method.

(3) He is in prison or detained for some other offence.

(4) He is already serving a term of imprisonment or detention. It is considered incorrect to impose a fine which the convicted person cannot afford. Fines given in magistrates' courts are limited to £400.

Probation

A court may make an order where a person is over 17, has been convicted of an offence, and is willing to be put on probation. An order may be made if the court is 'of the opinion that having regard to the circumstances, including the nature of the offence and the character of the offender, it is expedient to do so'. The order is made instead of any other sentence and the person put on probation must be under the supervision of a probation officer for a period of between 1 and 3 years. The probation order may require the person to comply with certain restrictions, e.g. residence in a probation home or hostel; usually these conditions may not include submitting to psychiatric treatment. Before making the order, the court must explain to the person in ordinary language the nature and terms of the order, and must tell him that if he fails to comply with the order or if he commits another offence he can be brought back and sentenced for the original offence.

The probation order may be discharged on the application of the probation officer or the probationer. The order can be discharged only by the court which made the original order. The court may, instead of discharging the order, substitute a conditional discharge for the same period as the original order.

It should be pointed out that a probation order is not only for young offenders but can be used for anyone where it is the most appropriate form of punishment and where some degree of supervision is required.

Imprisonment

Most offences have a maximum period for which a person can be imprisoned, although certain common law offences (e.g. conspiracy) have no maximum. It is not possible to discuss here the merits and demerits of prison sentences.

In a magistrates' court the maximum term of imprisonment that can be awarded is usually 6 months, but the court can also impose a period of imprisonment in default of payment of any fine. When a person is tried for more than one offence and the sentences are made to run consecutively, the total term of imprisonment should not exceed 6 months, or, in the case of offences which could have been tried in a higher court, 12 months.

No one under the age of 17 may be imprisoned, and a convicted person between 17 and 21 should be imprisoned only if there is no other appropriate punishment. The reasons for the choice of imprisonment must be recorded.

Suspended Sentence

When a court passes a prison sentence for 2 years or less, it can order that the sentence shall not take effect *unless*, during a specified period between one and 3 years, the convicted person commits a further offence punishable with imprisonment: if that happens, the court orders the original sentence to take effect.

Where a sentence is for not more than 6 months, the court must suspend the sentence unless certain conditions are present. These conditions relate either to the offence in question, e.g. assault and threat of violence, indecent conduct towards a person under 16; or to the offender, e.g. he has already served a term of imprisonment or been subjected to a suspended sentence (Criminal Justice Act 1967). These provisions apply to all courts but it is clear that the powers of the magistrates have been curtailed by them. In most circumstances a magistrate will be compelled to give a suspended sentence.

On passing a suspended sentence the court must explain to the offender in ordinary language that if he is convicted of a further offence during the period of his suspended sentence, he will be brought back to the court that gave him his suspended sentence and may be ordered to serve all or part of it. Not every conviction will result in the suspended sentence being brought into operation. Although a person should not receive a suspended sentence unless the appropriate punishment in the first place was a term of imprisonment, there is a tendency for people to be given suspended sentences where before the 1967 Act they would have been fined, put on probation, or given conditional discharges.

Young People

Young people between 17 and 21 are not, except in very rare circumstances, sentenced to a term of imprisonment ($\diamond$ p. 31). They can be fined, put on probation, or discharged, but special forms of punishment can also be given, such as detention centre and Borstal training, supervision or care orders.

Detention Centre

Detention may be ordered in the case of an offender aged between 17 and 21 where the court would otherwise have power to pass a sentence of imprisonment. Where the maximum term of imprisonment for the offence is more than 3 months, the sentence of detention must be between 3 and 6 months. In all other cases it must be for 3 months.

Borstal Training

Sentence of Borstal training may be passed where a young person is convicted of an offence punishable with imprisonment 'where the court is of the opinion having regard to the circumstances of the offence and after taking into account the offender's character and previous conduct, it is expedient that he should be detained for training for not less than six months'. Before passing a sentence of Borstal training the court must consider any report prepared by the prison department but there is no obligation to obtain such a report. A person may be detained for any period between 6 months and 2 years unless the Home Secretary directs his release earlier. He must remain under supervision for two years from the date of his release. If during that period he fails to comply with any conditions on which he is released, he may be recalled to Borstal.

Supervision and Care Orders (⬧ p. 154)

Pleas of Mitigation

The main purpose of a plea of mitigation is to draw the attention of the court to factors which are in favour of the convicted and normally the court will consider letters or other written documents in the person's favour. Where a person is legally represented, he should be allowed to add to what has been said by his lawyer if he wants to, although it is a matter for the judge's discretion. Where a person is not represented and wishes to submit a plea of mitigation in writing the court must accept the document and give it full consideration.

Further Information

D. A. Thomas, *Principles of Sentencing*, Heinemann, London, 1970

J. D. McClean and J. C. Wood, *Criminal Justice and the Treatment of Offenders*, Sweet & Maxwell, London, 1969

33

K. Devlin, *Sentencing Offenders in Magistrates' Courts*, Sweet &
Maxwell, London, 1970

Appeals

General Points

A convicted person may appeal against conviction and/or the
severity of his sentence. As a rule he may appeal against conviction only if he pleaded not guilty at the trial; but if he pleaded
guilty he may still appeal against sentence. In certain circumstances, however, he may be allowed to appeal against conviction
after pleading guilty: e.g., if he was under pressure from his advisers to plead guilty or if he did so by mistake.

In theory, every legally aided person who has been tried and
convicted has the right to further advice from the lawyer who
represented him at his trial. The lawyer should advise him
whether he has grounds for an appeal and, if so, should help him
prepare his case.

If you have been convicted, you should insist on receiving
adequate advice and, if you do not receive it, you should inform
the Registrar of Criminal Appeals, who will do what he can to see
that it is given to you. Prisoners should inform the prison authorities, who will provide a special letter to be sent to the trial
solicitor requesting advice.

Appeal after Conviction by a Magistrate's Court

If you have been sentenced by a magistrate's court, you may
appeal to Quarter Sessions within 14 days of your conviction.
You may be allowed to appeal later than this if you can give
convincing reasons for the delay.

The grounds for your appeal should be written out clearly and
precisely, signed by you and sent to the clerk of the magistrate's
court where you were tried, and to the prosecutor.

It is sometimes possible to appeal directly to the High Court, but only on a point of law. Legal advice and representation are essential for this type of appeal.

Legal Aid and Advice

If possible, you should get legal advice before submitting your appeal. It is equally important to have legal representation when the appeal is heard, as an appeal to Quarter Sessions means that the whole case must be heard again. Application for Legal Aid (⬦ pp. 18–20) should be made to the magistrate's court where you were tried or to Quarter Sessions.

Bail

You may appeal to the magistrate's court to be released on bail until your appeal is heard. If bail is refused, you may renew your application to a judge in chambers (i.e. a single High Court judge), but Legal Aid is not available for this. Bail is rarely granted at this stage.

Appeal after Conviction on Indictment (i.e. after Trial at Assizes, the Central Criminal Court, a Crown Court, or Quarter Sessions)

The first step is to apply for leave to appeal. Your application should be sent to the Registrar of Criminal Appeals within 28 days of your conviction, together with the grounds for your appeal. (If you are waiting for more detailed advice, you may submit general reasons first and make them more specific later, but on the whole the courts take a dim view of this.) Application forms are available from the Registrar, or from prison authorities. The appeal may be based on a question of law and/or fact, i.e. alleging that the trial court has misinterpreted the law or has made an error in its findings of fact.

Applications for leave to appeal on a point of law are usually treated as full appeals and sent straight to the Court of Appeals. Other applications are sent to a single judge, who considers the short transcript of the court proceedings, the grounds submitted by the appellant, and other papers such as doctors' reports. If your application is refused, you may renew it within 14 days to a full Appeal Court, which consists of three other judges.

If the judge grants leave to appeal, he also considers applications for:

(1) Legal Aid, which is normally granted, depending, of course, on the appellant's means. Normally Legal Aid is granted only for a barrister and the appellant is given the same barrister who represented him at his trial. But if he objects to this barrister, he has the right to suggest another. In complicated cases he may ask for both a solicitor and a barrister to be assigned to him under Legal Aid.

(2) Bail, which is rarely granted.

(3) The calling of witnesses who did not give evidence at the trial – there must be good reason for granting this.

There is often a long delay before an appeal is heard: the main reason is that it takes a long time to obtain the transcript of the court proceedings from the shorthand writers.

Appeals are heard by the Court of Appeal, Criminal Division, which consists of three judges. The Court hears argument from counsel, but it does not re-try the case or consider all the evidence again. It has the power to reverse a conviction or to reduce sentence or to order a new trial, but not to increase sentence.

Appeal to the House of Lords

Permission to appeal to the House of Lords can be granted only if a full appeal has been heard by the Court of Appeal and if the Court certifies that a point of law of public importance is involved. If an application is not made at the Court of Appeal hearing, it should be made within the following 14 days.

Provision for Legal Aid, bail, etc. is the same as for appeals to the Court of Appeal. Costs are extremely high: an appeal to the House of Lords without Legal Aid would be impossible for all but the very rich.

Prisoners on Appeal

If a prisoner wants to appeal against his conviction or sentence, or if he is already on appeal when he arrives in prison, he should inform the governor. There should be an officer delegated to help prisoners with their appeals.

A prisoner on appeal may:

(1) Be visited by anyone connected with his appeal in the sight and hearing of a prison officer.

(2) Have meetings with his legal adviser in the sight but not in the hearing of an officer.

(3) Be examined by his own doctor, if medical evidence is relevant to the appeal.

(4) Correspond with his legal adviser and with anyone else connected with his appeal (he should be given writing materials for this). Letters to his legal adviser are not read by the prison authorities.

A prisoner may be ordered to spend extra time in prison to cover the time taken up by an unsuccessful appeal. Orders for more than 90 days have been made, but a single judge does not normally make orders for more than 42 days. These do not count as part of the prisoner's sentence and their object is to deter 'frivolous' appeals.

Prisoners

A prisoner has no absolute rights, he has only privileges. The Prison Rules state what he may and may not do in ideal circumstances, but the privileges he is granted may be withdrawn by the Prison Governor for a variety of reasons, e.g. for a breach of prison discipline or for administrative reasons such as difficulties due to overcrowding.

If a prisoner's privileges are withdrawn unjustly, and a complaint to prison authorities has no effect, he should petition the

Home Secretary, or write to his M.P. or to the NCCL, to Justice, or to NACRO (◊ p. 337). Unfortunately, his attempt to do so may fail, as his letters are censored and he is not allowed to petition the Home Secretary without the consent of the Prison Governor. It may prove much more effective to get a friend or relative to write on his behalf.

Reception into Prison

Every person is searched on his reception into prison. He may also be photographed. Anything he is not allowed to keep for his own use (apart from cash) is taken into the Governor's custody. An inventory of the property in custody must be kept by the prison authorities and the prisoner must sign it after he has had a reasonable opportunity to see that it is correct. All cash must be paid into an account under the control of the Governor.

Every prisoner must be given a written account of the Prison Rules in his own room or cell, which includes information about earnings, privileges and the method of making complaints. A prison official must make sure that each prisoner has read and understood the information as soon as possible or, at the latest, within 24 hours of his reception.

Access to Prison Authorities

A prisoner may visit the Prison Governor, the Chaplain, or the Medical Officer, usually by arrangement with his landing officer. All prisons have Welfare Officers and prisoners are referred to them quite frequently. Relatives and friends of prisoners may arrange to see these officers for help and advice; if they want to complain about the way they themselves have been treated by prison authorities, they should write to the Home Secretary.

Unconvicted Prisoners

A person who is remanded in custody to await trial is treated somewhat differently from convicted prisoners:

(1) He may wear his own clothes and may arrange for clothes to be sent by his family or friends. He should not be made to have his hair cut or beard shaved except for reasons of hygiene.

(2) He does not have to work, although he may apply to work in the same way as convicted prisoners. On the whole, he does not participate in prison life, but this can be a disadvantage as boredom becomes a greater problem.

(3) He may send and receive as many letters as he likes, but they are censored like those of ordinary prisoners. He may not conduct business from prison – and this includes writing business letters – but he may apply to the Prison Governor for permission to do so. He may give someone else power of attorney to conduct business for him.

(4) He may receive as many visits as he likes, although he is usually limited to one visit a day.

(5) He may receive food, but apart from fruit, chocolate and similar 'extras', he may only receive complete meals, which are then substituted for prison meals. He may not be given one course to supplement a prison meal.

(6) He may buy or be given books, papers and writing materials, unless they are considered 'objectionable' by the prison authorities.

(7) He may ask for a visit from a doctor or dentist who is not attached to the prison if he is willing to pay any expenses incurred.

(8) He may see his legal adviser during normal working hours, as often as is necessary, in the sight but not in the hearing of a prison officer.

In many cases, the treatment of unconvicted prisoners is grossly inadequate and belies the principle that a person is innocent until proved guilty.

Convicted Prisoners

Visits

Under the Prison Rules, convicted prisoners may receive only one visit every 8 weeks; in practice, visits are usually allowed once every 4 weeks. Prisoners under 21 may normally be visited once a fortnight.

Anyone who wants to visit must first obtain a visiting order from the Prison Governor. This is usually done by post and the order covers up to three visitors. Visits take place within the sight and hearing of a prison officer, and last for at least 30 minutes.

Visits are not always allowed immediately after the prisoner's conviction, but young prisoners and those with more than 2-month sentences may normally apply for reception visits.

Visits by voluntary prison visitors count as ordinary visits, but prisoners may receive extra visits from ministers of their religion. Visits from legal advisers do not require a visiting order, except when the prisoner is not involved in any legal proceedings; these visits take place in the sight but not in the hearing of a prison officer.

A police officer may, on production of an order from a chief police officer, interview any prisoner who is willing to see him.

A prisoner is not allowed to accumulate visits and receive several in a short period of time, unless he is a long way from home and his relatives are in real difficulty. Some prisoners may obtain temporary transfers in order to be visited near home, but this is not normally allowed unless they have already served 4 years.

If a prisoner is punished for breach of prison discipline, his right to receive visits may be withdrawn. Extra visits are allowed by the Governor or by the Visiting Committee if they are considered necessary for the welfare of the prisoner's family, or for other special reasons.

Visitors may give prisoners cigarettes to smoke during visits, but this privilege may be withdrawn; they are liable to a fine if they give anything else and if they give alcohol or tobacco they are liable to imprisonment. They may not take notes of the conversation.

Letters

Prisoners may send and receive one letter a week, but this may be increased to two per week if postage is paid out of the prisoner's money.

The prison authorities read all letters to and from prisoners (except correspondence between prisoners on appeal and their legal advisers). The Governor may stop any letter he considers to be objectionable or too long. Letters are often arbitrarily censored. 'Objectionable' can be widely interpreted, e.g. letters mentioning other prisoners' offences; complaints about the police or the courts; matters which may attract press publicity; complaints of prison treatment. Prisoners are normally given the opportunity to re-write letters which have been stopped.

Generally, a prisoner may write letters only to relatives and friends, but the Governor may allow him to write to his doctor or M.P., to the NCCL, to Justice, or to NACRO. He must get special permission from the Home Secretary, via the Prison Governor, to write business letters: the European Commission on Human Rights has ruled that this is contrary to the Declaration of Human Rights, but the practice remains.

A prisoner may write to his M.P. after he has spent 2 months in prison. He may not complain about the prison staff or the way he is treated, unless his complaint has already been investigated within the prison. He may ask his M.P. to visit him, but the object of the visit must be given: again, it may not concern a complaint unless there has already been an investigation within the prison. As with other letters, the Governor may stop a letter to an M.P. if he considers it 'objectionable'; but there is no reason why friends or relatives should not write on the prisoner's behalf.

The Home Secretary has ultimate responsibility for prisons: prisoners may petition him on a limited number of matters, e.g. applications to re-open a case after all rights of appeal have been exhausted, applications to attend court proceedings or to conduct business, etc. Friends and relatives of prisoners may petition the Home Secretary.

Food

A prisoner is entitled to 3 meals a day unless he is put on a restricted diet as a punishment: this consists of one pound of bread and sufficient water for 3 consecutive days, then ordinary food for 3 days, then bread and water for 3 days, and so on, until the punishment ends.

Work

A prisoner who has no outdoor work and is not in an open prison is entitled to one hour's exercise a day. He must work if required.

Books, etc.

A prisoner may receive library books and educational textbooks from the prison; friends and relatives may send him books, newspapers and periodicals, but these are often subject to unreasonable censorship. *Private Eye*, *International Times* and *Black Dwarf* are banned from some prisons. Books sent to prisoners are eventually given to the prison library. Prisoners are not allowed to be sent money.

Money

If money is sent to a prisoner from outside it will either be returned to the sender or, if the sender's name and address is not known, paid into a special account for the benefit of discharged prisoners.

National Insurance

A prisoner may arrange to pay National Insurance stamps from his prison earnings or from his private money. It is sensible to do this, as it makes it easier to obtain employment on release. A prisoner's dependants may benefit from income tax rebates after his conviction, and the Office of the Inspector of Taxes should be consulted.

Marriage

A prisoner receives permission to marry while in prison only if his girl-friend is pregnant.

Women

A woman's hair must not be cut without her consent. She may have her baby with her in prison, if the Home Secretary's consent is obtained, although he may make it subject to conditions.

Religion

If a prisoner asks to be visited by a minister of his religion and there is no such minister attached to the prison, the Governor should arrange for an appropriate minister to visit him.

Discipline

Privileges may be withdrawn if the prisoner commits a breach of discipline. If a prisoner commits an offence in prison, his case is heard by the Visiting Committee. He is not entitled to have representation or to appeal against the Committee's decision.

Category 'A' Prisoners

Following Lord Mountbatten's report, 'Prison Escapes and Security', severe restrictions were imposed on certain long-term prisoners considered to be a particular security or social risk and classified by the Home Office as category 'A'. This has had two unpleasant and undesirable effects.

(1) People wishing to visit category 'A' prisoners, even close relatives, must first complete a personal inquiry form and submit it with photographs to the authorities for approval: this has caused great resentment, particularly among prisoners' wives, because it constitutes a fresh curb on visiting rights which are already far more restrictive than in many other countries.

(2) The special security precautions have had a bad effect on prison regimen and on the morale of all inmates of prisons which

take category 'A' prisoners: there has been a reduction of outside working parties and of educational classes, closure of some hostels and an admitted deterioration of staff–prisoner relationships.

There is a special Home Office committee which decides whether a prisoner should be classified as category 'A'; it also reviews and reclassifies cases. There is no appeal, but if it is felt that there are grounds for reclassification, representations should be made to the Home Office by the prisoner's relatives or solicitor, by his M.P. or by the NCCL. Unfortunately the committee does not have to give its reasons for classifying a prisoner as category 'A'. At present there are over 200 category 'A' prisoners.

Release from Prison

Remission

A person sentenced to more than one month's imprisonment is entitled, by good conduct in prison, to remission of up to one third of his sentence. The sentence cannot be reduced to less than one month. Release with remission means that the sentence has ended and the prisoner cannot be recalled. Prisoners not eligible for remission are those imprisoned for non-payment of fines, prisoners under 21, and prisoners with extended sentences (extended sentences, i.e. those above the maximum laid down by law, may be given by the court in certain specified circumstances to those convicted who have very bad records).

Release on Licence

Prisoners under 21 and those with extended sentences may be released on licence after they have served two thirds or more of their sentence. Release on licence means that the prisoner may be recalled to prison if he fails to comply with certain conditions.

Parole

A prisoner becomes eligible for parole after serving one third of his sentence or after one year, whichever is the longer period. The

Parole Board considers the prisoner's written application; reports from the Governor, from probation officers and medical officers; and representations from other people interested in the case. Relatives and friends should write to the Board, giving reasons why they feel parole should be granted. If necessary, the prisoner will be interviewed by a member of the Board.

The Board may, at its discretion, recommend to the Home Secretary that the prisoner be released on parole. There is no appeal against the decision of the Board. Once on parole, the prisoner may be recalled to prison at any time if he fails to abide by certain conditions. The parole ends when the prisoner would otherwise have been released on remission.

Entitlements on Release

(1) If a prisoner has served a sentence of more than 3 months, he is entitled to £4 on his release if his savings do not exceed £5. For every penny that his savings exceed £5, the amount given to him by the prison will be reduced by the same sum.

(2) The prisoner will be given a travel warrant to cover the cost of his journey from prison to home. If he has no home, he may select any destination within a reasonable distance of the prison.

(3) If the prisoner is worried about the state of his clothing, he should see the Discharge Officer who may arrange for a replacement.

(4) *Employment:* A prisoner who is soon to be released may ask to see the officer from the Department of Employment who visits the prison once a week. If he manages to find a job before he is released and he needs to buy equipment for it, he should see the prison Welfare Officer, who may arrange for him to be given the necessary money.

(5) *Accommodation:* The prisoner should apply to the Welfare Officer as soon as his release date is confirmed. The officer may be able to find him accommodation, but he is under no obligation to do so.

Further Information and Advice

Apex Trust
Howard League for Penal Reform
NACRO (National Association for the Care and Resettlement of Offenders)
NCCL
RAP (Radical Alternatives to Prison), 104 Newgate Street, London, EC 1

5. Search and Seizure

Search

Search before Arrest

As a general rule, the police have no right to search a person who has not been arrested, but there are three important exceptions:

(1) When they are searching for drugs (Misuse of Drugs Act 1971).

(2) When they are searching for firearms (Firearms Act 1968).

(3) In the Metropolitan Police area (most of Greater London, except the City and the Temples), when they are searching for goods which have been stolen or unlawfully obtained (Metropolitan Police Act 1839); and outside London there are similar provisions under local Acts.

In all three of these cases, the police must have reasonable grounds for suspecting that you possess what they are looking for. If a policeman asks to search you or your vehicle, remember that he has no general right to do so. Generally, you need not let a policeman search you unless you think he has reasonable grounds for suspecting that you possess drugs or firearms. In Greater London and in many towns, however, the police have wide powers to search if they reasonably suspect unlawful activity. You may always ask them what they are looking for, but unless you think their suspicion is unfounded, it is advisable to let them search. If you refuse to allow the police to search you, you may be arrested and you are likely to be searched at the police station. The matter will then be decided by a court and you may be found guilty of obstructing a policeman in the execution of his duty. ($\Diamond$ p. 58)

The fact that a policeman does not find what he is looking for does not necessarily mean that he had no reasonable grounds for searching.

Search after Arrest

If you have been arrested without a warrant, the police may search you and seize any weapons and anything which can be used as material evidence for the prosecution. But they may *not* search your premises without your permission, unless they get a warrant for that purpose or unless they have entered your house with your permission in the course of making the arrest.

Entry and Search of Premises without a Warrant

Generally the police have no power to enter or search private premises without a warrant from a Magistrate. There is one important exception: a police officer of or above the rank of Superintendent may give written authority to a policeman to search any premises for stolen goods if:

(1) The person occupying the premises has, within the last 5 years, been convicted of handling stolen goods, or of any other offence involving dishonesty and punishable by imprisonment.

(2) A person who has been convicted of handling stolen goods within the last 5 years has been occupying the premises within the last 12 months (Theft Act 1968).

This means that the police can easily get permission to search any house if, within the last 12 months, someone with the right kind of criminal record lived there. The Act does not even specify that they must have reasonable suspicion that there are stolen goods on the premises.

Apart from this and another important exception which resulted from the case of Ghani v. Jones (1970) ($\Diamond$ p. 50), the police may not enter and search your premises without a warrant, unless they have your consent. Once you withdraw your consent and ask them to leave, they must do so. If they refuse, you may use as much force as is reasonably necessary to make them leave (Davis *v.* Lisle, 1936). A policeman who remains on your premises without your consent is trespassing and therefore is not acting in the course of his duty, so you cannot be arrested for obstructing him (Bailey *v.* Wilson, 1958).

A policeman has a right to walk up your garden path and knock on your front door only because it is generally assumed that anyone may do this. But if your gate had a notice saying 'No hawkers, no circulars, no trespassers', he would probably not be able to walk up to your front door without trespassing – unless he had a warrant, or was acting in order to avert an immediate public danger, or had reasonable suspicion that an arrestable offence had been committed.

Entry and Search with a Warrant

A warrant to enter and search premises can only be obtained from a magistrate on the strength of a statement sworn by a police officer that he has reasonable grounds for searching.

Police may obtain warrants to search for a huge range of things – from stolen goods and drugs, to evidence of sexual offences and neglect of children. Powers given under different warrants vary considerably, and may include the power to search people found on the premises or to seize goods even when they are not specified in the warrant. Powers of arrest are often contained in a warrant.

Most warrants expire after they have been used once, so the police cannot demand re-entry on the same warrant, but some warrants authorize entry at any time and may be used more than once.

If you are in doubt as to the search powers of the police, ask to see their warrant and read it carefully. It will tell you what they may or may not do. You have the right to read it, and you need not admit the police to your premises until you have read it. If the police are making a search, they have no right to take general photographs of the premises, inside or outside, without your consent.

49

Seizure

Without a Warrant

If the police search you without a warrant, either after arresting you or when searching for drugs, firearms, or, in London, for stolen goods (⟡ p. 47), they may seize anything relevant to the offence in question. But if they find something which is not relevant to the offence of which you are suspected, they may not, in theory, seize the goods. In the recent case of Ghani *v.* Jones (1970) the Court of Appeal laid down the circumstances that had to be established to justify seizure by the police where no one has been arrested or charged.

(1) The police must have reasonable grounds for believing:

(i) That the offence which has been committed is so serious that it is of great importance that the offenders are caught and brought to justice.

(ii) That the article is either the fruit of the crime or the instrument used to commit the crime, or material evidence to prove the commission of the crime.

(iii) That the person who has possession of the article has himself committed the crime, is accessory to it or is implicated in it, or that his refusal to hand it over is unreasonable.

(2) The police must not keep the article for any longer than is reasonably necessary to complete their investigations or to preserve it as evidence. If a copy will do, it should be made, and the original returned. As soon as the case is over or it is decided to abandon it, the article must be returned.

(3) The lawfulness of the conduct of the police must be judged at the time and not by what happened afterwards.

With a Warrant

If the police have a warrant to search your premises, it may give them power to seize goods relevant to the crime in question.

If, for example, the police are looking for stolen radios and their warrant empowers them to seize any stolen goods found, they may also seize any other goods which they believe to have been stolen, because the category is the same – stolen goods (Chic Fashions (West Wales) Ltd *v.* Jones, 1968). If, however, they find something quite different, for example, obscene literature, they will need a separate warrant to make the seizure lawful. The correct procedure in this case is for the police to send a colleague away to get another warrant. Despite this rule, it has been shown in the past that if the police seize goods unconnected with the crime they are investigating, and these goods are subsequently used as evidence, successfully, for another prosecution, the seizure is lawful (Elias *v.* Pasmore, 1934).

Remember: if in doubt, read the warrant. If you believe that the police have acted illegally in entering, searching or seizing, it is advisable to consult a solicitor about the possibility of taking legal action against them.

Other Powers of Search and Seizure

The following powers are contained in various Acts of Parliament and differ considerably.

(1) Customs and Excise Officers have wide powers to search and seize, including power to intercept what they consider to be obscene or pornographic literature. (◊ p. 270)

(2) An Immigration Officer may, with a warrant, search premises to look for someone who is suspected of contravening the Immigration Act 1971. (◊ p. 255)

(3) Certain officials of local and national government, and gas and electricity boards, may enter private premises without permission. (◊ pp. 217–19)

(4) A Bailiff or Sheriff's Officer, with a court order, may seize goods or money from the person named by the court order.

Summary of Rights Concerning Search and Seizure

You have the right:

(1) To know what the police are looking for.

(2) To know under what authority the police are stopping or searching you, or searching your premises.

(3) To refuse the police admission to your premises unless you are satisfied that they have the authority to enter.

(4) To refuse to let the police search you and your premises unless they satisfy you of their authority.

(5) To read carefully any warrant the police may produce.

(6) To withdraw your consent for the police to remain on your premises and ask them to leave at any time (unless they have a warrant).

(7) To use as much force as is reasonably necessary to remove unauthorized police from your premises.

If you have no objection to being searched, you may help the police by agreeing, even though they cannot force you to do so – there is no sense in insisting on your rights just to be obstructive. If, however, you think the police are exceeding their authority and you object, you may insist upon your rights and refuse to be searched.

Never be afraid to question the police. If in doubt, get advice from a solicitor. If the police have acted unlawfully, you may have grounds for a complaint or a civil action. (◊ pp. 88 ff.)

6. Breach of the Peace and Similar Offences

This chapter describes some of the most common ways in which your freedom of action can be restricted by the law. You may be charged with one of the following offences when your behaviour is not in itself harmful, but merely disorderly or unconventional – e.g. when you are demonstrating, picketing, or even celebrating.

Conduct Likely to Cause a Breach of the Peace

A 'breach of the peace' means an intentional use or threat of violence by one person against another. But you do not have to be committing a breach of the peace to be charged with this offence: all you need to be doing is acting in a way which gives reasonable grounds for suspicion that you or someone else *might* commit a breach of the peace.

In theory, you may not be arrested just because your behaviour might lead to disorderly conduct, abusive language, or excessive noise: it must be suspected of leading to a genuine use or threat of force. However, in a number of cases, the courts have applied the concept of 'breach of the peace' to any form of disturbance in the presence of a large gathering of people.

An explanation of how a policeman may decide that a breach of the peace is likely to occur was given by Lord Chief Justice Parker:

> First, the mere statement by a constable that he anticipated a breach of the peace is clearly not enough. There must exist

proved facts from which a constable could reasonably have anticipated such a breach. Secondly, it is not enough that he believed there was a remote possibility, but there must be a real possibility of the breach of the peace (Piddington *v.* Bates, 1960; ◊ pp. 134–5).

Binding Over

If you are arrested on this charge, you may be 'bound over'. This means that the magistrate will ask you to enter into a recognizance, with or without sureties (◊ p. 4), to keep the peace or to be of good behaviour. If you fail to do this, you may be imprisoned for up to 6 months.

You can be taken to court and bound over for a wide variety of reasons, even when you have committed no criminal offence. Your rights vary according to whether you are bound over under the Magistrates Court Act 1952; or under the Justice of the Peace Act 1361. Under the 1952 Act, the courts must first prove that the complaint against you which led to a demand for binding over was justified. Under the 1361 Act, they need not prove this, but there must be sufficient evidence that there is likely to be a further breach of the peace. Under both Acts, you should be warned, and given a chance to defend yourself.

Magistrates sometimes impose unreasonable binding over orders as a form of punishment. You have the right to appeal against a binding over order to the Quarter Sessions (Magistrates Court (Appeal from Binding Over Order) Act 1956).

Insulting Words and Behaviour

A person is guilty of an offence if, at any public place or public meeting, he (1) uses threatening, abusive, or insulting words or behaviour, or (2) distributes or displays any writing, sign, or visible representation which is threatening, abusive, or insulting, with intent to provoke a breach of the peace or which is likely to cause a breach of the peace (Public Order Act 1936 as amended by the Race Relations Act 1965, s.7; Metropolitan Police Act 1839, s.54, and other local Acts).

'Threatening' is defined as any behaviour which causes people of ordinary firmness or maturity to fear physical harm to themselves or their property. *'Abusive'* is a much vaguer term: it is possible to be abusive to a particular person without committing the offence of 'abusive words or behaviour'; it is generally related to the provocation of disorder and any verbal hostility may amount to the offence of 'abuse'.

The maximum penalties under the Public Order Act are a fine up to £100 and/or 3 months' imprisonment if tried in a magistrate's court, or a fine up to £500 and/or 12 months' imprisonment if tried in a higher court. There is a separate penalty under the Metropolitan Police Act of a fine up to £20.

You can be found guilty if your words and behaviour are threatening, abusive, or insulting only to certain people in your audience whom you had not expected to be present. This is an important point which was upheld in the following case:

In 1963, the National Socialist movement held a meeting in Trafalgar Square which attracted groups including Jews and Socialists. There was disorder throughout the meeting. Colin Jordan in a speech said, '. . . our real enemies, the people we should have fought, were not Hitler and the National Socialists of Germany, but world Jewry and its associates in this country'. At this point there was complete disorder and a surge towards the platform, and the police stopped the meeting. The Divisional Court held that the speaker must take his audience as he finds them and that Jordan was guilty of the offence (Jordan *v.* Burgoyne, 1963).

Unlawful Assembly and Riotous Assembly

'Unlawful assembly' means an assembly of 3 or more people in order to commit a crime; or in order to do something (legal or illegal) together in a way which endangers public peace or makes 'firm and courageous' people fear a breach of the peace.

'Riot' is defined as a 'tumultuous disturbance' by 3 or more people who have assembled in order to carry out some common purpose and to help each other, by force if necessary, against anyone who opposes them; and who then do what they have planned, using enough force or violence to alarm at least one person of reasonable firmness.

There has recently been a tendency to prosecute demonstrators on charges of 'unlawful assembly' or 'riotous assembly' (i.e. riot), where normally they might have faced lesser charges such as 'threatening, abusive or insulting behaviour'. This tendency is disturbing because the charges carry considerable penalties and because it is apparently quite easy for the prosecution to establish the ingredients of these offences.

In the Garden House case (1970), four Cambridge students were found guilty of riot and three of unlawful assembly. Lord Justice Sachs, who upheld these convictions in the Court of Appeal, made two important statements:

(i) That the difference between unlawful and riotous assembly was as follows: the moment persons in a crowd, however peaceful their original intentions, came together to act for some common purpose in such a way as to make reasonable citizens fear a breach of the peace, the assembly became unlawful. It became riotous when alarming force or violence began to be used; and anyone who actively encouraged such an assembly by words, signs or actions or by participating in it was guilty of an offence.

(ii) That each individual who took part in tumultuous disturbances of the public peace was guilty of an offence. Those who chose to do so did so at their peril.

These pronouncements have dangerous implications: a person who takes part in a demonstration cannot know in advance whether or not the crowd will act 'for some common purpose' or whether the disturbance will be 'tumultuous'. He therefore cannot anticipate that he may break the law, still less that he may be charged with riotous or unlawful assembly.

Rout

This is a disturbance of the peace by people who intend to do something which, if they did, would amount to riot, but who fail to achieve their purpose. There have been no recent prosecutions for rout, but it may be revived, since there have recently been prosecutions for riot, and rout is a lesser offence.

Affray

This is defined as a fight between 2 or more people 'to the terror of Her Majesty's subjects'. It is therefore sufficient for the prosecution to show that 2 or more people were fighting in the presence of others who were neither encouraging nor participating and that some of them were frightened by the fighting. The affray need not have occurred in a public place.

Sedition

An enormous range of actions might be interpreted as sedition. It has been defined as follows:

'It embraces all those practices, whether by word, deed or writing, which fall short of high treason but tend to have for their object to excite discontent or dissatisfaction; to excite ill-will between different classes of the Sovereign's subjects; to create public disturbance or to lead to civil war; to bring into hatred or contempt the Sovereign or the Government, the laws or constitution of the realm, and generally all endeavours to promote public disorder' (Archbold).

It is a serious offence, carrying heavy penalties. Fortunately since 1909 there have been few prosecutions for sedition and most of these were unsuccessful. But it is always possible that the offence may be revived.

Incitement to Racial Hatred

It is also an offence to use threatening, abusive, or insulting language at any public place or public meeting, with intent to stir up hatred against any section of the British public distinguished by colour, race, or ethnic origins (Race Relations Act 1965, s.6; ▷ p. 266).

You can be charged with this offence even when there is no likelihood of a breach of the peace; but the consent of the Attorney General is needed before a prosecution is started. The maximum penalty is a fine of £200 and/or 6 months' imprisonment on summary conviction and up to £1,000 and/or 2 years' imprisonment on indictment.

Obstruction and Assault of a Police Officer in the Execution of His Duty

Anything you do which is intended to prevent a policeman from carrying out his duty is an obstruction. The penalty is a fine up to £20 and/or one month's imprisonment.

Obstruction may not necessarily include assault. An assault on a policeman means any intentional hitting, kicking, or striking. The penalties for this are: (1) in a magistrate's court up to 6 months' imprisonment on first conviction, and up to 9 months' on a subsequent conviction, and/or a fine up to £100; (2) in a higher court up to 2 years' imprisonment with or without a fine (Police Act 1964, s. 51).

It is a defence if you can prove that you did not intend to assault the policeman, but this is not easy (a man is presumed to intend the natural consequences of his actions). It is no defence to say that you did not know that he was a policeman.

It seems that if a policeman thinks you are obstructing him, he need not give you a reasonable time to stop doing so, but can arrest you immediately. You can be arrested without a warrant for assaulting a policeman, but not merely for obstructing him, unless the obstruction is physical.

'In the execution of his duty' means when a policeman is preventing any kind of crime, including a breach of the peace and minor offences such as obstruction of the highway. But it is not the duty of the policeman to interfere without good reason with people who are peacefully and lawfully exercising their rights. Therefore, if you are charged with obstructing the police by continuing a meeting which the police have said is obstructing the highway, it is a good defence to *both* charges if you can prove that you were not obstructing the highway.

You have no legal duty to answer a policeman's questions, although questions about motoring are an exception (◊ pp. 231, 233), and if you are unwilling to do so, it will not be considered an obstruction.

Aiding and Abetting

It is an offence to help bring about any offence by helping the person who is committing it (aiding and abetting); by procuring a person to commit an offence (accessory before the fact); or by sheltering or *actively* helping a person after he has committed an offence (accessory after the fact).

Incitement

Incitement to crime is also illegal, even when the crime is not committed, or when the person who has been incited is not influenced by it. If the crime is committed, then the inciter becomes the principal offender and is liable to a heavier penalty. There are a number of specific Acts concerning incitement of which the most important are:

(1) *Incitement to Mutiny Act 1797* which makes it an offence punishable by life imprisonment if a person intentionally 'endeavour(s) to seduce' those serving in the armed forces from their 'duty *and* allegiance' to the Crown, or incites them to commit any act of mutiny.

(2) *Incitement to Disaffection Act 1934* which makes it an offence 'maliciously and advisedly' to endeavour to seduce any member of the forces from his 'duty *or* allegiance'. The Act has a wide application, but as a matter of prosecuting policy there have been no recent charges. Conviction of the offence is punishable on indictment with up to 2 years' imprisonment and/or a fine of up to £200; or on summary conviction, up to 4 months' imprisonment and/or a fine up to £20.

(3) *Police Act 1964, s. 53,* which makes it an offence to cause or to attempt to cause disaffection amongst members of any police force. It is not certain whether a person can be guilty of these offences if his acts were unintentional. On summary conviction the maximum penalty is imprisonment for up to 6 months and/or a fine of up to £100; and on indictment, imprisonment up to 2 years and/or an unlimited fine.

Conspiracy

If a person commits an offence alone, he is not guilty of conspiracy. But if he agrees with anyone else to do an unlawful act, then they are both guilty of the crime of conspiracy, even if nothing at all is done towards carrying out the agreed act.

A conspiracy is an agreement between two or more people to do something illegal, or to do something legal by illegal means. It is not even necessary to establish that the act they contemplated was criminal. There are two categories of conspiracy which are criminal even though the agreed objective would not be criminal if done by one person alone:

(1) Conspiracy to commit a civil wrong (i.e. to commit an act for which you can be sued by a private citizen). Usually, this

involves fraud, but because the offence is vague and the sentence is unlimited, there is a tendency to use it as a convenient charge where it is not clear what individual offence has been committed. An example of this was the Greek Embassy case in 1967, where a charge was initially brought of 'conspiracy to trespass'.

(2) Conspiracy to commit an act which is neither a crime nor a civil wrong, but which seems calculated to 'injure the public'. An example of this is the *Ladies' Directory* case. (◊ p. 121)

The court has the power to try one conspirator in the absence of the others if the jury can be persuaded that the absent conspirators would have been found guilty, had they been there. But if all the conspirators are tried together, the court must reach the same verdict for all of them. Once any agreement or common action has been shown, evidence against one conspirator amounts to evidence against all the others.

Wherever possible, people should be charged with the actual offence, rather than with conspiracy (this principle has been established by judicial statements). However, there is an increasing tendency to use the blanket charge of conspiracy, especially in 'political' cases. In a trial for conspiracy, a conviction can be reached where much of the evidence is established by implication, and where the accused have done nothing at all except come to an agreement.

The penalties for conspiracy are a fine or imprisonment. There is no limit. A court can pass a heavier sentence for conspiracy to commit an offence than for the offence itself, if it has grounds for treating the conspiracy as a more serious crime. However, this can only be justified in very exceptional cases.

Further Information

◊ p. 81.

7. Public Meetings

General Outline

Generally the holding of a public meeting is not in itself a criminal offence. However, there is no unlimited right to hold meetings in public places such as streets, roads, squares, etc.; these are 'public' only in the sense that the general public has the right to 'pass and repass' along them. Technically, the sub-soil always belongs to somebody and the use of it for any purpose other than passing and repassing could lead to a civil action for trespass. Where criminal law is concerned, a meeting in a public place is not unlawful so long as no specific criminal offence is committed.

The expression 'public place' is defined in the Public Order Act 1936 as 'any highway, public park or garden, any sea bridge, road, lane, footway, square, court, alley or passage, whether a thoroughfare or not', and includes any open space to which the public have access for the time being, whether on payment or not.

Prosecutions resulting from public meetings will normally be based on one of two main offences: (1) causing an obstruction; (2) causing a breach of the peace. Such conduct may be illegal under local by-laws, local Acts, common law or some statutory provision such as the Public Order Act 1936.

(1) Local By-Laws

By-laws which govern some public parks and public places lay down special conditions for holding meetings; others prohibit them altogether.

If you intend to hold a meeting, first find out what the by-laws are. (You can usually find out at the local Borough or County Council, but if you want to hold a meeting in Hyde Park or Trafalgar Square, you must inquire at the Department of the Environment.) If a policeman tells you that such by-laws exist, it is still advisable to check up: make a copy of the by-law and find out from the NCCL or from a solicitor exactly what the by-law forbids or demands. Some local Acts impose penalties on people who organize meetings without authorization.

(2) Notifying the Local Authority and the Police

Local Acts often require that the organizers of a meeting or procession give advance notice to the local authority and the police station. This notice must be in writing, and must state the time of the meeting and the route of the procession. It should be delivered at least 36 hours before the meeting is due to start.

Even if local Acts do not insist on this, it may be wiser to notify the police in advance about any public meeting – especially if you are planning a large meeting with advance publicity which they are bound to know about anyway, or if your organization enjoys good relations with the police. If they raise no objections, you can safely assume that there will not be any police interference on any pretext unless the meeting causes some unexpected disturbance.

If your organization is not on good terms with the police and you notify them in advance, you might find yourself in difficulties if they object to your holding it or suggest that you do so subject to certain conditions. However, they do not have the power to forbid you to hold meetings, nor to lay down conditions – they can only give advice. You are under no obligation to follow their advice, but if you ignore it, you are obviously more likely to meet with police interference. The only time when the police are entitled to lay down conditions is when they decide to exercise their powers under the Public Order Act 1936, s.3; they can do so only if they have reasonable grounds to suspect that 'serious public disorder' may occur. (◇ p. 74)

(3) Obstruction of the Highway

If you take part in a procession or street meeting, you may be charged with 'obstructing the highway': this means acting in a way which is likely to prevent members of the public from freely crossing or passing along the street.

Any street meeting is likely to be technically an obstruction, but for an obstruction to constitute an offence, there must be an *unreasonable* use of the highway. On the whole, a moving procession is less likely to amount to an unreasonable use of the highway than a stationary meeting. The practical test is whether you are using the street reasonably, taking into consideration factors such as the time of day, the amount of traffic, the width of the road, and the number of people present.

The prosecution does not have to prove that you actually prevented someone from using the road, but it must show that your action was intentional or reckless.

If you plan to use a site which has been used frequently for public meetings and has become a traditional meeting-place, you can normally assume that there is no danger of causing an obstruction at that place – but do not rely on this, as there have been some notable exceptions.

Obstruction of the highway is a common law offence, punishable by a fine and imprisonment at the discretion of the court; and an offence under the Highways Act 1959, s.121, punishable with a maximum fine of £50.

(4) Breach of the Peace

The police sometimes object to the holding of a meeting on the grounds that it is likely to cause a breach of the peace (◊ pp. 53 ff.). 'Breach of the peace' is very loosely interpreted by the courts: it is only necessary to show that it was 'reasonable' to suspect that the behaviour in question would lead to a disturbance involving physical force. One case which illustrates how loosely this can be interpreted is Duncan *v.* Jones (1936).

Here are the facts of the case. A speaker was about to hold a public meeting near the entrance to a training centre. A policeman told her she could not hold it there but could hold it in another street about 175 yards away. She nevertheless began to address the meeting and was arrested. There was no allegation that anyone there had committed, incited or provoked a breach of the peace, but a meeting held at the same place by the same speaker 14 months earlier had been stopped by a disturbance. The superintendent of the centre thought that the meeting had caused the disturbance and that further meetings in the same place might have the same results. It was held that the policeman 'reasonably' feared a breach of the peace. The speaker was convicted of obstructing a police officer in the execution of his duty.

The effect of this decision was to create an offence based on a 'reasonable' (but in practice usually very subjective) apprehension of a danger to the peace.

(5) Words Used at Meetings

The words used by speakers at meetings may result in court action. The most likely charges are:

(a) The criminal charge of 'threatening, abusive or insulting words'. (◊ pp. 54–5)

(b) *Defamation:* You may be faced with a civil action for slander if you accuse individuals or identifiable groups of a serious crime, or of being unfit for their jobs. It is a defence if everything you say about them can be shown to be true, but this can be very difficult as the burden of proof is on the defence. (◊ pp. 124 ff.)

(6) Wearing Uniforms

It is an offence to wear a uniform in a public place or at a public meeting if the uniform signifies that you are associated with a political organization or the promotion of a political object. However, if a chief officer of police is satisfied that there is no

65

risk to public order involved in wearing a uniform on a special occasion he may, with the Home Secretary's consent, allow the uniform to be worn, subject to whatever conditions he sees fit.

The offence of wearing a uniform is punishable by imprisonment for up to 3 months or a fine of up to £50. Once a person has been charged with the offence, no further proceedings can be taken without the consent of the Attorney General. If consent is not given, the accused should be discharged and bound over (◊ p. 54) (Public Order Act 1936).

(7) Behaviour at Meetings

(a) Political meetings sometimes result in charges of 'threatening, abusive or insulting behaviour'. (◊ pp. 54–5)

It is an offence to use 'threatening, abusive or insulting' words or behaviour, or to distribute or display any 'threatening, abusive or insulting' writing or picture, if it is likely or intended to provoke a breach of the peace. As explained above (p. 62), a place or meeting is 'public' whenever members of the public are admitted, regardless of whether they have paid to get in. So the kind of behaviour covered by this provision is extremely wide. In one case it was used to obtain a conviction where only one obscene word had been used in shouting a political slogan, without any evidence that there was, or might have been, a breach of the peace.

There must be some reasonable likelihood of a breach of the peace and the words or behaviour must be serious. But magistrates tend to be very subjective and ignore the necessity for evidence of a real or probable breach of the peace.

(b) Unlawful and riotous assembly, rout, sedition. (◊ pp. 55–7)

(8) Restrictions on Meetings near the Houses of Parliament

(a) *Political Meetings and Processions:* Open-air meetings and processions may not be held within one mile of the Houses of Parliament, north of the Thames, if:

(i) There are more than 50 participants, and

(ii) Parliament is sitting on that day, and

(iii) The purpose of the meeting is to consider or prepare 'any Petition, Complaint, Remonstrance, Declaration or other Address' to the Crown or to either House, 'for alteration in matters of Church or State' (Seditious Meetings Act 1817).

This, in effect, would ban any meeting dealing with a subject which is the concern of the Crown or Parliament and would apply to almost any ordinary political meeting.

(b) *Other Meetings and Processions:* At the beginning of each Parliamentary session, the Commissioner of Police makes an order banning *all* open-air meetings and processions within a certain distance of Westminster on any day when Parliament is sitting (Metropolitan Police Act 1839, s.52).

The banned area is roughly within a mile radius of Parliament, north of the Thames. It is bounded by the south side of the Thames, from Waterloo Bridge to Vauxhall Bridge, along Vauxhall Bridge Road to Victoria Street and from there to Grosvenor Gardens and Grosvenor Place to Hyde Park Corner, along Piccadilly, Coventry Street and the north side of Leicester Square, through Cranbourne Street, Long Acre, Bow Street and Wellington Street and over Waterloo Bridge.

The ban only applies to meetings and processions which actually obstruct the free passage of M.P.s to and from the Houses of Parliament, or which cause disorder or annoyance in the neighbourhood. The police have no right to forbid meetings in this area on days when Parliament is not sitting.

(9) Meetings in Trafalgar Square

Meetings in Trafalgar Square (the most important traditional meeting-place in Britain) are governed by special regulations made by the Department of the Environment. The following acts are prohibited unless permission is first obtained from the Department:

(i) Making or giving a public speech or address.

  (ii) Placing or exhibiting any display or representation.

 (iii) Using loudspeakers, etc.

 (iv) Causing any obstruction to free passage.

  (v) Using artificial light or a tripod or stand for photography.

 (vi) Organizing, conducting or taking part in any assembly, parade or procession (Trafalgar Square Regulations 1952).

In theory, the Department does not exercise any discrimination and the only facts that should be considered when granting permission are:

(i) Whether or not the meeting will interfere with the ordinary life of London by causing traffic congestion.

(ii) What advice is received from the police (who must be consulted in each case) on the maintenance of public order.

Despite this, there have in the past been a number of refusals which appeared to amount to political discrimination. It is vitally important that Trafalgar Square is available for the free expression of public opinion.

Less conventional forms of presentation such as music, drama and display have been included in a number of meetings recently – and the Department of the Environment has occasionally raised objections. If you are planning this kind of activity, it is best to negotiate in advance and, if necessary, seek advice and assistance from the NCCL at an early stage.

(10) Meetings on Private Premises

The right to hold a meeting on private premises (in or out of doors) depends on getting the permission of the owner or occupier. If you fail to do this, you may be accused of trespass, although this is only a civil wrong, not a criminal offence.

For this reason, people often think that bomb sites and other derelict land are good places to hold meetings, since the owner is hardly likely to come along and enforce his rights. But bear in mind that the owner may at any time insist that you leave his land and he may use reasonable force to get you out.

If you intend to hold a meeting on land which is not completely derelict, or in a private building, it is always advisable to get permission. Otherwise, you may find yourself charged with more serious criminal offences, such as burglary or wilful damage to property.

Conduct of Meetings

Heckling and Breaking Up Meetings

It is illegal to try to break up a meeting (Public Meeting Act 1908); penalties are especially severe if the meeting is in connection with an election (Representation of the People Act 1949).

Anyone has the right to heckle, provided that it is kept within reasonable limits. If a heckler goes too far and acts in a disorderly way, he may be charged with trying to break up the meeting, or with some other offence. (◊ p. 65–6)

Taking Names and Addresses

If a policeman reasonably suspects a person of trying to disrupt a public meeting, or of inciting others to do so, he may, at the request of the chairman of the meeting, ask that person to give him his name and address and, if he refuses, arrest him. In practice, the police sometimes allow the person to leave the meeting instead (Public Order Act 1936).

The police have claimed that under the Public Order Act 1936, names and addresses may be given to the chairman as well as to the policeman – hence the objectionable practice of informing the chairman of the interrupter's name and address, which sometimes leads to his victimization. It has not yet been decided by the courts if the chairman does have a right to these particulars.

The police often ask for the names and addresses of the organizers of meetings and of speakers: they have no right to this information unless they give a valid reason, nor do they have the right to demand names and addresses of members of deputations visiting embassies. Some people may see little point in refusing on principle to give the police this information. However there may be a tendency to use it for the purposes of intimidation, and this should be discouraged.

Stewards

At meetings held on private premises, a reasonable number of stewards may be employed to help keep order and they may be assigned certain duties and given badges, but this is an exception. At all other meetings (i.e. nearly all outdoor meetings), it is illegal to train or equip stewards so that they might be able to take over the functions of the police; or to train or equip them to make a show of force to promote a political objective (Public Order Act 1936).

If this law were strictly enforced, no one would be able to use stewards at outdoor meetings, except perhaps to take round collection boxes or to sell literature. This seems an unreasonable restriction, but there is some safeguard in the fact that no prosecution may be brought without the consent of the Attorney General.

Quite apart from this, it is worth remembering that stewards have no right to ask people to leave if the meeting is held in a public place.

Meetings on Private Premises

(1) *The Right to Attend Council Meetings*

Any meeting of a local authority or local authority committee is open to the public (Public Bodies (Admission to Meetings) Act 1960). However, an authority may pass a resolution excluding the public from any meeting if it feels that it would be in the public interest to exclude them, due to the confidential nature of the business or for some other reason. The reason must be stated in the resolution.

(2) *The Right to Remove Members of an Audience*

People who attend a meeting held on private premises (e.g. in a hall hired for the purpose) do so technically at the invitation of the organizers. Therefore the organizers have the right to refuse admission to anyone without giving a reason, whether or not there is an admission charge. If someone forces his way in after being forbidden to enter, he is trespassing and the stewards may throw him out, provided that they do not use unreasonable force.

When it comes to getting rid of a member of the audience once he has been allowed in, the rules differ according to whether or not he has paid an entrance fee:

(a) If he has not paid an entrance fee (or if there has been only a voluntary collection), the organizers have the right to ask him to leave and, if he refuses, the stewards may use reasonable force to make him leave.

(b) If he has paid to go in, the organizers cannot normally make him leave without the risk of being sued for breach of contract. But they may reserve the right to exclude any person after he has been admitted by displaying a notice to this effect on the tickets or in the entrance hall.

If a member of the audience acts in a disorderly way during the meeting, the organizers can certainly ask him to leave and throw him out if necessary, on the grounds that they fear a breach of the peace.

(3) *Rights of the Police*

The police have no right to attend meetings held on private premises unless they are invited by the organizers. It is, however, their duty to prevent crime (including breach of the peace), and if they reasonably believe that a breach of the peace is likely to be committed at a meeting to which the public have been invited, they have the right to enter without a warrant to prevent this happening.

Recently there has been a disturbing tendency for plain-clothes policemen to turn up without authorization, and for prosecutions to be launched based on their evidence. Organizers and speakers should bear this possibility in mind.

(4) *Refusals by Owners to Let Halls*

Owners of halls have every right to refuse to let their property whenever they like – it is purely a matter of private contract. But there are certain exceptions:

(a) During general and local elections, candidates have rights (subject to conditions) to use rooms in publicly owned schools and certain other publicly owned meeting places (Representation of the People Act 1949).

(b) Where halls have been established under trust deeds, the powers of the trustees to refuse lettings may be limited – it is usually worth looking into this possibility.

It sometimes happens that owners agree to let out a hall and then try to reverse the decision. Unless it is written into the contract that they reserve the right to do this, a civil action may be brought against them for an injunction and damages. But proceedings could be costly and it is best to get legal advice first.

Experience has shown that when owners of halls show unreasonable bias in refusing to let their property, local publicity and pressure can sometimes persuade them to change their policy.

Further Information

⇨ p. 81

8. Processions

Most processions are lawful, as they simply consist of people exercising their legal right to move along the highway. But there are a number of exceptions.

(1) Obstruction

If a procession is large and unwieldy, it may be obstructing the traffic, which is an offence (▷ p. 64). If a policeman orders marchers to disperse, their leader should point out that they are exercising their right to use the highway. If the policeman persists, the marchers must then decide whether they are causing a genuine obstruction (i.e. their use of the highway is unreasonable), in which case they should disperse; or whether the policeman is exceeding his duty, in which case it may be worth continuing the procession and risking arrest.

(2) Police Conditions

The police have a long-established right to regulate the route of processions. In addition, if a chief officer has grounds for suspecting that a procession is likely to cause 'serious public disorder', he may impose whatever rules or directions he considers necessary to preserve order. But he may not restrict the use of banners and flags, etc., unless this is necessary to prevent a risk of breach of the peace (Public Order Act 1936).

(3) Special Powers to Ban Processions

In very special circumstances, the chief officer may apply to the local authority for a temporary ban on processions, if he can satisfy them that the powers described above are insufficient to enable him to prevent a 'serious public disorder'. The local authority may then, with the consent of the Secretary of State, make an order prohibiting some or all processions in that area for up to 3 months. In London, the Commissioner of Police for the Metropolis or of the City of London can make the order, with the consent of the Home Secretary (Public Order Act 1936).

Police Commissioners have power to make an order laying down which routes may be taken by all people and vehicles 'in all times of public processions, rejoicings or illuminations and in any case where the streets are thronged or liable to be obstructed' (Metropolitan Police Act 1839, s. 52; Town Police Clauses Act 1847, s. 21). The Divisional Court has made it clear that the Acts are strictly limited in their application and that they should only be used to prevent obstruction.

(4) Police Advice

Remember that the police only have the right to lay down conditions if they anticipate 'serious public disorder'. Sometimes they try to enforce restrictions indirectly by saying that an obstruction or some other offence may be caused, or by giving 'advice'. If this happens, the organizers must decide whether or not the police requirements are reasonable, in which case they should be obeyed, or whether they are so far-fetched that it is possible to ignore them.

(5) Advance Notice to the Police

Some local Acts require advance notice of processions to be given to the police; and in some circumstances, it is advisable to do so anyway. ($\Diamond$ p. 63)

(6) Processions near Parliament

Most processions are banned within a certain distance of Westminster while Parliament is sitting. (♢ pp. 66–7)

Further Information

♢ p. 81

9. Propaganda

Poster Parades

The police have no special power to censor the wording on posters, but they have been known to interfere with poster parades for two reasons:

(1) That they are likely to cause a breach of the peace.
(2) That the wording on the posters is 'threatening, abusive or insulting' (Public Order Act 1936, s. 5 as amended by the Race Relations Act 1965, s.7).

This kind of interference is justified only if the wording on the poster is extremely offensive, or if there are other very exceptional circumstances.

On occasions, the police have used this provision in a way that is quite contrary to its purpose. The following case is an example – it seemed that the police considered that people practising racial discrimination were doing nothing wrong, whereas those trying to end it were potential criminals:

In 1967, eight members of the Oxford Committee for Racial Integration picketed a ladies' hairdresser which had refused to serve coloured customers. They carried placards saying 'This shop has a colour bar' and 'Other Oxford hairdressers serve everyone'. They were arrested and charged with displaying insulting signs contrary to Section 7 of the Race Relations Act 1965. The magistrate dismissed the charge without hearing the defence evidence.

If the police put a ban on processions (◊ p. 74), poster parades are usually allowed, as long as the participants walk in single file in the gutter and are widely spaced out.

Flyposting

Flyposting (i.e. sticking up posters in public places) is illegal – and that applies to any words, letters, signs, placards, notices, or anything else that might be considered as an advertisement, announcement or direction (Town and Country Planning Act 1962). The fine is a maximum of £100 on a first conviction, and £5 for every day after that until the offending poster is removed.

You cannot put up a poster anywhere without the consent of the local planning authority, which is usually the County Council or, in London, the Borough Council. However, advertisements for local non-commercial events (those of a religious, political, educational, cultural, social, or recreational character, and parliamentary or local elections) can be displayed without the consent of the planning authority, provided the following conditions are observed:

(1) You have the consent of the site-owner.

(2) The poster does not block or obscure the view of a road.

(3) The poster is no bigger than 6 feet square (except election posters).

(4) Election posters are taken down 14 days after the poll.

(5) You comply with other minor conditions.

These conditions do not apply to advertisements displayed on vehicles, but it is illegal to use a vehicle purely for advertising purposes within 6 miles of Charing Cross (Metropolitan Streets Act 1867).

Local regulations also forbid flyposting. In the London area, for example, it is illegal to put up posters in any public place or to deface or write or paint on any building, wall, or fence (Metropolitan Police Act 1839; City of London Police Act 1839).

It is illegal to display any advertisement or notice which might be understood as 'indicating an intention to do an act of discrimination' (Race Relations Act 1968). You cannot be prosecuted by the police for this, only sued by the Race Relations Board. (⇨ p. 264)

Loudspeakers and Bands

If you are planning to use a loudspeaker or a band, first check up on the local Acts and by-laws, which often include special regulations to limit noise. You can get this information from your local authority.

To use loudspeakers for non-commercial purposes, you must usually give at least 48 hours' advance notice to the local police station. It is usually illegal to use loudspeakers in the streets for the purpose of advertising a trade or business. Loudspeakers, megaphones and all amplifiers are forbidden in any public place between 9 p.m. and 8 a.m. They are forbidden at all times if used to advertise an organized entertainment, trade, or business. Bands are usually allowed, provided they are not too loud or continuous, nor used at an unreasonable time so as to be a public nuisance (Noise Abatement Act 1960). But remember that something which is allowed by this Act may still be prohibited by a local Act or by-law.

In the London area, it is illegal to use any noisy instrument, including a loudspeaker, for the purpose of calling people together, announcing a show or entertainment, selling, distributing or collecting any article, or collecting money. However, this does not prevent you from using a loudspeaker at a meeting, provided that you are not calling people together or taking a collection. You can also announce a meeting, since this cannot be classed as a show or entertainment. Be careful how you phrase the announcement: if you say, 'Come to a meeting at the Town Hall tonight', you may be accused of calling people together, but you can quite legally say, 'There will be a meeting at the Town Hall tonight' (Metropolitan Police Act 1839; City of London Police Act 1839).

Before you use a loudspeaker or band in a park or similar open space, make sure you know the local regulations. In Hyde Park, for instance, you cannot use loudspeakers without the prior consent of the Department of the Environment.

Selling and Distributing Literature in the Street

Non-commercial organizations who are selling or distributing literature for propaganda are not usually covered by local regulations which control street trading and the distribution of advertising matter in the streets. Even when they are, they can often get a special exemption. 'Distribution' means distributing to the public at large, not to one individual, or to an association of which the publisher or distributor is a member.

You may not carry or distribute any print, board, placard, notice, or leaflet in any street within 6 miles of Charing Cross, unless you do so in a way which is approved by the Commissioner of Police (Metropolitan Streets Act 1867). Obviously, a lot depends on how the police exercise their discretion.

Literature may be sold at public meetings in Trafalgar Square, but only with written permission from the Department of the Environment. You must apply in advance. Permission applies to the period of the meeting but is not limited to one specific day.

It is illegal to distribute leaflets on which the wording is 'threatening, abusive or insulting' with the intention of creating a breach of the peace or in circumstances where it is likely to create a breach (Public Order Act 1936, as amended by the Race Relations Act 1965). This section was given an unusual twist by the court's decision in the following case:

In 1968, Gwyneth Williams was prosecuted for distributing leaflets to American servicemen. The leaflet criticized the US Government for its involvement in Vietnam in restrained and unprovocative language. Yet the court held that it was 'insulting' because it invited its readers to consider deserting if they agreed with its arguments: it was 'insulting' to ask a soldier even to consider such a thing.

The main difficulty you are likely to meet when selling or distributing literature is that you may be accused of causing an obstruction. Try to keep to the kerb and be careful not to get in the way of cars or pedestrians. If a policeman thinks that you are causing a real obstruction, he should only ask you to move on. He has no right to confiscate your literature. If he asks you to move on, do so immediately, at a reasonable walking pace, keeping to the kerb to avoid obstruction. As long as you do this, the policeman has no right to follow you and tell you to go away. There is nothing to stop you selling or distributing your literature as you go.

After you have left the congested area you may, if it seems reasonable, stop again. The policeman may then, at his discretion, tell you to move on and it is advisable to do as he says. But if he seems to be following you around and ordering you to move on even in uncongested areas, take his number. You may wish to make a formal complaint later.

You may also find that the police interfere on the grounds that, owing to the content of the literature, your behaviour is likely to cause a breach of the peace. This charge may be justifiable, depending on the circumstances. If, for example, someone persists in distributing anti-immigrant leaflets in a predominantly immigrant area, he may justly be charged with this offence.

Written Material

Any printed book or paper intended for publication or distribution (including duplicated sheets) must bear the name and address of the printer. If this is not done, both the printer and the distributor can be prosecuted. Printers must keep for 6 months a copy of everything they print, and must write on each article the name and address of the person who commissioned the work.

The publication and distribution of written material is also controlled by the libel laws (◇ p. 124) and the Race Relations Acts. (◇ p. 264)

Collecting Signatures in the Street

There are no laws or regulations which forbid you to collect signatures in any street or public place, although you may be accused of causing an obstruction. (◊ p. 64)

Further Information

I. Brownlie, *The Law Relating to Public Order*, Butterworth, London, 1968

J. F. Archbold, *Pleading, Evidence and Practice in Criminal Cases*, Sweet & Maxwell, London, 1969

Stone's Justice's Manual, Butterworth, London, published annually

NCCL

10. Fund-Raising, Gaming, and Lotteries

Fund-Raising

Street Collections

You may take a collection in the street with a police permit, but these are extremely hard to get, unless you are collecting for a big charity.

Find out from the local authority the regulations controlling collections. In the Metropolitan Police District (most of Greater London, excluding the City of London), no collections may be made without the consent of the Commissioner of Police. As a general rule, not more than one collection is allowed per week in one locality and the aim is to keep the number of street collections as low as possible. There is no system of appeal against the Commissioner's decision. The following conditions are also imposed:

(1) Collectors should not be under 16.

(2) They must remain in one place, at least 30 yards from one another.

(3) They must carry written authorization, which must be shown to a policeman on demand.

(4) No tables may be used if they are bigger than 30 inches by 20 inches.

(5) Collectors must not be accompanied by animals.

(6) Tins must be labelled.

(7) Accounts of the collection must be submitted within one month.

You may make a collection at an open-air meeting without a

police permit, provided that you operate within a reasonable distance of the meeting. A 'reasonable distance' has not been defined, but as long as you are walking around near the meeting, you have the right to collect from passers-by and from the audience. If the meeting is being held in a park or similar open space, collections may be prohibited by the by-laws of the park.

House-to-House Collections

It is illegal to travel from house to house appealing to the public to give money or property to a charity, without a licence from the local police (House to House Collections Act 1939).

The Act applies even if the collector gives something in exchange for what he gets. It has also been known to apply in the case of a genuine sale of articles, when the salesman has made it known that part of the purchase price is to go to a charity. It does not apply to collections made by one member of an organization among other members of the same body.

Collectors must not be under 16, they must carry a collection box or receipt book, and wear a badge, and they must not receive payment for their work.

A policeman may ask anyone whom he believes to be collecting for a charitable purpose to give his name, address, and signature.

The Act only applies to charitable collections, i.e. all benevolent and philanthropic concerns, such as relief of poverty and the advancement of religion and education at home and abroad; it would probably include fund-raising for a local club or for the relief of strikers. But an appeal for funds for a political party would not be subject to these regulations.

Borderline cases, of course, are determined by the views of the magistrate, but unlicensed door-to-door collectors have not normally been prosecuted unless they were not collecting for a 'charity' in the conventional sense of the word.

You can apply for a licence to the local chief officer of police. The procedure and conditions are rather complicated, but you can get information about this from your local police station. If the collection is confined to only one locality and is not likely to continue for long, you can sometimes get a certificate of exemption by a much simpler procedure; but it is left to the discretion of the chief of police as to whether or not to grant one.

If a charitable collection is made without a licence, both the organizer and the collector can be prosecuted and fined. The organizer is liable to a maximum fine of £100 and/or 6 months' imprisonment, but the collector can only be fined £5 for a first offence.

The House to House Collections Act 1939 also applies to the door-to-door sale of literature.

Gaming and Lotteries

Gaming

The gaming laws are very complicated. This chapter deals only with non-commercial gaming for the purpose of charitable or political fund-raising, which is bound by a separate set of regulations.

'Gaming' is defined as games of pure chance (dice, roulette, bingo, etc.) and games of chance combined with skill (card games, chess, etc.).

Gaming on Unlicensed Premises

(a) In private homes or semi-private institutions, any gaming may be carried on, provided that no one is charged a fee for taking part.

(b) Elsewhere, games which involve playing or staking against a 'bank' and games in which chances are not equal are not allowed. Therefore in unlicensed clubs, for example, only games such as whist, cribbage, poker, and bingo may be played. There may be an inclusive charge of up to 50p. No levies may be made on the stake or on the winnings.

(c) Games and amusements with prizes require a special permit. This may be obtained from the local licensing authority. Any kind of game may be played, provided that the following conditions are obeyed: the maximum charge for one attempt is 5p;

no more than £2·50 may be taken in one game; £2·50 is the maximum amount of prize winnings at one time; the proceeds must not be devoted to private gain; the games or amusements must not be the sole or major attraction at the entertainment where they are carried on.

(d) If slot machines are installed at non-commercial entertainments, the person who sells or supplies them must have a permit. There is no limit to the number of machines or prizes at one event. The proceeds must not be for private gain.

(e) For any other gaming at entertainments held for a good cause, an all-in charge of 50p is allowed. The total value of prizes distributed at one event must not be more than £50. The proceeds must go towards the 'good cause'.

(f) Other general regulations: no one under 18 may take part; the prohibition of public advertising of gaming does not apply to non-commercial entertainments or those held for a good cause.

Gaming on Licensed Premises

If gaming is carried on in licensed premises, most of the above regulations, with the important exception of (f), do not apply. A person applying for a licence must first obtain a certificate from the Gaming Board and then apply to the local licensing authority.

Inspectors appointed under the Gaming Act 1968 have the power to enter licensed premises without a warrant to inspect equipment and books.

Lotteries

Most lotteries are illegal and anyone connected with them may be liable to prosecution. Listed below are three types of lottery which are lawful and the main regulations which must be obeyed. In all three cases, the winner may not be determined by more than three factors: each factor must be either the result of a draw or similar means of selection; or the outcome of an event.

(1) Registered Lotteries

Non-commercial organizations, such as charities and cultural or sports societies, may apply to the local authority for registration. The application may only be turned down on specified grounds and there is a right of appeal to Quarter Sessions against refusal. The registration fee is £1·25. Non-members may take part.

(a) The organizers must make accounts to the local authority as to how much money has been raised; in certain cases, duty may be payable on the proceeds.

(b) The person who organizes the lottery must be a member of the society, authorized in writing by the committee. He may not be paid for this work.

(c) Proceeds must be devoted to the purposes of the society. No more than 10 per cent may be deducted as expenses and no more than half the proceeds may be spent on prizes.

(d) No prize may be worth more than £100.

(e) Tickets may not be sold for more than 5p each and the total value of all tickets sold must not exceed £750.

(f) Each ticket must cost the same and must be printed with the price of the ticket, the name and address of the organizers, and a statement that no prize will be given to anyone except the person with the winning ticket.

(g) Tickets may not be sent through the post, except to members of the society.

(h) All tickets must be sold at their face value.

(i) No one under 16 may buy a ticket.

(j) The lottery may not be advertised.

(2) *Lotteries Promoted as Part of an Entertainment*

These include lotteries held at bazaars, fêtes, dances, and sporting events.

(a) The lottery may not be the major attraction of the event.

(b) Proceeds, after expenses are deducted, may not be devoted to private gain.

(c) Expenses are limited; not more than £10 may be spent on prizes.

(d) Money prizes are not allowed.

(e) Both the sale of tickets and the announcement of the winners must take place during the entertainment.

(3) *Private Lotteries*

These are lotteries organized exclusively for people who work or live in the same premises, or belong to the same society (but not if the society exists for the purpose of gambling).

(a) Only the cost of stationery and of printing tickets may be deducted as expenses. The rest of the proceeds must be spent on prizes or on the purposes of the society.

(b) Regulations for registered lotteries (f), (g), (h) and (j) also apply to private lotteries.

Further Information and Advice

Charity Commission
Charities Act 1960 Betting, Gaming and Lotteries Act 1963
Gaming Act 1968
Eddy and Loewe, The New Law of Gaming, Butterworth, 1970

11. Complaints Against the Police

There are a number of ways of pursuing a complaint against the police:

(1) Official complaints to police.
(2) Complaints in court.
(3) Complaints to M.P. and Press.
(4) Complaints to the NCCL.
(5) Civil proceedings.
(6) Criminal proceedings.
(7) Independent inquiry.

The remedies are not mutually exclusive. For example, it is possible to make an official complaint and to bring civil proceedings at the same time.

(1) Official Complaints

You can make a complaint to the chief officer of police in the appropriate area. (He is known as the Chief Constable in areas outside London and as the Commissioner of Police in the Metropolitan area.) He is obliged to record your complaint and have it investigated. He can ask a senior police officer from another area to conduct an official inquiry, and he must do so if directed by the Home Secretary. When he receives the report from the inquiry, he must send it to the Director of Public Prosecutions unless he is satisfied that no criminal offence has been committed (Police Act 1964, s.49).

Although a chief officer is not obliged to let inquiries be made by officers from other police areas (Section 49 says that he 'may' ask for such inquiries), it is usual for him to do so.

In theory, leaflets which explain how to make complaints should be provided at every police station, and a copy should be sent to anyone who makes a complaint and to any other person who asks for one. In practice, police stations do not always have these leaflets available and are occasionally reluctant to hand them out to anyone.

How to Make a Complaint

You may call at any police station and make your complaint in person, but generally it is better to submit a detailed report of your complaint in a letter. An investigating officer will contact you and ask to interview you. You can ask for the interview to take place at your home or at another place, such as a lawyer's office, rather than at the police station, and this has obvious psychological advantages. Remember to keep a copy of your letter of complaint.

When you make a statement to the investigating officer, make sure that the final written version of the statement represents accurately what you have said and also represents the substance of your complaint. Ask for a copy to be made and given to you. It is unlikely that a copy will be handed to you unless you ask for it, and difficulties have been experienced by complainants in obtaining copies later. If you are not satisfied with the statement, do not sign it. Check that the emphasis is correct.

If there are any witnesses, give their names and addresses to the police so that they may be interviewed, and make sure that they also keep copies of their statements. (As you will see, this is most important if you later decide to take civil proceedings.)

When the investigating officer has completed his inquiries by interviewing you, your witnesses, and the police officers concerned, he will draw up a report and make one of four conclusions:

(a) *That the complaint is unsubstantiated.* If so, the complainant will be informed of this in a brief letter. The report is treated as

89

confidential and no evidence will be given for the decision.

(b) *That the complaint is substantiated but trivial.* The complainant will be given an apology. This happens rarely since the police are unwilling to admit even minor faults. If there were more apologies, complainants might be less suspicious that the whole method of inquiry is unreliable.

(c) *That there are reasonable grounds for a complaint under the Police Discipline Code* (i.e. there is a *prima facie* case). There will be a quasi-legal inquiry, held in private. The complainant should be present but he may be excluded when confidential matters are discussed. He may be accompanied by a friend, but not by a lawyer or any other professional representative. He should be called as first witness and told what the charges arising from his complaint are, and whether the accused officer admits or denies the charge. He should also be assured that nothing has taken place before his arrival that might have an effect on the case.

The complainant may question the accused officer, but the chief officer may forbid him to ask questions that he considers to be irrelevant. (According to regulations, questions concerning previous disputes between the complainant and the officer might be considered irrelevant: this seems most irrational.)

If the officer is found guilty, he can be punished in a number of ways, ranging from a caution to dismissal. The complainant is allowed to hear what decision is reached, but not what penalty is given.

(d) *That there are reasonable grounds for a criminal prosecution.* If so, all papers must be sent to the Director of Public Prosecutions. The vast majority of these cases are dismissed by the DPP and only about 10 per cent of them lead to prosecution. According to Home Office Regulations, when it is decided that criminal proceedings will not be taken, there should still be disciplinary proceedings if there is adequate evidence to justify a charge under the disciplinary code. This happens very rarely: all too often, chief officers use the DPP's decision as an excuse to dismiss the whole matter.

Trivial Complaints

Remember that the police often work under considerable pressure and while you should never be discouraged from bringing a complaint if you feel you have a genuine grievance, trivial complaints are a waste of time.

(2) Complaints in Court

Magistrates in criminal courts seldom seem to take complaints against the police very seriously. They either refuse to listen altogether, or they tend to say that they do not believe the complaints are true. Nevertheless, if you feel it necessary to make a complaint in court, you should do so. If a sufficient number of defendants made similar complaints in court, even the most unsympathetic magistrates should begin to take notice.

If you have been charged with an offence and you want to make a complaint against the police in connection with this, do not do so without legal advice: it may have an adverse effect on your case. Your lawyer can make a complaint on your behalf at the most suitable time. Usually complaints are not investigated until after the case has been completed but it is better to give notice at the earliest opportunity that you intend to complain when the case is over. In practice, complaints rarely succeed if you are found guilty.

(3) Complaints to M.P.s and the Press

In certain cases, it might be worth complaining to your M.P. or publicizing your complaint through the Press: police are naturally sensitive to public opinion. However, they are also extremely prompt to take legal action against any form of defamation, and the Police Federation will finance libel suits.

(4) Complaints to the NCCL

The NCCL has had experience over a number of years of taking up police complaints. It will always examine any complaint against the police and will assist in pursuing it where there is a substantial case.

Because of the amount of time and money involved in civil proceedings, people often prefer to make an official complaint first, knowing that they can take civil action if this fails. But in practice, it is nearly always impossible to succeed in a civil action once the police have dismissed a complaint. The main reasons for this are:

(a) The police are well prepared to fight the case, since they have all the statements made by you and your witnesses during the inquiry.

(b) You have no knowledge of their case, since you have not seen any police statements, nor the report of the inquiry.

(c) You may not remember exactly what you said to the investigating officer unless you have kept copies of your statements and those of your witnesses.

In addition, you will be told that disciplinary action will not be taken against the accused officer until the case has been concluded.

It is worth noting that a chief officer can be held responsible if one of his officers commits a tort, e.g. assault or false imprisonment. Therefore, in such cases you do not have to identify one particular constable before taking action.

(5) Civil Proceedings

In certain cases you can sue the police for damages instead of, or in addition to, making an official complaint, but it is essential to get legal advice on this. (It is possible, but not easy, to obtain Legal Aid.)

There is little point in pursuing a complaint by this method unless you have satisfactory supporting evidence. It will be necessary to show that the police have committed a tort (a civil wrong). For example, if you are wrongfully arrested you have a specific right, laid down by law, to claim damages for 'false imprisonment'. This phrase not only means being put into prison, but also being wrongfully detained or deprived of freedom when the police have no reasonable grounds for suspecting that you have committed or are likely to commit an offence. Similarly, in other circumstances, you may have an action for damages for trespass, assault, or even negligence.

(6) Criminal Proceedings

It is possible to bring criminal proceedings if your complaint involves a police officer having committed a criminal offence. False imprisonment is a criminal offence, in addition to being a civil wrong. Similarly, assault is criminal.

You should obtain legal advice before commencing criminal proceedings, as again you will need considerable evidence if you are to succeed with your case. You should remember that the purpose of criminal proceedings is to punish the offender and you will not be able to obtain compensation by this method.

An important point to remember is that if a prosecution is brought for assault you may be precluded later from bringing civil proceedings, whatever the outcome of the criminal case.

(7) Independent Inquiry

The only form of independent inquiry provided by law is a 'local inquiry' which the Home Secretary may order 'into any matter concerned with the policing of the area' (Police Act 1964, s.32). This inquiry may be held in public or in private, and should be given as much publicity as the Home Secretary considers to be in the public interest. Only one 'local inquiry' has been held since 1964.

(8) Proposals for Change

The present system of investigating complaints from within the force is highly unsatisfactory. The NCCL set out detailed proposals in a memorandum to the Home Secretary in October 1969 for a system of Independent Review Tribunals to examine complaints against the police. In June 1971 the Home Secretary was still engaged in re-examining the existing procedures.

Notes on Other Police Forces

(1) Docks and Railway Police and Other Special Forces

Docks and railways and similar public bodies have the right to raise their own police forces for the protection of their property. Members of these forces have the same powers as members of the regular police forces, subject to certain limitations. The most important of these limitations is territorial: they can use their police powers only within the area controlled by their employers or within a certain distance from it (usually a mile or less).

Complaints should be made to the chief constable of the particular force. Information can be obtained from any office of the docks, railways, etc.

(2) Private Police Forces

The recent increase in private security organizations has given rise to many complaints, particularly when these organizations try to interfere in industrial spheres by using plain-clothes informers, and when they employ large numbers of uniformed men, many of whom are ex-policemen, on private 'security' jobs.

A private security organization is employed by the Home Office to take care of potential immigrants at ports of entry, to ensure their safe custody and attendance at Immigration Appeal Tribunals. This is an objectionable extension of power.

Private police forces have no powers in addition to those of ordinary citizens.

12. Tribunals

Administrative tribunals have been set up by the Government to settle disputes between citizens and Government officials without the formality, cost and complication of the ordinary courts of law.

The following tribunals will be described individually in this chapter:

National Insurance Local Tribunals
Supplementary Benefit Appeal Tribunals
Local Valuation Courts
Rent Tribunals and Rent Assessment Committees
Industrial Tribunals
Medical Appeal Tribunals
National Health Disciplinary Bodies (Service Committees, Executive Councils and National Health Service Tribunals)
Mental Health Review Tribunals
Immigration Appeal Tribunals

General Description of Tribunals

Nearly all tribunals have a number of features in common.

(1) Openness

Most tribunal hearings are open to the public and the Press – the idea being that people should have confidence in the system if its activities are not kept secret. If the case involves disclosing highly personal information, the applicant may ask for a private hearing. Supplementary Benefit Appeal Tribunals are always in private for this reason, and Mental Health Review Tribunals are held in private unless the applicant asks for a public hearing.

(2) Informality

One of the great advantages of tribunals is that, unlike ordinary law courts, their atmosphere and procedure is informal, without any pretentious judicial trappings. Some tribunals are more informal than others, depending on the views of the chairman. This informality helps to put the applicant at ease and when he presents his case, he does not have to follow any strict rules. Where the parties are not represented, the chairman will usually ask most of the questions and he will control the hearing to prevent it being disrupted by unnecessary bickering or interruption.

(3) Cheapness

An applicant does not have to pay any fees to a tribunal and with the exception of a few tribunals not considered here, e.g. the Lands Tribunal, he cannot be made to pay costs if he loses the case (except, of course, his own if he chooses to employ a lawyer). Tribunals do not have the power to award costs to either party, but at welfare tribunals the applicant can usually claim travelling expenses. The informality of the proceedings is intended to make it unnecessary for anyone to have legal representation. In practice, this is not strictly true, but it is nevertheless easier and cheaper to appeal to a tribunal than to a court of law.

(4) Speed

Complex cases seldom take more than three hours to be settled; most cases are settled far more quickly than that. This should encourage applicants who might be put off by the idea of having to take a whole day, or more, off work.

(5) Expertise of Tribunal Members

Both chairman and members usually have an expert knowledge of the subject of their particular tribunal: in some cases they are professionally qualified, and in others they have had long experience of the work of their tribunal. Consequently, tribunals are better equipped than are the ordinary courts of law to deal with the cases which are brought before them.

(6) Appeals

You may appeal to the High Court against a tribunal's decision, but only on a point of law or incorrect procedure. If you do appeal, you will need expert legal advice and representation, but you may be able to obtain legal advice and aid (◊ pp. 14 ff.).

(7) Attendance

It is always advisable to attend the hearing in person, rather than submit your case in writing. At some tribunals, attendance is compulsory.

(8) Advice and Representation

At nearly all tribunals you are allowed to be represented by someone who may or may not be a lawyer. However, although you may be able to obtain legal advice, you cannot get Legal Aid for a tribunal hearing. This can be a severe setback for two reasons: (a) the law surrounding some tribunal cases is extremely complex; (b) the opposition (Government official, employer, landlord, etc.) is usually either an expert on the subject or well able to afford a lawyer. Legal Aid *is* available for appeals to the Land Tribunal, but this is far more like a law court and legal representation is usually essential.

There are various voluntary organizations from which you can obtain advice and, in some cases, representation. Many specialize in giving advice on a limited number of subjects, and these will be mentioned in the descriptions of individual tribunals which follow.

You can get advice on all tribunals from your Citizens' Advice Bureau, and if you are a member of a trade union, you should be able to get help from your local branch secretary. In many cases, trade unions provide free representation if their members apply to National Insurance Tribunals, Medical Appeal Tribunals and Industrial Tribunals.

In addition, there are local advice centres. Those in London include the Mary Ward Centre, Toynbee Hall, Cambridge House, the Neighbourhood Law Centre, the Claimants Union and the Citizens' Rights Office.

Individual Tribunals

The following descriptions are concerned only with procedure, not with your legal rights.

National Insurance Local Tribunals

Functions: To consider appeals against the decisions of local National Insurance Officers concerning the following National Insurance benefits: unemployment benefit; sickness benefit; maternity grants and allowances; widows' allowances, widowed mothers' allowances, and widows' pensions; guardians' allowances; retirement pensions and graduated retirement benefit; children's allowances; death grants ($\Diamond$ p. 178); and to consider industrial injury benefit appeals when the issue in dispute is not within the jurisdiction of the medical appeal tribunals.

How to Apply: If you disagree with the Officer's decision whether you are entitled to one of these benefits, or how much you should receive, you may appeal to the tribunal. Application forms are available from your local National Insurance Office.

Advice: If you belong to a trade union and you are claiming unemployment benefit, sickness benefit, or any other National Insurance benefit connected with your work, you should seek advice and, if possible, representation, from your local branch secretary. You may be able to get advice from your local Welfare Officer, or from the Child Poverty Action Group (particularly if you are claiming widow's or child's benefit).

Character: The tribunal consists of three members: a chairman, who is usually a lawyer, and two others, drawn from two panels representing employers and employees. Members of these two panels are appointed by the Department of Health and Social Security, but none of the members is an employee of the Department. The atmosphere is very informal – the applicant sits at the same table as the tribunal, and does not have to take an oath or stand up when giving evidence.

Procedure: The tribunal knows the basic facts of your case before the hearing, as its members have read your statement of appeal and the National Insurance Officer's statement supporting his decision. You present your case first. You or your representative may call witnesses, and may produce documentary evidence such as letters, docors' certificates, payslips, time sheets, etc. The tribunal asks you a number of questions and the Insurance Officer also questions you. You may question witnesses and inspect documents produced by the Insurance Officer.

Decision: The tribunal tells you its decision either at the hearing, or by post. It is not bound to give reasons unless you ask for them and you should do this at the time or immediately after you hear the decision. It is best to ask for a written decision with reasons in case you decide to appeal.

Appeal: You may appeal against the tribunal's decision to the National Insurance Commissioner, but before you do so you should get expert advice, either from a solicitor or from your trade union.

Expenses: You are entitled to travelling expenses. The clerk of the tribunal usually deals with this.

(The National Insurance Tribunals were set up under the National Insurance Act 1965.)

Supplementary Benefit Appeal Tribunals

Function: To hear and determine appeals from people claiming or receiving supplementary benefit and family income supplement, against decisions of local Officers of the Supplementary Benefits Commission.

How to Apply: If you are not satisfied with the local Officer's decision as to whether you are entitled to receive supplementary benefit, or as to how much you should receive, you may appeal to the tribunal, but you must do so within 21 days of the decision (or later if the tribunal agrees). Application forms are available at the local office of the Supplementary Benefits Commission, but a letter merely stating 'I wish to appeal against the decision of ... (date) as to my benefit' is enough.

Advice: You may be able to get help with filling in the forms from your local Welfare Officer, from the Child Poverty Action Group, or from a claimants' union, if there is one in your area. One of these may also be able to provide you with a representative. You are entitled to be accompanied by not more than 2 persons at the hearing, either or both of whom may represent you, take notes or simply sit with you.

If you cannot get help from one of these sources, you should obtain a copy of the *Supplementary Benefit Handbook* from the local office of the Supplementary Benefits Commission, the Stationery Office or your local authority.

Character: The tribunal consists of a chairman and 2 other members, one from a panel representing workers, and the other appointed by the Minister for Social Security. The chairman is often a lawyer. The hearing, which is extremely informal, is always held in private except that research workers may, with your consent, be permitted to attend hearings.

Procedure: You will rarely win your case simply by going along to the tribunal and proving that you do not have enough money to live on: the statutes and regulations governing the Supplementary Benefits Scheme are very complex, and you or your representative must know and understand them; otherwise, the Officer from the Supplementary Benefits Commission will have more influence with the tribunal, as he is bound to have a thorough knowledge of the laws and practices of the scheme. You may produce witnesses and documents to back up your case and you may speak on your own behalf if you want to. You may be questioned by the chairman and sometimes by the other members of the tribunal; the Officer from the Supplementary Benefits Commission may also want to question you and your witnesses. You are entitled to question the Commission and any other witnesses.

Decision: You are told of the tribunal's decision either at the end of the hearing or later, by post. The tribunal must give you reasons for its decision, in writing, as soon as is practicable after the hearing.

Appeal: If the tribunal has made a mistake on a point of law, or if there has been a breach of the rules of natural justice, it may be possible to have your case reviewed by the High Court.

Expenses: You and your witnesses are entitled to travelling expenses and compensation for loss of wages. The clerk of the tribunal is responsible for this.

(Supplementary Benefit Appeal Tribunals were set up under the Ministry of Social Security Act 1966.)

Local Valuation Courts

Functions: To hear and judge objections to the proposals of Valuation Officers, who assess the rateable value of property for the Inland Revenue Department.

How to Apply: When you receive notice from your local Valuation Officer as to the proposed rateable value of your property, you will also receive the necessary forms for making an objection, should you wish to do so. There is an enormous backlog of cases, so the hearing of your objection may be postponed for anything up to 2 years.

Advice: You may be able to get help from the Surveyors Aid Scheme or from Shelter. Your case must be prepared thoroughly in advance, because rating valuation law and practice is a complex subject.

Character: Members of the court are selected from local panels, made up of councillors from local authorities. To ensure that the court is impartial, no councillor is allowed to sit at a hearing of an objection concerning property in his area. The hearing is fairly informal – more so than the Rent Tribunal.

Procedure: The Valuation Officer presents his case first, as an appeal against your objection. This is a great advantage to you, as you discover the grounds of his case and thus have a chance to present your own case more effectively. You may call witnesses, produce relevant documents, and question your witnesses after they have given evidence. When you have presented your case, the Valuation Officer may comment on any points in your argument.

Decision: If the case is not too complex, the court's decision will be given shortly after the hearing. However, the court may want to inspect your property and therefore postpone its decision until a later date. If so, you will be notified later on. You should always ask the reasons for its decision, in case you want to appeal.

Appeal: You may appeal to the Lands Tribunal, as long as you do so within 8 days of the original decision. You will need expert legal advice for this.

(Local Valuation Courts were set up under the General Rate Act 1967.)

Rent Tribunals

Function: Dealing only with furnished accommodation, the tribunal determines what is reasonable rent and whether or not tenants should have security of tenure. (◊ p. 184)

How to Apply: You may apply at any time to have a fair rent fixed, although tenants usually apply after they have received notice to quit. The tribunal cannot deal with an application for security of tenure alone, but only as part of an application to fix rent. The necessary forms are available from your Citizens' Advice Bureau or from the tribunal office. (Landlords and local authorities may also refer cases to the Rent Tribunal.)

Advice: You may be able to get advice, but not representation, from the Surveyors' Aid Scheme or from Shelter, as well as from your Citizens' Advice Bureau. It is important to get help with preparing your case and, if possible, representation – the law is complex and your landlord will probably be represented by a lawyer.

Character: Members of the tribunal are selected from panels nominated by the Minister for the Environment; the chairman is almost always a lawyer. Although less formal than a law court, the Rent Tribunal in some ways resembles a normal judicial hearing. The chairman and members sit at one table and the parties with their representatives sit at two separate tables. But do not be intimidated by this formality, as you will have your turn to put your case and argue against the other person's statements.

Procedure: The tribunal visits your home, often on the morning of the hearing. You should be there, so that you can draw their attention to relevant details. At the hearing, you may call witnesses and produce documentary evidence such as letters, plans, rent books, and agreements. You are questioned by the tribunal and by the landlord or his representative, and you or your representative may question the landlord and his witnesses. The tribunal does not have the power to make witnesses give evidence on oath.

Decision: The tribunal gives its decision either at the end of the hearing or later, by post. You should always ask for its reasons, in case you have grounds for an appeal.

Appeal: You may appeal to the High Court, but only on a point of law.

(Rent Tribunals hold jurisdiction under the Rent Act 1968.)

Rent Officer and Rent Assessment Committee

Function: To determine and register what is fair rent for unfurnished accommodation. (⟡ p. 186)

(1) *Rent Officer*

How to Apply: You should first apply to the Rent Officer. Application forms are available from the Rent Office or from your Citizens' Advice Bureau. The landlord and tenant may apply separately or jointly.

Advice: It is a good idea to consult the register of rents at your local Rent Office, to find out what rents are charged for accommodation similar to yours. You may be able to get help from the Surveyors' Aid Scheme.

Character: The Rent Officer is an independent statutory officer. If you have a consultation with him, it will be an informal discussion round a table.

Procedure: The Rent Officer informs the other party (i.e. the landlord if it is the tenant who has applied) that an application has been made and that a new rent has been proposed. He may ask either party to give him further information and he usually inspects the accommodation in question. If the other party does not agree to the proposed rent, he may submit his objections in writing. If there is no objection, the Rent Officer may then register the proposed rent as fair rent. If there is an objection, the Rent

Officer notifies the landlord and tenant that he proposes to hold a consultation: both may be present and both may be represented. At the consultation, witnesses are not usually called, but documentary evidence may be produced.

Decision: The Rent Officer decides on a fair rent and notifies the landlord and tenant. He then registers the rent.

Appeal: If you object to the Rent Officer's decision, you may appeal to the Rent Assessment Committee.

(2) *Rent Assessment Committee*

How to Apply: You must send a written objection to the Rent Officer within 28 days of receiving his decision. The case is then referred to the Assessment Committee.

Advice: You would be well advised to get expert advice from a valuer, land agent, or surveyor, if you can afford it; if not, you may be able to get voluntary help from the Surveyors' Aid Scheme. Failing this, you should consult your local register of rents, if you have not already done so.

Character: Members are chosen from panels nominated by the Minister for the Environment; the chairman is almost always a lawyer. The hearing is fairly formal – comparable to a Rent Tribunal.

Procedure: The Committee may ask the parties for further information. It notifies them of a certain date (at least 2 weeks ahead) before which they may submit their case in writing or ask for an oral hearing. If either party asks for an oral hearing, the Committee must agree to it and must give each party the chance to argue against the other's case. It usually inspects the premises in question before the hearing. There is no automatic right to call witnesses, but in practice, if you ask to call an expert witness such as a surveyor, you are allowed to do so, and if the other party calls witnesses, you may question them.

Decision: The Committee either confirms the Rent Officer's decision or determines a new 'fair rent', which is then registered.

You should always ask the reasons for its decision, in case you have grounds for an appeal.

Appeal: You may appeal to the High Court, but only on a point of law.

Industrial Tribunals

Function: The majority of cases deal with claims for redundancy payments, although the tribunal also has powers to deal with cases concerning selective employment payments, contracts of employment ($\diamond$ pp. 129–30) and industrial training.

How to Apply: If you are made redundant – i.e. if you are dismissed from your job because there is no longer any work for you – you may be entitled to redundancy payment; the amount you receive depends on how long you were employed in that job before you were dismissed, but you must have been employed there for at least two years. If your employer refuses to give you redundancy payment or if there is a dispute about the amount, you may appeal to the tribunal. You can get the application forms from the tribunal offices or from the local office of the Department of Employment.

Advice: If you are a member of a trade union, you should consult your local area organizer or branch secretary, or the legal department of your union, before you fill in the forms. It is important to get legal advice and, if possible, representation, because the law on redundancy is very complex and your employer will almost certainly be represented.

Character: The tribunal consists of a legally qualified chairman, and two other members drawn from two panels representing employers and employees. It usually takes place in a special Industrial Tribunals building; never in premises of the Department of Employment. (This independence is essential because the Department has a direct financial interest in the decisions of the tribunal: when employers have to make redundancy payments, they receive a rebate from the Department.) The hearing is more formal than many tribunals.

Procedure: You are sent a copy of your employer's written statement and notified of the date of the hearing. If you do not turn up and if you do not write asking for an adjournment, the tribunal may hear the case in your absence. If your employer does not attend the hearing, the Department of Employment may send someone to represent him.

Your case is presented first. You are asked to describe your job and the circumstances leading up to your dismissal; you may call witnesses and produce documentary evidence to support your case. The tribunal and the employer's representative question you. Do not be intimidated by the formality of the hearing. If you are not represented, the chairman will usually question you in a way that will allow you to explain your case fully and clearly.

Next, the employer presents his case. You or your representative may question him and his witnesses. Each party sums up its case, and at the end of the hearing you will be allowed to argue against the employer's summing-up.

Decision: The tribunal makes its decision in private and usually announces it, with reasons, at the end of the hearing. Typed copies are sent to both parties. If the tribunal does not give its reasons, you are entitled to ask for them and you should do this anyway as you may find you have grounds for an appeal.

Appeal: You have the right to appeal to the High Court, but only if there has been a legal error.

(Industrial Tribunals were set up under the Industrial Tribunals Regulations 1965, with jurisdiction under the Redundancy Payments Act 1965, the Selective Employment Payments Act 1966, and the Industrial Training Act 1964, the Contracts of Employment Act 1963 and the Docks and Harbours Act 1966. Their jurisdiction will be further extended to include claims for wrongful dismissal under the Industrial Relations Act 1971.)

Medical Appeal Tribunals

Function: To decide certain matters concerning industrial accidents and diseases. This involves: (a) determining whether an accident has resulted in loss of any physical or mental ability; and (b) if so, assessing the degree of disablement and the length of time which should be taken into account. (⋄ p. 138–9)

How to Apply: If one of these questions arises when a local National Insurance Officer is deciding a claim for industrial injuries, he must refer the case to a Medical Board, or directly to a Medical Appeal Tribunal. If you are dissatisfied with the decision of the Medical Board, you may appeal to the Medical Appeal Tribunal. Application forms can be obtained from your local National Insurance Office.

Advice: If you belong to a trade union, you should seek advice, and, if possible, representation, from your local branch secretary.

Character: The tribunal consists of a chairman, who is usually a lawyer, and two doctors. The hearing is very informal.

Procedure: The tribunal questions you about your injury or illness and asks how you are handicapped by it. The doctors examine you. You may call witnesses, including your doctor, to speak on your behalf, and you may produce documentary evidence such as a medical consultant's report. You may question witnesses and inspect documents produced by the Insurance Officer.

Decision: In most cases, notice of the decision is sent by post. You may ask for a written decision, with reasons, either at the end of the hearing or soon after you hear the decision. Make sure you do this if you are considering an appeal.

Appeal: You may appeal against the tribunal's decision to the Industrial Injuries Commissioner, but it is best to get legal advice first.

Expenses: You are entitled to travelling expenses: the clerk of the tribunal is responsible for this.

(Medical Appeal Tribunals were set up under the National Insurance (Industrial Injuries) Act 1965.)

Tribunals of the National Health Service

If a complaint is made against a doctor or dentist practising under the National Health Service, there is a complex system, involving 4 tribunals, for hearing and judging the complaint. Briefly, this is what happens:

(1) A complaint is first put to the local Service Committee, which holds a hearing and decides whether the practitioner has committed a breach of his contract under the National Health Service.

(2) The Service Committee makes a report to the local Executive Council, which decides what disciplinary action, if any, should be recommended to the Minister for Health.

(3) If the Executive Council makes a recommendation to the Minister, there is a right of appeal by either party to the Minister, who appoints a tribunal to hear the appeal.

(4) If the Executive Council believes that the practitioner should be struck off the register, it may refer the case directly to the National Health Service Tribunal.

(5) The National Health Service Tribunal holds a hearing and decides the case.

(6) If the decision is against the practitioner, he alone has a right of appeal to the Minister for Health. If the decision goes against the practitioner the final result will be disciplinary action, ranging from a warning, to withholding payments, to expulsion from the National Health Service.

Advice: Since the procedure is so complicated, you should get expert legal and medical advice if you intend to pursue your complaint. Unfortunately there are no organizations which can provide voluntary help, although Citizens' Advice Bureaux may be able to give advice as to how to present your complaint in the first place. Otherwise, there is not much help available, unless you can afford to pay for it.

(1) *Service Committees*

Function: To investigate complaints about doctors and dentists failing to comply with their terms of service under the National Health Service and to decide whether they are guilty of a breach of contract.

How to Apply: You should submit your complaint in writing to the Service Committee's clerk, within 6 weeks of the incident you are complaining about (or 8 weeks in certain cases). If you delay longer than this, you must get permission, either from the practitioner himself or from the Minister for Health, to waive the time limit.

The complaint is first sent to the Committee's chairman: he may decide that it is frivolous or unfounded and not worth pursuing. If so, he refers it to the Committee who must give their consent before the case is dismissed.

Character: Every local Executive Council of the National Health Service sets up medical, pharmaceutical, and dental Service Committees. Each Committee consists of three lay members from the Executive Council, three professional members from the appropriate branch of the profession, and a lay chairman appointed by the Committee.

Hearings are held in private and the procedure is fairly formal. The Press is excluded, but a member of the local professional committee – which may want to take action against the practitioner – is allowed to attend.

Procedure: The clerk of the Committee notifies the complainant and the practitioner of the time and place of the hearing and sends them copies of the complainant's written statement. Both parties may have representatives to help them, but they are not allowed to have a paid counsel or solicitor to conduct the case for them. The practitioner is nearly always represented by an expert member of his own profession who is entitled to address the Committee and cross-examine witnesses. Evidence is not taken on oath; you may call witnesses, but the Committee has no power to order them to attend.

When presenting your case, it is important to remember that the point you must prove is that the practitioner's conduct amounts to a breach of his National Health Service contract. You should therefore know the precise terms of the contract.

Decision: The Committee comes to a decision after the hearing and sends a full report to the Executive Council.

Decision by the Executive Council: The Council must accept the Service Committee's findings, but decides independently what action should be taken. Copies of its decision and the Committee's report are sent to both parties and to the Minister for Health. Occasionally, the Executive Council refers the case directly to the Minister for him to take the decision. If the case is sufficiently serious, it is referred to the National Health Service Tribunal.

The Executive Council's hearing is in private. All that is published of the case is a summary of the facts, the Council's recommendations, and the Minister's decision. The practitioner's name is not published.

Appeal: There is a right of appeal to the Minister against the Executive Council's decision (unless the Council has referred the case directly to the National Health Service Tribunal). However, the complainant cannot appeal if the decision is against the practitioner, even if he feels that the proposed disciplinary action is inadequate. The practitioner cannot appeal if the proposed disciplinary action amounts to no more than a warning. The Minister may dismiss the complainant's appeal without a hearing if he decides that it is frivolous or unfounded.

(2) *Hearing of an Appeal to the Minister*

Character: The Minister appoints a tribunal of three to hear the appeal. The chairman is a member of the Minister's legal staff, and the other members are chosen from the same profession as the practitioner – one from the Minister's staff and the other from a panel selected by the practitioner's professional association. The hearing is in private and very formal.

111

Procedure: Evidence is taken on oath. The tribunal may compel witnesses to attend. Both parties may have legal or lay representatives.

Decision: If, as a result of the hearing, it is decided to withhold part of the practitioner's payment, the Minister refers the evidence to an advisory professional committee. After that, he makes a decision and copies are sent to the Executive Council, the complainant and the practitioner.

Expenses: Travelling expenses are reimbursed and the Minister has power to award costs to the complainant if it is considered that he acted in the public interest.

(3) *The National Health Service Tribunal*

Function: To consider recommendations that doctors or dentists should be struck off the register of National Health Service practitioners. Such recommendations usually come from an Executive Council or Service Committee, but they may be made by anyone.

Character: The chairman of the tribunal is appointed by the Lord Chancellor and must be a barrister of at least ten years' standing. The other two members are appointed by the Minister for Health – one is a layman, and the other is a member of the same profession as the practitioner. The hearing, which is held in private, is as formal as a court of law.

Procedure: The tribunal may conduct proceedings more or less as it likes, within a general framework laid down in the regulations. It hears all the evidence as if the case were being heard for the first time. The parties may have legal or lay representatives; evidence is taken on oath; witnesses may be compelled to attend; legal rules of evidence are strictly followed.

Decision: When the tribunal has reached its decision, it draws up a complete report, including its findings of fact, conclusions, and an estimate of what costs, if any, should be awarded. Copies are sent to the Minister, the complainant, and the practitioner.

Appeal: There is a right of appeal to the High Court, but only on a point of law. The practitioner alone has a further right of appeal to the Minister, who will then appoint a committee to hear the appeal and make a recommendation.

Mental Health Review Tribunals

Function: To hear appeals by mental patients or their nearest relatives for discharge from mental hospitals and institutions. (⋗ pp. 192 ff.)

How to Apply: Application forms can be obtained from the patient's hospital, from the tribunal, or from the local health authority if the patient is in the care of a guardian (⋗ p. 197). The application may also be made by letter, as long as the intention to apply is clearly stated.

Advice: It is most important that a patient should receive advice and representation when appealing to the tribunal. He may be able to get help from the NCCL, which operates a scheme to provide trained representatives at Mental Health Tribunals, or from a welfare officer. Failing that, a relative can be of considerable help to the patient, by helping him understand what the tribunal wants to know and by making arrangements for his care and accommodation if he is discharged (an important factor which affects the tribunal's decision).

Character: The tribunal consists of three members, chosen from three panels representing (a) lawyers, (b) doctors, and (c) lay members with some knowledge of social welfare work. All three must be independent of the hospital and local health authority concerned in the case. The hearings are normally held in private at the patient's hospital. The patient may ask for a public hearing, but this may be refused on the grounds that it would be harmful to him or for some other reason.

Procedure: The applicant may ask for a 'formal hearing' (which means that everyone concerned must be present and everyone can speak and question the others), but the tribunal may refuse this. At a 'formal hearing', both the patient and the nearest relative can call witnesses, but otherwise the tribunal conducts proceedings more or less as it likes.

The tribunal has the power to take evidence on oath, to order witnesses to appear and to produce documentary evidence. It inquires into the conditions under which the patient will be living, if discharged. The medical member examines the patient and inquires into all aspects of his health. The patient and the nearest relative both have the right to be heard.

If an application is made to the tribunal and it considers that the patient is not suffering from mental disorder, or that he is not a danger to himself or others, he *must* be discharged. (This does not apply to cases referred to the Home Secretary for advice.)

Decision: The tribunal may limit the reasons for its decision on the grounds that it may harm the patient to give a fuller explanation, and the patient will not always be allowed to see medical reports.

Appeal: There is a right of appeal to the High Court, but only on a point of law.

Expenses: Expenses may be paid to the nearest relative, representatives of the patient and of the nearest relative (unless they are lawyers), and any witnesses that the tribunal feels have been really useful in helping to decide the case. Expenses consist of rail fare, subsistence, and loss of earnings (if any), but some negotiation with the tribunal may be necessary.

(Mental Health Review Tribunals were set up under the Mental Health Act 1959; their procedure is regulated under the Mental Health Tribunal Rules 1960.)

Immigration Appeal Tribunals

Function: To decide appeals arising from decisions of the Home Office or Immigration Officers, including appeals against refusal of an entry certificate, variation of conditions of admission, refusal to revoke or vary conditions of admission, refusal to revoke a deportation order, and place of destination under a deportation order. (▷pp. 248 ff.)

There is a two-tier system of appeal. The case is first heard by an *adjudicator*. If the adjudicator's decision is not accepted by either party, there is a limited right of appeal to the *Immigration Appeal Tribunal* itself.

The Adjudicator

How to Apply: If a decision is made against you and you are allowed to appeal, the Home Office or the Immigration Officer should inform you of your right of appeal, and you may be advised of the services of the UK Immigration Advisory Service (◊ p. 254), but it is always advisable to check the extent to which you have the right of appeal, as there are changes about to be made to the law at the time of going to press.

The time limit for appealing in most cases is either 14 or 28 days, depending on the circumstances. If you have a right of appeal it is essential to find out immediately the length of time available for you to give notice of appeal. You will be asked to state your grounds for appeal to the Home Office.

As soon as possible after notice is given, the Home Office must prepare a written statement of the facts relating to the case, giving reasons for their decision, and send a copy to you and to the adjudicator.

There are no provisions for permitting appeals outside the time limit.

Advice and Representation: You can obtain advice from the Immigration Advisory Service (UKIAS), who will provide representation at the hearing before the adjudicator or the full tribunal in certain circumstances. The Joint Council for the Welfare of Immigrants (JCWI) also gives advice and provides representation. The NCCL provides representation in a limited number of cases.

Many solicitors have no experience of immigration appeal cases and, in any event, Legal Aid is not available.

Character: There are a number of adjudicators in all major ports of entry and in some towns. Adjudicators are either lawyers or former civil servants. Proceedings are fairly formal.

Procedure: In a number of circumstances you will only be allowed to appeal from outside the United Kingdom and will not be permitted to attend the hearing. A representative (legal or otherwise) may attend on your behalf. He may present your case and, if necessary, submit written evidence and call witnesses. If you are able to attend, you will be expected to give evidence. This is advisable, but not compulsory. You and your witnesses can be asked questions by the Home Office representative and the adjudicator (or members of the tribunal). When your evidence is completed, the Home Office will give their evidence. Usually they rely on a written statement and no direct evidence will be called. You will therefore not be able to question anyone from the Home Office about your case.

You or your representative (if you have one) can then address the adjudicator; the Home Office also has this right.

Decision: The decision is usually given immediately, but in any event written reasons will be sent to you or your representative.

The Tribunal

You can *appeal* against the decision of the adjudicator in a limited number of cases. The Home Office also has this right.

If you are dissatisfied with the decision of the adjudicator you can appeal to the *tribunal*, with the consent of the adjudicator or the tribunal. Permission must be granted if the adjudicator or the tribunal is satisfied that the decision depends on an arguable point of law. An application to the adjudicator must be made immediately after the decision, although in practice 7 days will be allowed if a request is made immediately after the hearing. An application to the tribunal must be made no later than 7 days after the decision. If the person who is appealing is outside the United Kingdom when the decision is made, he has 28 days in which to appeal. The tribunal consists of a chairman, who is a qualified lawyer, and two other persons. The hearing is usually informal. New evidence can be called but normally the appeal involves legal argument as to why the adjudicator reached his decision. The tribunal does not re-hear the case. The decision is usually given immediately with written reasons following.

13. Censorship

Obscene Publications

The right to publish, sell, exhibit, and possess any book, picture, magazine, or other written or illustrated material depends initially on whether or not it is judged to be 'obscene'.

The Obscene Publications Act of 1959 makes it illegal to publish 'obscene' matter, whether for gain or not. The Obscene Publications Act of 1964 has made it illegal to possess any 'obscene' article with the intention of making a profit out of it; this includes books, pictures, films and photographic negatives.

A number of other laws, listed below, further limit the individual's rights in this field.

What is Obscene?

The fairness and effectiveness of the law is sadly impaired by the fact that no two people can be counted on to agree about the meaning of 'obscenity'. Distinguished judges have contradicted one another in their attempts to define it. To add to the confusion, the word has changed its meaning as the climate of opinion in this country has become less Victorian. Until 1970, it was considered indecent or obscene, and therefore an offence, to display the words 'venereal disease' in public. Very recently, pubic hair was thought to be obscene; now it is depicted freely – even in *Playboy* magazine – and few people complain. The 1959 Act gave this definition: an article 'if taken as a whole, such as to tend to deprave and corrupt persons who are likely having regard to all relevant circumstances, to read, see or hear the matter contained or embodied in it'.

Unfortunately, the words 'deprave and corrupt' are equally hard to define; some attempt has been made. According to Mr Justice Stable, in 1956, 'to deprave and corrupt' should not just mean 'to shock and disgust'; i.e. to shock and disgust someone is not enough to constitute an offence. The most important attempt at definition came from Lord Justice Salmon in 1968. According to this, 'corruption' may be to induce or promote:

(1) Erotic desires of a heterosexual kind.
(2) Homosexuality or other sexual perversions.
(3) Drug-taking.
(4) Brutal violence.

Lord Justice Salmon later said, 'The jury must set standards of what is acceptable, what is for the public good in the age in which we live.'

What Does This Imply?

The whole definition is unreliable because no one has been able to prove that drug-taking, violence, or sexual perversions can be induced by any books, pictures, films, or magazines; and there are strong arguments against this possibility.

According to sections (1) and (2), it seems to be a crime to induce perfectly acceptable, pleasurable sexual desires which are clearly not crimes in themselves. The inclusion of sections (3) and (4) is rather superfluous, since legal restrictions against incitement to drug-taking or brutal violence would exist even if the obscenity laws were repealed. Therefore one is left with the absurd conclusion that the obscenity laws exist in order to repress normal sexual desires which are somehow equated with depravity.

'This attitude was reflected by a Treasury Counsel (their advice to the DPP as to the wisdom of launching a trial is usually decisive). He was asked privately what guided him in recommending a book for prosecution. He replied . . . that the test he used was whether the book had made him feel randy. "Entirely subjective," he said, "but what else is there?" . . .

'Yet three comments suggest themselves. (1) It is doubtful whether this gentleman's revulsion at randiness is shared by a "significant number" of Her Majesty's subjects and at least arguable whether it ought to be. (2) Even accepting that more randiness may lead to more love-making, we must then decide whether that is an activity to be contained at a desirable level and, if so (harder still), at what level. And (3), if human randiness is a social evil and the object of the obscenity laws is to extirpate it, then the task of formulating effective legislation for the purpose may as well be abandoned at once as, to say the least of it, unpromising.' (Report of the Arts Council's Working Party on the Obscenity Laws)

How Are the Laws Carried Out?

The police may obtain a search warrant for any premises, stall, or vehicle, and may seize and remove any obscene articles and documents relating to a business carried on there.

The consent of the Director of Public Prosecutions is not necessary to start proceedings. There are two methods of procedure: the defendant may be tried summarily before a magistrate and fined up to £100 and/or imprisoned for up to 6 months; alternatively, he may be tried before a judge and jury and fined an unlimited amount and/or imprisoned for up to 3 years. A defendant who wishes to contest charges always has the right to be tried before judge and jury.

In addition, the authorities can proceed simply by seizing alleged obscene matter with a warrant from a magistrate and requiring the owner of the premises to show cause before a magistrate why it should not be forfeited (Section 3 of the 1959 Act). This procedure does not allow the defendant to be tried by a jury; it also gives the police powers to seize any documents found on the premises which relate to a business being carried on. The police have often used this against the 'underground' press.

'Obscenity' has been so inadequately defined that the decision as to whether or not an article is obscene rests with the jury in each individual case. Consequently, a person cannot protect himself by finding out in advance if he is in danger of breaking the law.

Lack of intention is not a defence under the 1959 Act. Mere depiction of crime (or even non-crime), regardless of intention, is looked upon as incitement and sufficient grounds for conviction. However, it is a defence, if charged with possession under the 1964 Act, to prove that the accused had not examined the article and had no reasonable cause to suspect that it was obscene.

Expert witnesses may be called to prove to the jury that the publication is justified as being in the interests of science, literature, art, learning, or other areas of general concern.

Ultimately, the jurors are expected to decide what may or may not be depraving or corrupting, with no possible guidance except from sociologists or 'experts', who may well disagree among themselves; to assess artistic merit although they probably have no qualifications for doing so; to judge how many people are likely to be depraved and whether or not that number is too many; and to work out whether the estimated amount of 'depravity' might be outweighed by the amount of 'public good' issuing from the offending material. To do this equitably is virtually an impossible task.

Other Laws Dealing with Obscenity

Exposure to Public View

It is an offence to expose to view any obscene print, picture or other indecent exhibition, in any street, public place, shop window, or part of a building where the public can see it (Vagrancy Acts 1824, 1838). Under these Acts, it is only necessary to prove that something is 'indecent' – and while 'indecent' is as hard to define as 'obscene', it is certainly less extreme, and therefore easier to establish in a court than 'obscenity'.

Sale, Distribution, Singing, Swearing

Every person who publicly offers for sale or distribution, or exhibition to public view, any profane, indecent or obscene article, sings any profane or obscene songs, or uses profane or obscene language – to the obstruction, annoyance or danger of other people in the vicinity – shall be liable to a penalty of up to £2 with, at the magistrates' discretion, up to 14 days' imprisonment (Town Police Clauses Act 1847).

Conspiracy to Corrupt Public Morals

This is an obscure common law offence, upheld in 1961 when a Mr Shaw, who had published *The Ladies' Directory*, a guide to Soho's prostitutes, was found guilty on this charge. It has recently come into more frequent use, although the defendants in the *OZ* trial were acquitted of this charge.

Importation

It is illegal to import indecent or obscene articles. Customs officers may seize books which have not yet been published, and they are supplied with a black list drawn up in consultation with the Home Office. A person whose books are seized has a month to notify the Commissioners of Customs and Excise that he objects, after which time the books are automatically forfeited (▷ p. 271). If he objects within one month, the case goes before a magistrate. The defences available under the Obscene Publications Acts are not available here (Customs Consolidation Act 1876).

Mailing

It is an offence to send through the post a packet which contains obscene or indecent material, or has obscene, indecent, grossly offensive, or libellous words or designs on the cover. It is also an offence for a person to order such a packet to be sent to him. The Post Office has power to detain and destroy material of this sort. The penalty is a fine of up to £100 or imprisonment for up to 12 months (Post Office Act 1953).

It is now an offence to send unsolicited books, magazines or leaflets (or advertising material relating to them) describing or illustrating human sexual techniques. A prosecution must be instigated with the consent of the Director of Public Prosecutions. The penalty is a fine of up to £400. (Unsolicited Goods and Services Act 1971.)

Corruption of Children

It is an offence to produce, sell, or hire any book, magazine, or other work which is likely to fall into the hands of children and corrupt them: that is, work which consists mainly of stories told in pictures and portraying crimes, violence, cruelty, or incidents of a horrible or repulsive nature. The police must have the consent of the Attorney General before prosecuting. The penalty is a fine up to £100 or up to 4 months' imprisonment. It is a defence to prove that the accused person had not examined the work and had no reasonable cause to suspect that it fell into this category (The Children and Young Persons (Harmful Publications) Act 1955).

The working party, set up by the Arts Council in 1968 to investigate the working of the Obscene Publications Acts of 1959 and 1964 and other relevant Acts, reached the conclusion that all legislation on this subject should be abolished, except the Children and Young Persons (Harmful Publications) Act 1955, and a section of the Post Office Act 1953, concerning unsolicited and offensive postal packets. They proposed a single law to protect people from being affronted by offensive displays or behaviour in public places. So far, nothing has been done to implement this recommendation.

Film and Theatre Censorship

Films

Commercial Film Shows

These must take place in premises licensed by the local authority, and must comply with certain safety regulations (Cinematograph Acts 1909 and 1952).

The Government has no direct power to censor films. The only censoring body that exists is the British Board of Film Censors, which was set up by the film industry in 1912 and has no statutory authority. Local authorities have the power to censor films, but this has been almost totally delegated to the BBFC: it has become standard practice throughout the country that no one may show a film which has not been passed by the BBFC without the express consent of the local authority. From time to time, local authorities do allow such films to be shown, but permission does not extend outside their own particular area. They have also been known to ban films which have been passed by the BBFC.

Non-Commercial Film Shows

These include free showings, private showings, and public showings by non-profit-making organizations and film clubs. They do not require a special licence from the local authority and they are not subject to censorship. They must comply with certain safety regulations. Children's cinema clubs come under special control.

The Obscene Publications Act ($\diamond$ p. 117) applies to films, although there is some doubt whether Section 3 (search and seizure) is applicable to films shown in a non-commercial club.

Theatre

Theatres must be licensed by the local authority. If a licence is refused, the applicant has the right to appeal. Local authorities may impose conditions in the interests of public safety, but they may not impose any conditions or restrictions as to the content of plays or the way in which they are performed (Theatres Act 1968).

However, the Act lays down the following offences which may give rise to prosecution:

(1) To present or direct an obscene performance of a play unless it is justified as being for the public good, in the interests of the arts, literature, or learning. Expert witnesses may be called by the defence and the prosecution.

(2) To stage a public performance involving the use of threatening, abusive, or insulting words, intended to incite racial hatred, if the play is likely to do so when considered as a whole.

(3) To put on a performance with the intent of causing a breach of the peace, or one which is likely to do so, whether intended or not.

(4) To use defamatory words in the course of a play.

Prosecution requires the consent of the Attorney General.

A copy of the script of any new play which is publicly performed must be handed to the British Museum.

The police may, with a warrant from a magistrate, enter any premises if they have reasonable grounds to suspect that a play is being performed which constitutes an offence under the Act. A licensing authority or a policeman in uniform may enter licensed premises without a warrant.

Defamation (Libel and Slander)

Definition

Defamation means the publication of something untruthful about a person in such a way that it tends:

(a) to lower him in the estimation of society; or

(b) to bring him into hatred, ridicule, contempt or dislike by society; or

(c) to make him shunned, avoided or cut off from society.

'Society' is taken to mean members of the public who are 'right-thinking' in the conventional sense.

There are two kinds of defamation: 'slander', which is transitory and usually means the spoken word; and 'libel' which is permanent and includes writing, printing, drawings, photography and other art work, and broadcasting. The rest of this chapter is concerned mainly with libel, which is the most common form of defamation.

Publication of a libel can result in a civil action for damages against all the people responsible: these include the writer (or artist or photographer), the printers, the publishers, and the editor. Libel as a criminal offence is rare now and there is no such thing as criminal slander.

When a case is contested, either side can ask for trial by jury; the jury awards damages which often amount to substantial sums. The laws of defamation can and do limit the extent of political discussion in this country, because the need to protect people from defamation is not adequately balanced with the need to preserve the free exchange of information and expression of opinion. Legal Aid is not available for either side in a defamation case.

Material is 'published' when it is communicated to anyone else apart from the person it concerns. Therefore it is technically published as soon as the manuscript reaches the publisher and before it is distributed to the public at large. However, the scope of publication is taken into account when the jury assesses damages.

The plaintiff (i.e. the person who claims he has been libelled) does not have to present proof of the actual harm done to him: it is presumed in law that libel results in damage.

The plaintiff must show that the material refers to him, and the use of a nickname or a recognizable distortion of his name would be sufficient proof; this fact is established objectively, regardless of whether the publisher intended to refer to the plaintiff. A generalization cannot be proved to be libellous unless a person's name is mentioned in conjunction with it or there is a clear innuendo from which a name can be deduced. If libellous material is published about one unnamed person who belongs to a small identifiable group, then each person in that group may bring an action for damages.

Material may be judged libellous in its ironical sense or by innuendo, even when the actual words appear to be harmless; and it need not imply that the plaintiff is at fault – e.g., to say that a woman was raped by a man who is mentally ill does not imply that either of them is at fault, but it may be defamatory to both.

Defence

There are five major defences against an action for libel:

(1) *Justification*

It is a defence to prove that the offending words were true, but this is not easy. Substantiating details, dates, and places must be given. It is not sufficient for the defendant to prove that he accurately repeated the words of a third person: he must also prove that the words were true. It is not a defence to show that the defendant genuinely believed that the offending words were true (if they were not), although this may lessen the amount of damages awarded against him.

(2) *Fair Comment*

It is a defence to prove that the offending words were fair comment, i.e. an honest opinion made without malice on a matter of public interest. This defence only applies when the words complained of constitute an opinion, not a statement of fact, and members of the public may exercise their own judgement about it, to agree or disagree. The case for the defence will be strengthened if the opinion is backed up by a number of substantiated facts, but it will not necessarily fail if some of these facts are not proved to be true, as long as the comment is fair.

Criticisms which have been invited, either expressly or by implication, such as criticisms of books and films, can normally be defended as 'fair comment'. On the other hand, 'fair comment' is not regarded as a reasonable defence for an opinion about a person's moral character.

(3) *Privilege*

In certain circumstances, people are protected from being sued for libel or slander. This is known as privilege and falls into two categories: 'absolute' which gives complete immunity; and 'qualified' which gives protection only if the material is published without malice.

(a) *Absolute Privilege:* This covers all statements made in the course of parliamentary proceedings and by M.P.s in the course of their duty; parliamentary papers published by the direction of the House, or complete republications of them; judicial proceedings, including the acts and words of the judge, defendant, prosecutor, and all others taking part; fair, accurate, and contemporaneous reports of public judicial proceedings in newspapers; and reports of the Ombudsman and relevant communications made to him by M.P.s.

(b) *Qualified Privilege:* This covers fair, accurate, and non-contemporaneous reports of judicial proceedings in any publication; extracts from parliamentary papers; fair and accurate reports of parliamentary proceedings; and fair and accurate reports of public meetings. Where public meetings are concerned, this defence is not available if the defendant has refused, when asked by the plaintiff, to publish a letter of explanation. It also covers certain cases where there is a public interest in free communication, e.g., where an M.P. passes on to the Law Society complaints by some of his constituents against a firm of solicitors.

(4) *Innocent Defamation*

If the defendant claims that the words were not intended to be defamatory towards the plaintiff and he exercised all reasonable care to avoid making such a mistake, he may make an offer of amends (usually a suitable correction and apology). The plaintiff may refuse to accept this and proceed with his action, but it is then a defence if the defendant can prove that the words were published innocently (Defamation Act 1952, s.4).

(5) *Apology*

It is a defence to plead that the libel was inserted without malice and without gross negligence, and to publish a full apology in the newspaper where the original words appeared; or, if that is published less than once a week, to offer to publish in another newspaper chosen by the plaintiff. This defence is used rarely because apologies tend to be accepted before the matter goes to court.

127

Other Restrictions

The publication of indecent matter and medical, surgical and physiological detail in court proceedings is prohibited, where publication is calculated to injure public morals. Where matrimonial cases are concerned lawful publication is limited to the names of people involved and a discreet outline of the proceedings (Judicial Proceedings (Regulation of Reports) Act 1926).

The publication of written details or pictures, identifying children who are involved in court cases as defendants or witnesses, is restricted. The court may waive this restriction if it is in the interests of justice to do so (Children and Young Persons Acts 1933 and 1963).

Further Information

Defence of Literature and the Arts Society

The Obscenity Laws, report from the Arts Council's Working Party, André Deutsch, London, 1969

14. Law and the Worker

The Contract of Employment

Your rights as a worker depend partly on the terms of your contract of employment and partly on the general law laid down by Acts of Parliament. The position will be greatly complicated by the Industrial Relations Act 1971 when it is brought into force. (Although it has now been passed, various parts of it may be brought into operation on different dates by Orders made by the Secretary of State for Employment.) The Act is extremely complex and it cannot be set out or even usefully summarized here. Nevertheless it is important that you should know what your legal rights and liabilities are.

A contract of employment need not be in writing. It may be made orally, or partly in writing and partly orally. It may even be made by a gesture: if a group of men turn up at a building site on Monday morning and apply for jobs, the foreman may engage them by handing them each a shovel. Even if it is not written down it is perfectly possible to enforce a contract in court if you can prove what its terms were: if you have no other witness it may of course be a question of who is believed – you or the other party.

The terms of the contract may be set out in full, but normally most of them are implied. If your contract refers to a collective agreement made between your trade union and the employer, these terms will be incorporated as far as possible into your contract. (The collective agreement is not usually a contract in itself; even if it were, an individual worker could not be a party to it and could not sue the employer for a breach of it.)

129

The terms of your contract may be fixed according to the particular customs of the trade and the locality of the individual factory. If so, it will be assumed that you know these customs, whether you do or not.

Your employer is bound by law to give you, within 13 weeks of starting work, a memorandum setting out in some detail what the terms of your contract are. But remember – this document is *not* the contract: it is only a record of what the employer thinks the terms are. If you disagree with it, you can apply to an Industrial Tribunal to have it put right (Contracts of Employment Act 1963). ($\Diamond$ pp. 106–7)

Dismissal and Redundancy

If you are dismissed you have the right to certain minimum periods of notice (unless your contract provides for longer). These will be: 1 week's notice after 13 weeks' continuous service; 2 weeks' notice after 104 weeks; 4 weeks' notice after 5 years; 6 weeks' notice after 10 years; and 8 weeks' notice after 15 years (Industrial Relations Act, s.17). If you are dismissed without proper notice you can sue your employer for breach of contract; though the maximum amount of damages you can get will usually amount to what you would have earned in the period of notice to which you were entitled. It would be a defence if the employer could show that he had sacked you for a serious act of misconduct.

If you want to leave you must give 1 week's notice after 13 weeks' continuous service, but not more unless your contract requires it.

If you are dismissed *by reason of redundancy*, you are entitled to a lump sum payment (Redundancy Payments Act 1965). The amount depends on your age, length of service and final rate of pay. Disputes over redundancy payments go before the Industrial Tribunals: procedure is fairly informal and it is not always necessary to be represented by a lawyer, but you should consult your trade union or solicitor for advice. ($\Diamond$ p. 106)

If you are dismissed *unfairly* (whether in breach of contract or not) you may have a remedy under the Industrial Relations Act, s.20. In this case you may apply to an Industrial Tribunal, which has power to recommend (but not to order) that your employer should re-engage you. Alternatively you may be awarded a sum in compensation for the loss of your job. The amount is in the discretion of the tribunal but cannot in any case exceed 104 weeks' pay, or £4,160 – that is, 104 × £40. In most cases it is very unlikely to be anything approaching this sum. Also, you cannot get both compensation and a redundancy payment for the same dismissal. You may find that your trade union and your employer or his association have an agreement by which these cases go to a Joint Council or the like instead of the Industrial Tribunal.

The Right to Strike

For more than 60 years your right to strike has been protected by the Trade Disputes Act 1906; though its effectiveness has been greatly reduced by recent decisions of the courts (Rookes *v.* Barnard, Stratford *v.* Lindley, Morgan *v.* Fry, etc.). The whole situation has now been radically changed by the Industrial Relations Act, which repeals the Act of 1906 entirely while re-enacting some, but not all, of its protective sections. These however are now of comparatively minor importance for two reasons.

First, they only apply to acts done 'in contemplation or furtherance of an industrial dispute'. For the exact meaning of this term you must look at the definition section of the Act (s.157). But it means broadly a dispute concerning the terms and conditions of employment; so that a political strike of any kind, or a strike to enable workers to go on a political demonstration, would clearly not be covered whatever the issue might be. In such a case the strikers would be left at the mercy of the common law and in particular of the 'labour injunction' which employers have made frequent use of in recent years.

In the second place, even if the strike is an industrial dispute, the Act sets out a long list of 'unfair industrial practices', one or more of which you may easily find yourself committing. Again, this is complex but the list certainly includes:

(1) A strike in breach of a collective agreement if this is itself a contract. (When the Act is in force some collective agreements will be enforceable contracts which would not have been before; either because the parties are presumed to have intended that result or because the new National Industrial Relations Court has made an order to that effect – ss. 32, 39.)

(2) Any strike to enforce a closed shop.

(3) A strike for recognition of a trade union, in particular where it cuts across the procedure provided in the Act.

(4) A strike against any 'extraneous party' – that is, where pressure is put on an employer by getting his suppliers' or his customers' work-people to come out in sympathy.

(5) Any act which induces or threatens to induce a breach of contract (very many strikes inevitably do so) unless the person doing the act is officially authorized to do it by a registered trade union.

(6) Almost any action taken to support (which includes financing) strikers who are themselves committing an unfair industrial practice. (Their dispute may of course be at the other end of the country. If someone passes the hat round in your trade union branch to help them, it is hard to see how you can be expected to know whether they are committing an unfair industrial practice or not.)

All this applies not merely to a strike but to any 'irregular industrial action short of a strike' – this is the lawyers' new jargon for the old go-slow or work-to-rule – provided only that the employer can show that just one workman did something in breach of his contract of employment. For any of these practices your trade union or you personally (if you take any part in calling or leading the strike) may be ordered to pay 'compensation' to your employer or to a non-unionist who claims to have suffered from your activities. This will not technically be a fine or damages but it will feel very much the same if you are called upon to pay it. As if all this were not enough, there are further provisions in the Act (in Part VIII) by which the Secretary of State can apply in certain circumstances to the NIRC for an order restraining you or your union leaders from calling or organizing or carrying on a strike for a period of not more than 60 days. He can also, if he thinks fit, apply for an order that a ballot must be taken of all *workers* affected (not just union members) before a strike may be called. Failure to obey either of these orders can result in imprisonment for contempt of court. Finally, if you go on strike in breach of contract (and it is often difficult to decide whether a strike would be in breach of contract or not) it may still be a criminal offence if you have reasonable cause to believe that the probable consequence of your doing so will be 'to endanger human life, or cause serious bodily injury, or to expose valuable property whether real or personal to destruction or serious injury' (Conspiracy and Protection of Property Act 1875).

The law is so uncertain in this field that even a solicitor will have difficulty advising on the legal consequences of a strike. It can only be said that *from the legal point of view* it is probably, though not necessarily, safer to give 7 days' notice of intention to strike. But of course the legal point of view is not the only one worthy of consideration.

The Right to Picket

Picketing in itself is a perfectly normal, lawful activity whether it is done in the course of an industrial dispute or otherwise. The right of peaceful picketing was established by the Trade Disputes Act 1906 but this is now repealed and replaced by s.131 of the Industrial Relations Act which is much narrower. All this section says is that if pickets go to a place where a person works or carries on business; or any other place where a person happens to be, *not the place where he resides*; and they do so only for the purpose of peacefully obtaining information from him or communicating information to him or persuading him to work or not to work – then their action shall not of itself constitute any crime or tort. Since there is no crime or tort of 'picketing' known to the law, it is not easy at first sight to see what all this means.

133

The answer probably lies in s.7 of the Conspiracy and Protection of Property Act 1875, which is still in force. This makes it a crime punishable with a fine of £20 or 3 months' imprisonment if you do any of the following things:

(1) Use violence or intimidate another person or injure his property.

(2) Persistently follow another person about from place to place.

(3) Hide any tools, clothes or other property of his.

(4) Watch or beset his house or any other place were he lives or works, carries on business or happens to be.

(5) Follow him with two or more other persons in a disorderly manner in or through any street or road.

This curious list by no means exhausts the ways in which pickets may run into trouble if they are not careful. The law here is even more uncertain than the law concerning the right to strike Thus it is quite lawful *in itself* to picket the gates of an employer's factory at any time and the pickets cannot be sued for trespass or for creating a nuisance for that reason alone. There is no reason why they should not carry placards or banners, so long as the wording on them is not defamatory or insulting or likely to cause a breach of the peace. Likewise pickets can presumably stop anyone going into or coming out of the works so long as they do so solely to obtain or communicate information or peacefully to persuade him to work or not to work; though they would not be entitled to bar his path or detain him by physical force.

Obstruction

There are some other possible difficulties. In a case decided in 1965 it was held that pickets had no right to obstruct the highway even for the purpose of peacefully communicating with incoming lorry drivers or persuading them not to deliver to the firm (Tynan *v.* Balmer).

In an earlier case a picket was arrested because a police officer had formed the view that if more than two pickets were posted at the back entrance of a small printing works there was likely to be a breach of the peace. The defendant went to join the pickets who were already there and was convicted of obstructing the officer in the exercise of his duty under the Prevention of Crimes Act 1885. No violence was actually threatened or used (Piddington *v.* Bates).

Both these decisions appear to give the police a wide discretion to direct pickets how they are to behave. But it must be remembered that in every case obstruction of the highway is a question of fact; and the likelihood of a breach of the peace is very much a matter of opinion. It is certainly not enough in either case for a policeman to go to court and say what he *thought* the situation was. Pickets are by no means necessarily obstructing the highway; and if a policeman says that he feared that violence would occur he must also show that he had reasonable grounds for his fear. The difficulty is that cases of this kind are always brought before a bench of magistrates, and many of them accept police evidence uncritically.

It is also possible that words on placards used by pickets, or words used by them to exhort other workers to come out on strike, might be held to amount to inducing a breach of contract. It would then be an unfair industrial practice unless it was done officially on behalf of a registered trade union.

Suggestions for Pickets

So much of all this is uncertain that it is probably better not to try and foresee every possible legal consequence that may arise from picketing in the course of a strike. In practice the outcome usually depends much more on the overall situation than on legal niceties: in particular on the degree of organization and discipline of the workers involved and on whether the police are prepared to deal with the situation reasonably. Police officers will almost certainly be present, and while it is not suggested that pickets must always do as they say, it is often better to comply with their requests as long as these are reasonable. Failure to do so may of course lead to immediate arrest for obstruction. In practice the majority of prosecutions resulting from picketing are either for obstruction of the highway or of the police or for 'insulting words or behaviour' or the like.

It is almost always best before setting up a picket line to get advice from one or more experienced trade unionists and perhaps from a sympathetic lawyer as well. A few practical suggestions may be offered here:

(a) Wherever possible official pickets should be given badges, arm bands, or other means of visible identification.

(b) Pickets should be given precise instructions (written if necessary) so that they are left in no doubt as to what is expected from them.

(c) If slogans are to be used, care should be taken to see that everyone is familiar with the agreed wording and that they do not give rise to police action.

(d) If in spite of all precautions a picket is arrested, then it is of the greatest importance that the names and addresses of any possible witnesses be noted immediately.

Search

In some circumstances, employers insist that their employees be searched on entering or leaving the works. This might be a precaution against theft, or to prevent anything dangerous being brought into the works. These searches may be carried out by 'security guards', or by private works police employed by the firm.

A contract of employment seldom makes express provision for search. If you are searched without your consent – either express or implied – you may have the right to sue for assault, or, if you were detained on leaving, for false imprisonment. But the courts would usually find that your consent, however fictitious, had been given by implication. In any case, if you refused to give your consent, you would probably be told 'If you don't like it, you don't have to work here.'

Proper safeguards against abuse of this practice should be negotiated, e.g., by insisting that a trade union representative be present while searches are conducted.

Safety and Accidents

An employer is bound by law to take all reasonable steps to ensure the safety of every person working for him. In addition, there are many detailed requirements laid down in the Factories Act 1961 and in special regulations that have been made for different trades and industries.

Factory Inspectors have the task of enforcing the Act, but the inspectorate is grossly understaffed and can make only routine visits to a factory on average once every four years. And when they do discover breaches of the Act, their policy is usually to persuade rather than to prosecute the employer.

Any worker or trade union official who discovers a breach of the Act has the right to call in the Inspector and ask him to insist that it is remedied. If the Inspector fails to do so, anyone may prosecute the occupier of the factory. But it is often quicker and more effective to make strong representations to the foreman or manager of the part of the factory involved and, if the result is not satisfactory, to call a strike until the situation is put right. This is entirely justifiable and the employer is unlikely to succeed in any claim against the strikers. He would himself have been in breach of his contract if he allowed work to continue in dangerous conditions.

The first concern of trade unionists should always be to see that their working conditions are as safe as possible. But if an accident does occur, it is important to know what the rights of the injured person are and how he can best be protected.

(a) Obviously – summon first aid and an ambulance if necessary.

(b) Take the names and addresses of any witnesses.

(c) Make a careful note of what happened, preferably with a drawing or photograph of the place and plant involved.

(d) Make sure that any defective equipment is preserved for later examination.

(e) Make a report to the management; keep it brief and factual.

No one is obliged to give a statement of evidence, either to the employer's insurance company or to the injured person's representative. But if a witness makes a statement, he can insist on keeping a copy of it. The employer's insurance company is not entitled to approach the injured person and ask him questions about the accident.

Rights to Financial Compensation

If you are injured at work, you will have two main rights to financial compensation.

(1) Benefit from the Department of Health and Social Security

If your injury occurs as a result of your work, you are entitled to one or more of the following benefits from the DHSS under the Industrial Injuries Act, which greatly exceed what you would otherwise get under the National Insurance Act.

(i) *Injury benefit* while you are off work, for up to 26 weeks, including allowances for your wife and children.

(ii) *Disablement benefit* when you return to work, or after 26 weeks, if you are still suffering as a result of the accident. This is given on a percentage scale depending on the degree of your disability.

(iii) *Special hardship allowance:* you may be eligible for this if, as a result of the accident, you are unable to earn as much as you did before.

There are other benefits which are important in exceptional cases.

Your claim should be made to the local office of the Department of Health and Social Security as soon as possible after the accident. Claims are usually met without difficulty. You should keep in close touch with your trade union or solicitor and consult them if difficulties arise, as some of the provisions of the scheme are complicated. Disputes over entitlement to benefit go to a local appeal tribunal and disputes over assessment of the extent of disability go before a Medical Appeal Tribunal. (◊ pp. 108 ff.)

(2) Damages

You may be able to claim from your employer or from some other person by suing them for damages, if you can show that they were responsible for causing the accident through negligence (that is, by failing to observe the standards of safety which the law imposes). Negligence on the part of the employer includes failure in his duty to take reasonable care to provide a safe system of work, a safe place of work, and safe plant and equipment: he is also responsible for the negligence of any of his employees, provided that the employee was acting in the course of his employment at the time.

If you were careless for your own safety at the time you were injured, the value of your claim may be partially diminished – but this should not deter you from embarking on a claim for damages.

The employer will also be liable if the accident resulted from a breach of any of the safety provisions of the Factories Acts and similar legislation; except occasionally when the sole reason for the accident was the deliberate act of the employee (e.g., removing a guard from a machine).

The law on all these matters is complicated. Always get the advice of a solicitor (except in the most trivial accident cases), preferably a solicitor employed through your trade union, who will usually have extensive experience of such cases. He will be able to advise you on liability and on the amount of damages you can expect.

If a solicitor recovers damages for you, his costs (with the exception, perhaps, of a few pounds) should normally be paid by the insurance company, not by you.

Women in Employment

Equal Pay

It has at last been enacted that women and men will receive equal pay and conditions for work of equal value by 29 December 1975 (Equal Pay Act 1970). The Act attempts to define work of equal value:

> A woman is to be regarded as employed on like work with men if, but only if, her work and theirs is of the same or a broadly similar nature, and the differences (if any) between the things she does and the things they do are not of practical importance in relation to terms and conditions of employment.

This rather vague definition will not be clarified until the courts begin to interpret the Act. As K. W. Wedderburn says in *The Worker and the Law*:

> One can only gulp with apprehension at the work for industrial tribunals . . . and for the High Court on the points of law that could arise from this formula.

Women will also be regarded as doing work of equal value if their work is rated equally with men's work in a job evaluation study. This is a slightly more reliable means of assessment, but only one third of the jobs in industry are subject to such studies. Job evaluation studies are initiated and managed by the employer and it is very doubtful whether they will have any effect in upgrading female employees. As most women are employed in different sections or departments on different work from men, it will be extremely difficult for women to prove that their work is of equal value. Only when they work side by side with men on identical jobs will they have a clear claim.

If an employer fails to comply with the terms of the Act, claims may be made to an Industrial Tribunal (◇ p. 106) for equal pay, damages and up to 2 years' back payment. It will be up to the employer to prove that where a man is given a better reward, his work is materially different.

Collective Agreements

If a collective agreement between a trade union and an employer discriminates between men and women in terms of pay or conditions, a trade union can apply to an Industrial Tribunal to have it amended. This arrangement does not provide adequate protection for women because most women are employed in jobs that are not unionized: the TUC has 7 million male members but only 2 million female members and most trade union negotiating committees are made up of men. (Employers and the Secretary of State may also refer the matter to the tribunal, but they are less likely to do so.)

Exemptions and Omissions

The Act does not require a collective agreement to be extended to women if it previously applied to men only. It will therefore still be possible to reserve certain jobs for one sex, without contravening the Act.

A woman will not benefit from the Act if the terms of her employment are affected by protective legislation (see below) or by special conditions concerning pregnancy and childbirth. As the Act does not apply to employment provisions connected with retirement, marriage and death, it does not give women equal pension rights. In addition, it appears to require equality only in contractually binding 'terms and conditions' of employment and therefore does not prevent employers from paying discretionary bonuses to men only.

The Equal Pay Act does not deal with equal job opportunities for women nor with equal promotion prospects for women – both of which are of vital importance in achieving any real equality.

The Act does not apply to Northern Ireland.

Protective Legislation

In industry, women and young people under 18 are prohibited from working more than a certain number of hours per day, from doing night work, and from working on Sundays, Bank Holidays and during meal and rest intervals (Factories Act 1961). The same Act prohibits the employment of women and young people in certain jobs, mainly those connected with lead and paint manufacture.

It is possible to gain exemption from these restrictions if employers and employees agree to it, and if it is considered 'desirable in the public interest for the purpose of maintaining or increasing the efficiency of industry or transport' (Section 117). In July 1971, exemption orders applied to 152,600 women and 15,500 young workers between the ages of 16 and 18.

The restrictions do not apply to women holding responsible positions of management who are not engaged in manual work.

Women and young people under 18 are not allowed to work underground (Mines and Quarries Act 1954).

The Sex Disqualification (Removal) Act 1919

According to this Act,

A person shall not be disqualified by sex or marriage from the exercise of any public function, or from being appointed to or holding any civil or judicial office or post, or from entering or assuming or carrying on any civil profession or vocation, or from admission to any incorporated society.

Unfortunately, the Act does not make it a punishable offence to discriminate against women in employment, although it sets out that women should not be disqualified. It has only been used three times since its introduction and it has not yet been used for a prosecution.

Further Information and Advice

Consult your shop steward or trade union; then, if necessary, a solicitor

For the law of employment generally, see K. W. Wedderburn, *The Worker and the Law* (Penguin Books, second edition 1971), which itself contains many references to other books on more specialized topics

For the Factories Acts, etc., see *Redgrave's Factories Acts* and *Redgrave's Offices, Shops and Railway Premises Act* (both published by Butterworths)

Industrial Relations Act 1971 (HMSO)

15. Children

Registration and Naming

The birth of a child must be registered with the local registrar of births within 42 days. A birth certificate will be issued, either at the time of the registration or at any time in the future when requested. The certificate, which can be obtained in a full or shortened version, belongs to the person who has paid for it; and it gives the child the right to a name.

The full birth certificate of a legitimate child will show the father's and mother's name, the mother's maiden name and the name the parents have chosen for the child. If the child is illegitimate, the father's name will not be entered, unless he is present at the registration and wants his name to be on the certificate.

A legitimate child is normally given the father's name. An illegitimate child has no right to take his father's name, unless he changes his name after birth. If he does so, his new name will not appear on his birth certificate. Once a child's name is entered on his birth certificate, there is no way of changing the certificate at any time in the future.

A child cannot alter the forenames or surnames given to him by his parents without his father's consent if he is legitimate, or his mother's if he is illegitimate (until he is 18). A child over the age of 16 must give his consent if his name is to be changed by his parents. A mother cannot legally change the surname of a legitimate child without the father's consent.

When a child is 18, he can change his name without his parents' consent, either formally by deed poll or informally. Once a child has left home, even if he is under 18, there is nothing to stop him changing his name informally without his parents' consent.

Illegitimacy

A child is illegitimate if, at the time of his birth, his parents are not married and never have been. If his parents marry after he is born, he can be legitimized. An illegitimate child has equal right of inheritance with legitimate children if his parents should die without making a will.

A father has a duty to support his illegitimate child by making payments to the mother, either voluntarily or as a result of court proceedings and an affiliation order. But such orders are in favour of the mother, not the child: the child is merely the object of the court proceedings and has no right of his own to make a claim; therefore if the mother should die, the child has no right to claim economic support unless the father is prepared to pay voluntarily.

The mother of an illegitimate child has the rights and duties of a parent, regardless of her age. However, a person under 16 cannot in law be guilty of neglecting a child.

A mother under 16 is usually encouraged to have her child adopted, but if she keeps the child she can claim:

(1) Maintenance payments for the child from the father (see above).

(2) Supplementary benefit for herself and the child on the application of any adult in the household where she is living (although the money then officially belongs to the applicant, not to the mother).

Adoption

A child can be adopted through (1) local authorities; (2) adoption societies; or (3) private placements.

A child can be adopted formally only by means of a court

order. The law insists that two conditions are fulfilled: that the child's parents (or mother if the child is illegitimate) give their consent; and that no money changes hands. Illegitimacy, colour, race, and nationality should all be immaterial in deciding whether a child is eligible for adoption. An adoption order can be made by a juvenile, a county or the High Court. There is no law which insists that only married couples may adopt, but in practice courts rarely give consent in any other case.

Before an adoption order can be granted a child must have been in the 'care and possession' of the adopters for 3 months. If neither of the adopters is a parent of the child, the local authority must be informed. The child then becomes a 'protected' child and a child care officer (now known as a local authority social worker) visits the home. A guardian (usually a probation officer or a child care officer) is appointed during the 3-month period who checks that the application is in order and reports to the court.

When the court assesses the desirability of an adoption, the welfare of the child is not (as it should be) considered of paramount importance. It is simply one of the factors that must be taken into consideration.

In certain cases, the court has the power to dispense with the consent of the parents – e.g. where the parents have neglected or abandoned the child, or are withholding their consent unreasonably. Parents may make their consent subject to certain conditions, such as a stipulation that the child be brought up in a particular religion.

When a child enters a family by adoption, he severs all ties with his natural parents. All rights and responsibilities are taken over by the adoptive parents.

Registration

After the adoption, a certified entry is made in the registry of adoption, indicating that the child has been adopted and giving the names of the adoptive parents. There is no way of obtaining a certificate for an adopted child which shows the name of the adoptive parents, but does not show that the child has been adopted (apart from the shortened form of birth certificate). An adopted child cannot normally see his full birth certificate; but he has the right to apply to a court for details of the full certificate, and he may thus be able to find out information about his natural parents – this is a little known right that is rarely used.

An illegitimate child cannot be made legitimate by adoption. His original birth certificate and the certified copy of the entry in the registry of adopted children will clearly show this status.

Children are usually too young when they are adopted to be able to exercise any rights (if such rights existed). If a child is old enough to state a preference, his views will be considered but he will have no right to reject an adoption order if he disagrees with the decision of the court.

The right to adoption ceases when a child is 18, or when he marries, whichever is earlier.

Fostering

The fostering procedure is quite different from the adoption procedure. Foster parents look after a child on a temporary basis, sometimes for the length of his non-adult life, sometimes for a short period, for example whilst his mother is in hospital. The basis of foster care is to keep the child in touch with his natural parents wherever possible so that one day the family may be reunited.

Foster parents are required to sign an undertaking that they will allow a foster child to be withdrawn by the placing agency (local authority or voluntary organization). Normally, placing agencies are bound to return a fostered child to the natural parents when requested to do so. This would not be the case if the child were subject to a Care Order (placing him in the care of the local authority) or if the local authority had taken over the 'rights and powers' of a parent, in which case the local authority acting as the parent would decide where the child should be. It sometimes happens that foster parents are unwilling to allow a child they have looked after for many years to return to his parents and a tug-of-war develops.

Foster parents have one method of preventing the immediate removal of a child from their care – they can make the child a ward of court. Legal Aid is available for this purpose. Once the application is lodged, the child becomes a ward of court for a period of 28 days and the custody of the child is vested in the court. The foster parent may then ask for the care and control of the child and, so long as an appointment is made for a hearing within this period, the wardship continues until the issue is determined between the foster parent, local authority, and natural parents.

Religion

A young child cannot prevent his parents from making him a member of any particular faith or from going through formal ceremonies such as baptism. If he is living at home and they insist that he receive religious instruction, he has no legal right to prevent this.

The law requires that children in state schools receive religious instruction, but if the parents object to this and notify the school, the child may opt out (◊ p. 207). However, no child has the right to make this decision on his own behalf.

A child's religion may be altered after birth without his consent. This sometimes happens as a result of a dispute between the parents. The child's view will be taken into consideration if the court considers that he is old enough to hold an opinion; but his opinion is only one of those considered, and it may be overruled. As a rule, the court does not make comparative judgements between one faith and another, but it tends to take the view that a child should have some form of religious instruction rather than none at all.

Education

(◊ p. 201)

Sex

As far as the law is concerned, a girl under 16 cannot consent to any sexual act whatever. Any sexual caress is technically an indecent assault because in law a girl under 16 cannot given her consent to it.

In theory, the girl could be charged with being an accessory to the 'crime' but in practice she would almost certainly be dealt with under the Children and Young Persons Act – i.e. she would be judged in need of 'care and protection'. (◊ p. 154)

A girl over 16 can consent to sexual intercourse; neither she nor her partner should find themselves in legal difficulty unless action is taken under the Children and Young Persons Act.

Drinking on Licensed Premises

A child under 14 is not allowed to enter a pub or any licensed premises, unless he is the child of the occupier of the premises. A child is not allowed to drink until he is 18, nor can he be sent to buy drinks at a pub. He may have beer or wine with a meal if he is over 16.

Smoking

There is no law preventing a child from smoking in private, but it is an offence to sell tobacco to a child under 16 when it is for the child's consumption. A child between 10 and 16 can be charged with aiding and abetting the retailer who made the sale.

If a child under 16 is found smoking in a public place, a uniformed policeman (or park-keeper) may seize all tobacco and cigarette papers in his possession. However, a pipe or tobacco pouch may not be seized.

Betting and Gaming

A child can enter a betting shop when he is 17, but he cannot undertake any form of betting or gaming until he is 18. However, he may do so at any age in a private house in the presence of his parents or with their permission. A child over 14 can play dominoes or cribbage in a pub.

Cinema

Cinemas usually classify their films in a way which restricts the admission of children. The classifications are as follows:

'U' films are passed for general exhibition.

'A' films – parents are advised that they might prefer children under 14 not to see them.

'AA' films are restricted to people over 14.

'X' films are restricted to people over 18.

These classifications are made by the British Board of Film Censors. They have no legal effect, but local authorities can and do adopt the same classifications, thereby placing a legal obligation on the manager of the cinema (◊ p. 123). No criminal offence is committed by a child who goes to a cinema and sees a restricted film. The offence is committed by the exhibitor of the film who allows the child to enter.

Children who are too young to understand the nature of a film (probably children of 2 or under) may enter most cinemas, no matter what film is showing, provided the cinema manager has no objection.

Driving

A child of 16 may hold a licence to drive certain tractors and to ride motor cycles or invalid carriages. At 17, he may drive any vehicle, except certain heavy duty vehicles.

Driving while under age is punishable in a magistrates' court by a maximum fine of £50, and there is usually a further charge of driving without insurance. In addition, the child may be disqualified from obtaining a driving licence for a certain period. He may also have a future licence endorsed. If a child is charged with this offence, it is useful to have a lawyer to plead mitigating circumstances in order to prevent the child from being disqualified.

Work

All restrictions on work are lifted when a child reaches 21; a great many are lifted when he is 18. No child is allowed to work until he is 13, with two exceptions:

(1) His parents may allow him to do light agricultural or horticultural work if local by-laws permit this.

(2) He may, with a special licence, take part in entertainment (films, theatre, stage), but until he is 16 he cannot take part in a public performance if 'life or limb' is endangered.

At 13, a child may do light work if the local by-laws permit, but for no longer than 2 hours on school days and Sundays. On school days, a child may work for one hour, beginning not later than 7 a.m. and finishing before school begins. Consent of the school medical officer must be obtained first. On Sundays, a child may only work for one hour, before 7 p.m.

Local authorities may forbid anyone to employ a child, or may ask the employer or parent to give information about the employment. (◊ p. 207)

When a child has reached school-leaving age he may work full-

151

time. But there are a number of rules restricting hours and conditions for children working in factories.

A child may not normally work at night (10 p.m. to 5 a.m.) in a factory or any industrial undertaking. There are general rules covering hours of work, rest periods, holidays, and overtime. Children under 16 may only work a 9-hour day and a 40-hour week; those under 17 may work a 48-hour week. There are provisions for these limits to be extended under special circumstances. There are special rules forbidding children under 18 to work in certain industries, e.g. asbestos and lead processing.

Children under 16 may not work as street traders unless local by-laws permit them to be employed as such by their parents.

Trade Unions

A child under 16 may not join a registered trade union, and he may only join at 16 if the union rules permit. He will not be bound by any contract unless it is beneficial to him, and he may enjoy all the rights and privileges of union membership and carry out union duties but he may not join the union executive until he is 18.

Children in Court

A baby cannot be excluded from any court, criminal or civil. Restrictions are imposed on children over about 2 years, but there is no fixed age limit. A child cannot observe a criminal trial until he is 14. There are no restrictions in civil courts, but a judge may exclude a child at his discretion.

Witnesses

There is no age restriction on children giving evidence in court. A child may do so as soon as he is able to make himself understood and to understand the duty of speaking the truth. If a child does not understand the nature of the oath, he cannot give evidence.

Criminal Proceedings

In England and Wales a child under 10 cannot be charged with a criminal offence. Children over 10 can usually be charged with any offence, as an adult can, but children under 17 are tried by the juvenile courts.

Children under 14 cannot be subjected to criminal proceedings (except for murder and manslaughter) unless the prosecution alleges (1) that a child is being neglected, or is in some other kind of danger, or beyond control and (2) that 'he is in need of care or control, which he is unlikely to receive unless the court makes an order' (Children and Young Persons Act 1969). At the time of going to press these provisions have not yet been put into practice and it is unlikely that they will be introduced for some time.

Arrest and Bail

Children over 10 can be arrested by the police and detained for inquiries. They must be released on bail unless a policeman of or above the rank of Inspector considers that:

(1) It is in the child's own interest to be detained.

(2) There is reason to believe that the child has committed a serious crime and that his release would defeat the ends of justice or that he would fail to appear to answer the charge.

The terms 'in the child's own interest' and 'serious crimes' have not yet been defined by the courts.

A child who is arrested is detained by the local authority in what used to be called a Remand Home but is now called a Community Home. He may not be held for more than 72 hours without making a new application for bail. A child aged between 15 and 17 can be detained in prison if an Inspector certifies and a magistrate agrees that it is impracticable to hand the child over to the local authority because he is 'unruly of character'.

Questioning

A child should be interviewed only in the presence of his parent or guardian or, in their absence, of someone who is not a police officer and is of the same sex as the child. ($\diamond$ p. 11)

A child should not be arrested or interviewed at school if this can possibly be avoided. But if it is essential, the interview should take place only with the consent of the head teacher and in the presence of him or his nominee.

If a policewoman is not available, a policeman may take statements from a female child witness, but a male officer should never interview a girl on a matter that concerns sex.

The Hearing

A juvenile court hearing is conducted like a magistrates' court hearing, except that the language is simplified. A child has the right to consult his parents on any matter, unless the case puts him into conflict with them.

Sentencing

In addition to the powers of an ordinary court, a juvenile court may impose the following:

(1) *A Supervision Order:* This lasts for a fixed period – under the new Act it is anticipated to be for a maximum of 3 years or until the child's 18th birthday; the order can be repealed at an earlier stage. A supervisor is appointed from the children's department or the task may be given to a probation officer. Under a supervision order a child cannot be taken into care.

(2) *A Care Order:* This vests all parental power in the local authority. It expires at 18, unless it is imposed on a young person over 16, in which case it does not expire until he is 19. The local authority decides where the child shall live. This may be in a Community Home, with foster parents, in private lodgings or at

home. The case must be reviewed every 6 months. If a child runs away from a Community Home or commits an offence, he may be sent for Borstal training.

   (3) *Borstal Training*. (⬦ p. 33)

   (4) *Detention Centre Order*. (⬦ p. 32)

These orders may be varied on application to the court at a later date if the circumstances have changed.

Legal Aid

Where a child is financially dependent on his parents, assessment of legal aid will be on parental income and capital.
(⬦ pp. 18 ff.)

Civil Proceedings

A child has the same right as an adult to sue and to be sued. If a child is under 18, he may only do so through a 'next friend'. If he is sued by someone else, a 'next friend' is appointed by the court unless the parents volunteer. If a child wants to start civil proceedings, his 'next friend' must normally be his father; his mother may be accepted if a reasonable explanation is given to the court.

There is no way that a child can sue someone independently of his parents. He has no right or remedy if his parents refuse to apply for Legal Aid on his behalf or to give an undertaking as required of the 'next friend': this situation should be rectified.

Contract

A child under 18 is free to enter into a contract, but generally speaking such contracts are not enforceable by law. If, however, a child received essential goods or services as the result of an agreement or if it is otherwise for the child's benefit, he would be forced to abide by it.

Further Information and Advice

There is a serious lack of places where children can seek advice without fear that the matter may be referred to their parents.

The local welfare officer may help – he may be contacted through the town hall. Citizens' Advice Bureaux have the advantage of being independent of the local authority, but they may not be prepared to help. Otherwise, a sympathetic teacher (if there is one) may be a useful source of advice.

Child Poverty Action Group
NSPCC (National Society for the Prevention of Cruelty to Children)
The NCCL Children's Committee has published a series of papers on Children's Rights, including one which gives a description and critique of the Children and Young Persons Act 1969
A Draft Chapter of Children's Rights, Advisory Centre for Education, 1971
Paul Adams et al., *Children's Rights*, Elek Books, 1971

16. Students

Right of Admission to College and University

Throughout this chapter, 'college' means 'college and/or university'. There is no general right of admission. In nearly all colleges, the appropriate governing body or official (e.g. the Vice Chancellor) can refuse admission to any person without giving a reason.

Most (not all) colleges make certain academic requirements for each course of study. But the fact that an applicant meets these requirements does not give him the right to be admitted to the course. It merely makes him eligible to be considered for admission. There is no automatic right of admission for courses not leading to an examination (e.g. non-vocational part-time or evening courses) and for which there are no entrance requirements apart from the payment of a fee. A local authority is not obliged by law to run such courses, and can cancel them once they have been arranged if they are under-subscribed.

Grants

Local education authorities are obliged by law to award a grant to any person who: (a) is ordinarily resident in their area; and (b) possesses a 'prescribed qualification in respect of his attendance at a designated course'. A 'designated course' is a first degree course, (e.g., B.A., B.Sc., C.N.A.A., Ll.B., etc.) or a diploma or certificate of equivalent status. A full list of such

157

courses is published by the Department of Education and Science. These automatic 'mandatory' awards are given subject to certain requirements being fulfilled by the applicant – most of these are technical, involving the provision of all relevant information, etc.

Under the following circumstances, the local education authorities are not obliged to award a grant to someone who would otherwise qualify for a mandatory grant:

(1) The applicant 'has not been ordinarily resident in the United Kingdom for the 3 years immediately preceding 1 September of the year in which he starts his course; unless the authority is satisfied that he, his wife (or in the case of a woman student, her husband) or his parent was for the time being employed outside the United Kingdom'.

(2) The applicant has, in the opinion of the authority, shown himself by his conduct to be unfit to receive an award.

(3) The applicant has already attended a designated course; or

(4) He has attended a full-time course of initial training as a teacher or has successfully completed a part-time course of such training; or

(5) He has attended any full-time course of further education of not less than 2 years' duration, or a comparable course outside the UK (not counting courses in preparation for a prescribed qualification, e.g. 'O' and 'A' levels); or

(6) He has successfully completed certain part-time courses or comparable courses outside the UK.

The applicant will be considered to have taken a course if he has attended any part of it.

The amount of the award is fixed according to a parental means test. Parents are expected, though not legally obliged, to make up the grant to the prescribed maximum amount: currently £465 London/Oxford/Cambridge; £430 elsewhere; £345 if living at home.

Students whose parents do not have to be means tested are those over 25; women who are over 21 and married; students who have worked for 3 years between leaving school and going to college on a designated course (eligible for a full award as 'independent students'); and those in other special circumstances where parents cannot be found. Students over 26 may be eligible for a higher value mature students' award, depending on what they have earned in any 3 of the previous years. (In most cases the time is estimated from 1 September of the year in which the course starts.)

Grants for Married Students

A student who marries can gain exemption from the parental means test only if he marries before the start of the course, and is over 25 in the case of a male and over 21 in the case of a female. The grants structure seems designed to encourage students to live together rather than marry during their course. For example, two students living away from their parents' homes and attending college in the same town would each receive, before marriage, a means-tested grant at the 'away' rate of £465 maximum. On their marriage, they would continue to be means tested on their parents' incomes even though most parents would feel that their responsibility to support the wife had ceased.

A woman student who marries a non-student receives a special low rate of grant, means-tested on her parents' income.

Discretionary Grants

Education authorities are not legally obliged to pay grants to students not on designated courses. It is left to their discretion and the exercise of this discretion varies greatly. The NUS *Grants Handbook* details the attitudes of individual local education authorities to such awards.

Disciplinary Powers of Local Education Authorities

The grants structure can be a strong disciplinary weapon. Local education authorities have the power to withdraw a student's grant, which normally means terminating a student's career: this power is only limited by the provision that they must first consult the college authorities. The precise form of this consultation is not made clear. The education authority is not obliged to accept the advice of the college. Therefore in law, both the original initiative and the final decision rest with the discretion of the local education authority.

Education authorities may also require a student to 'provide from time to time such information as they consider necessary for the exercise of their functions . . .' This could be used to make inquiries about criminal convictions or penalties imposed by a disciplinary tribunal, on the basis of which the education authority may decide to withdraw a grant.

No education authority has yet made use of the above powers, but the possibility exists – a dangerous one, which could undermine the principle that responsibility for terminating a student's career should rest with the college, not with the local authority.

Rights within College

When a college makes an offer of a place and a student accepts this offer, the two have entered into a contract. The terms of the contract can be found in a number of different documents: prospectus, application form, letters between college and applicant, college regulations, etc. It would be a great deal simpler and fairer if all the terms were included in one document, but they are not.

The contract made between student and college is not a true contract in the traditional sense of the word: both parties do not have complete freedom to negotiate terms. What happens is that the weaker party (student) states willingness to adhere to the terms dictated by the stronger party (college). He has little option as to whether or not to contract, since his only alternative is to sacrifice his academic career for the sake of an abstract principle. He cannot shop around to find better terms. Under the terms of the contract:

(1) The student has the right to enter and use the various facilities of the college, but he has no legal right to control them.

He may not always be permitted to invite guests on to the premises.

(2) The student is only permitted to do those acts for which permission is given in the contract. The act cannot be considered in isolation from its purpose: e.g., a group of students may enter the administrative offices of a college to inquire about their vacation grants, but if the same group of students entered the same offices in order to paralyse the college administration by an occupation, they would be acting outside the terms of the contract and may be committing a trespass.

(3) If a college prospectus gives information about a course which bears no relation to the course given, the college would be acting in breach of its contract.

Discipline

Most colleges have some form of disciplinary code, but in many institutions a wide area of arbitrary discretion and power is reserved to the Vice Chancellor, the Principal, or the Governors. Normally courts of law will act to restore a legal right that has been denied by a college only if it is considered that the college acted in bad faith, or that the *procedure* adopted by the college was inadequate, e.g. if a student was expelled after a hearing which did not conform to the disciplinary procedure of that college, or for an offence not contained in the college's disciplinary code.

Unfortunately, there is nothing to prevent colleges meting out 'double discipline', i.e. punishing a student for an offence which has already been tried in a criminal court.

Intervention by the Police

If a group of students occupy a part of the college, they are trespassing. Trespass is a civil offence and the college authorities can take only civil action against them. This may include requesting the police to help remove students if they have refused to leave when asked. The police can only intervene when invited. *But*, if the police think it likely that criminal offences will be committed, they are duty bound to enter the premises to prevent such offences and to arrest offenders.

Even without a warrant, a policeman can enter and search a student's room in a hall of residence, if the warden has given him permission.

Representation

The facilities for representation vary enormously: there are no general rights, but you should always obtain advice and, where possible, representation if involved in a disciplinary offence. The National Union of Students will always give advice and in a limited number of circumstances the NCCL may be able to help.

Student Unions

In almost every institution of higher education where degree-level courses are taught, and in most Further Education colleges, membership of the Students' Union is automatic with college membership. In most cases, the local education authority will pay the union fees. The great majority of these unions are affili-ated to the National Union of Students.

Further Information and Advice

NUS (National Union of Students), 3 Endsleigh Street, London, wc 1

Academic Freedom and the Law, a joint publication of the NUS and the NCCL, 1970

17. Sex

Age of Consent

As far as the law is concerned a girl cannot consent to sexual intercourse until she is 16. Boys of any age can have sex without committing an offence, provided it is with a girl over 16 who consents (⟡ p. 149). Lesbianism over the age of 16 is lawful.

It is an offence, punishable with life imprisonment, for a man to have sex with a girl under 13. If she is between 13 and 16, the penalty is 2 years. It is not normally a defence to show that the girl consented or that the man was mistaken about her age. However, 3 defences are available if the girl is aged between 13 and 16:

(1) If the man is under 24, it is a defence to show that he had reasonable cause to believe that the girl was over 16 unless he has been charged with the offence before.

(2) If the man had gone through a form of marriage with the girl, it is a defence to show that he had reasonable cause to believe that the girl was his wife.

(3) There is a presumption in law that a child under 14 cannot be guilty of unlawful sexual intercourse with a female.

Contraception

There is no legal restriction on the right of men and women to obtain contraceptives, although doctors have the discretion to refuse to prescribe them. It is now the policy of the Family

Planning Association to provide contraceptives to married and unmarried women over the age of 16 and this applies to almost all their clinics. A woman cannot normally have an intra-uterine device installed nor can she have a hysterectomy or be sterilized without her husband's consent. A man cannot have a vasectomy operation without his wife's consent, though these restrictions are often ignored in practice.

Abortion

Abortion is legal if performed by a registered medical practitioner in a hospital or other approved place and if two doctors genuinely believe that:

(1) The continuance of the pregnancy would involve risk of the mother's life or injury to her or her existing children's physical or mental health (taking into account her actual or reasonably foreseeable environment); and that this risk would be greater than the risk involved in terminating the pregnancy; or

(2) There is a substantial risk that the child, if born, would suffer a serious handicap from physical or mental abnormalities.

If these conditions are not met, abortion is legal if performed by a registered medical practitioner who genuinely believes that the termination is immediately necessary to save the life or prevent grave permanent injury to the physical or mental health of the woman (Abortion Act 1967). If a woman is married, her husband's consent is normally required.

Affiliation Proceedings

If a woman wants to establish that a certain man is the father of her child (and therefore liable to help maintain it) she should make an application to a magistrate during the first 12 months after the birth of the child. She can do so at a later date if she can prove that the man paid maintenance for the child within the first 12 months after its birth. If the man left the country after the birth, she may start affiliation proceedings within 12 months following his return. Proceedings can only be brought by a woman who at the date of the birth of her child is single, i.e. unmarried, widowed or separated by a court order (Affiliation Proceedings Act 1957).

Prostitution

A woman may be prosecuted for being a 'common prostitute', but it is not a crime for a man to hire a prostitute for the purpose of intercourse. This contradiction is due to the fact that it is a criminal offence 'to loiter or solicit', and not actually to have sex (Street Offences Act 1959). Even so, it is not an offence for a man to solicit a woman, for example by 'kerb crawling'.

It is an offence for a man to solicit another man, either on behalf of a woman or on his own behalf (▷ p. 166). It is an offence for a man to live off a prostitute's 'immoral earnings'. If a man has no regular employment and lives with a prostitute, even if she is his wife, the onus is on him to prove that he is not living off her 'immoral earnings' (Sexual Offences Act 1956).

Homosexuals

Consenting male adults over 21 have the right to commit homosexual acts in private (Sexual Offences Act 1967).

There are no laws restricting lesbian behaviour and there never have been – apart from those which apply to heterosexual behaviour. (▷ p. 163)

The rights of male homosexuals are restricted in the following ways:

(1) They cannot legally have sex before their 21st birthday, although heterosexuals and lesbians can do so as soon as they are 16. Evidently the law was intended to protect adolescents from seduction by older men, and a youth under 21 cannot be prosecuted without the consent of the Director of Public Prosecu-

tions; but minors can still be prosecuted for committing homosexual acts with each other.

(2) 'In private' does not include in public lavatories, or in the company of more than 2 people.

(3) If 3 or more people are present, even if they are all over 21, consenting and in absolute privacy, homosexual acts are illegal.

(4) Members of the armed forces are not protected by the 1967 Act: they can still be court-martialled for homosexual behaviour, although they cannot be tried by civil courts.

(5) Homosexual acts are illegal if committed by 2 United Kingdom merchant seamen on board a ship where one of them is a crew member.

(6) The 1967 Act does not apply to Scotland or Northern Ireland, i.e. homosexual acts are illegal, even between 2 consenting male adults.

(7) Homosexual behaviour which would otherwise be legal can still be prosecuted under the Sexual Offences Act 1956, s.32: 'It is an offence for a man persistently to solicit or importune in a public place for immoral purposes.' In theory, this was intended to deal with men procuring customers for female prostitutes. However, in practice it has been used almost exclusively against male homosexuals, and in situations which have nothing to do with prostitution, but concern inoffensive meetings and pick-ups between two men.

(8) Policemen are entitled to exercise their discretion in order to carry out their duty of preserving the peace. Consequently, they can disrupt homosexuals' parties and close down their clubs more or less at will, if the people present are not behaving like heterosexuals.

'In September 1968, the Manchester magistrates fined a club owner for having allowed men to dance together. Evidence was given by the police who had visited the place in plain clothes that it was "a haunt of homosexuals". Presumably the homosexuals themselves were not outraged by single-sex dancing. Nevertheless, the owner pleaded guilty to having permitted dancing of a nature likely to cause a breach of the peace.'

166

(Anthony Grey, 'Homosexuals: New Law but no New Deal', reprinted from *New Society*.)

(9) There are still heavier penalties for homosexual than for heterosexual offences. Maximum penalties for some acts committed by older men with minors were increased by the 1967 Act.

Further Information and Advice

Brook Advisory Centre
Family Planning Association
Pregnancy Advisory Services
Simon Population Trust
Gay Liberation Front, 5 Caledonian Road, London N.1.
Campaign for Homosexual Reform, 28 Kennedy Street, Manchester 2.

18. Marriage and Divorce

Engagement

It is no longer possible to sue for breach of promise to marry. The gift of an engagement ring is assumed to be absolute (so it need not be returned if the engagement is broken) unless it can be proved that the ring was given on the condition that the marriage should take place (Law Reform (Miscellaneous Provisions) Act 1970).

Wedding Presents

If the marriage breaks up, it is assumed that wedding presents belong to the spouse whose parents or relations gave them to the couple.

Traditional Signs of Marriage

On marriage, nearly all women assume their husband's name, change their title from Miss to Mrs, and put on a wedding ring. But if they prefer not to, they are under no legal obligation to do so. They do, of course, have the right to keep their husband's surname after they are widowed or divorced.

Domicile

When a woman marries, she acquires her husband's domicile. 'Domicile' is a legal term which is important in the context of matrimonial proceedings (e.g. it determines where a divorce case may be tried); it does not affect a woman's right to choose her own country of residence. If a woman has been resident in one country (other than where she is domiciled) she may then sue for divorce in that country.

Citizenship

A woman who marries a citizen of the United Kingdom or Colonies may apply for registration as a citizen (this is not the same as naturalization which requires a long period of residence). A man has no equivalent right. (◊ pp. 258–9)

Insurance

When a woman marries, she may opt out of paying full National Insurance contributions. If so, she qualifies for a pension only under her husband's insurance and does not benefit until he reaches retiring age, 65, and receives a married couple's pension. (If, for example, she is 2 years younger than him, she will have to wait 3 years after she retires at the normal age of 60 until she qualifies for a pension.) She also loses any contributions she has made before marriage.

On the other hand, she may continue to pay full contributions (if she can afford it), in which case she qualifies for a pension in her own right, as does a single woman. Even so, she does not receive the full rate of sickness and unemployment benefit, but a special reduced rate for married women.

Credit

A married woman cannot normally open a credit account or enter into a hire purchase agreement without her husband's signature. Single women are often asked to provide male guarantors. There is no legal basis for this, beyond the fact that any firm has the discretion to refuse credit to a customer who does not agree to its terms. But if a woman feels that she is capable of entering into an agreement on her own – particularly if she is earning – she should insist on her right to do so. It is also difficult for a woman to obtain a mortgage unless she can show that she is past child-bearing age and that she is not a financial risk.

Sex in Marriage

Unless a separation order is in force it is assumed that a wife gives her consent to intercourse during marriage; therefore a husband can never be found guilty of raping his wife. But if he uses force or violence against her he may be found guilty of criminal assault.

If a man's wife is injured by another person's negligence, he may sue the wrongdoer for loss of his wife's services: he may claim medical and domestic expenses incurred as a result of her injury as well as a moderate sum for any 'loss of consortium' (i.e. sex); he may recover damages even when his wife's 'consortium' is only partially or temporarily impaired. A woman has no corresponding right to sue for loss of her husband's services or consortium – a ridiculous anomaly which dates back to the ancient assumption that a man has a proprietary right to his wife.

It is perhaps worth noting that a woman may sue for damages on her own behalf and if, as a result of her injuries, her husband leaves her, she may be able to claim damages for loss of his consortium.

Adultery

A man may no longer claim damages from a co-respondent in a divorce (his wife's lover). The co-respondent may still be liable for *costs* but while they could previously be awarded only against the wife's lover, they may now also be awarded against the husband's lover (Law Reform (Miscellaneous Provisions) Act 1970).

Matrimonial Home

When a married couple buys a house, it is advisable from the wife's point of view to have it registered in both names.

Joint Ownership

The most common way of holding property jointly is as 'joint tenants'. In this case, the property will pass automatically to the survivor on the death of one spouse, whether or not the deceased made provision to the contrary in his or her will, or left no will at all. Consequently the surviving spouse does not have to wait for the will to be proved or for Letters of Administration to be granted before becoming owner of the house. However, one party may sever the joint tenancy in a will or deed.

Neither party can sell the property without the consent of the other. If no agreement can be reached, a court order will be necessary to force a sale and for the proceeds to be shared.

Acquisition of an Interest in the Property

If the husband is the only legal owner of the property, the wife may acquire an interest in it which will give her a share of the

171

proceeds if it is sold. (The same applies to the husband if the wife is sole owner.) There are two ways of doing this:

(1) By contributing to the purchase money of the house.

(2) By contributing in money or in money's worth to the improvement of the property. The contribution must be a substantial one: the wife cannot acquire an interest merely by doing housework or minor repairs, paying domestic bills or looking after the children. But if there is a divorce, the court must take such contributions into consideration when deciding whether the husband should make financial provision for the wife. One way of ordering financial provision is to transfer property from the husband to the wife, regardless of whether she has acquired any interest in it. So the wife's 'moral' claim to the property by virtue of having cared for the welfare of the family and home may be recognized in some circumstances (Matrimonial Proceedings and Property Act 1971). Under the Act the courts have an unfettered discretion to determine the interests of both parties.

Wife's Right of Occupation

If the wife has acquired an interest in the home by either of the methods described above, she has a right of occupation. However, the husband is still entitled to sell the property, provided that he gives her a share in the proceeds.

Whether or not she has an interest in the property, the wife may 'register a charge' under the Matrimonial Homes Act 1967. This gives her the right to occupy the house until there is a court order for her eviction. (If she is the sole or joint owner of the property, she cannot register a charge under the Act.) If the husband then wants to sell or mortgage the property, the wife retains her right of occupation: in effect this means that he cannot sell or mortgage it until she agrees to withdraw the charge or until he obtains a court order, because no prospective buyer or mortgagee will take property with a charge on it.

Even if the wife does not register a charge, she has the right to stay in the home pending the hearing of a divorce petition. If necessary, the court can reinforce this right by ordering the husband to leave the home, but this would have no effect if the property were sold.

Children

Custody of Children

In common law, the father is the legal guardian of the children. They assume his name and he alone has the right to change it.

When a court decides whether to grant custody to the father or the mother, the welfare of the child must be its first consideration: it must not consider the common law right of the father, nor must it give preference to the mother's claim. In practice 'care and control' of the children is usually given to the mother; but in disputed cases the courts tend to award custody to the father. This means that the mother has the responsibility of bringing them up, while the father has legal control and the right to make major decisions concerning their upbringing.

In the case of an illegitimate child, the mother has prior claim to custody, in view of her obligation to maintain it.

Religious Upbringing

Unless there is a good reason to the contrary, the father has the right to determine the child's religion; but if the parents disagree and take the matter to court, the court must first consider what is best from the child's point of view. In one case a boy of 13 was allowed to choose his own religion against his father's wishes.

Appointment of Guardians

Either parent may appoint a guardian for a child to act after his or her death. (Where a child is illegitimate, only the mother may do so.)

Adoption

The consent of both parents is needed before a legitimate child can be offered for adoption.

Liability to Maintain Children

Both parents are equally liable to protect their children and both are liable to maintain them. If the Supplementary Benefits Commission gives assistance for maintaining a child, it may recover the cost from the father and/or the mother. If the child is taken into care by the local authority, both parents may be called upon to contribute to its maintenance.

Court Cases

Either spouse may sue the other in tort (i.e. for a civil wrong), but the court may refuse to proceed with the case if it appears that 'no substantial benefit could accrue to either spouse from a continuation of the action'.

In criminal cases, a wife may give evidence against her husband (and vice versa) but cannot be forced to do so; neither she (nor he) can be forced to give evidence for the prosecution, except in special cases.

Divorce

The Divorce Reform Act 1969 came into force on 1 January 1971. Under the new law, the courts recognize only one reason for granting divorce: *irretrievable breakdown of marriage*. In order to satisfy the court that this is so, the husband or wife applying for divorce (i.e. the petitioner) must establish one of 5 facts:

(1) The petitioner finds it intolerable to live with the respondent because he (or she) has committed adultery.

(2) Because of the respondent's behaviour, it would be unreasonable to expect the petitioner to go on living with him (or her).

(3) The respondent has deserted the petitioner for 2 years immediately before the petition was presented.

(4) Husband and wife have lived apart continuously for at least 2 years immediately before the petition was presented and both of them consent to divorce.

(5) Husband and wife have lived apart continuously for at least 5 years immediately before the petition was presented, when only one party consents to divorce.

A divorce petition cannot be presented until 3 years after the marriage. Only in cases of *exceptional* hardship may a judge give permission to do so at an earlier date (Matrimonial Causes Act 1965).

There are now only two reasons for refusing to grant a divorce:

(1) The court is not satisfied that the marriage has broken down irretrievably, e.g., where the petitioner has failed to establish one of the 5 necessary facts.

(2) In cases where the petitioner is relying on the 5-year separation to prove irretrievable breakdown, the respondent may oppose the granting of divorce on the ground that 'dissolution of the marriage would result in grave financial or other hardship to him and that it would in all the circumstances be wrong to dissolve the marriage' (s. 4, Divorce Reform Act 1969).

Judicial Separation

Any one of the 5 bases for divorce described above will provide a sufficient reason for establishing judicial separation. Husband and wife remain married, but their duty to live together ends. The consent to sexual intercourse implied in the marriage contract is revoked, so a husband may be found guilty of raping his wife if he is judicially separated from her. Either party may apply for judicial separation at any time – there is no 3-year rule.

Nullity

A decree of nullity declares that there has never been a marriage. There are two kinds:

(1) Void marriage – where there is not and never has been a marriage.

(2) Voidable marriage – where there is a valid marriage until a decree of nullity is pronounced.

Grounds for Declaring a Marriage Void

(1) One party is already married.

(2) One party was under 16 at the time of the marriage.

(3) Insanity (of the respondent).

(4) Consanguinity: the parties were too closely related to be legally married – e.g., you cannot marry your parent, child, uncle, aunt, niece, nephew, sister or brother (Marriage Act 1949).

(5) Lack of consent – e.g., there was a mistake about the identity of the other party or about the nature of the ceremony; or the marriage was induced by threats.

(6) The marriage ceremony failed to comply with the formalities laid down in the Marriage Act 1949.

The marriage is not normally invalid unless both parties knew of the defect.

Grounds for Declaring a Marriage Voidable

(1) Inability to consummate the marriage.

(2) Wilful refusal by the respondent to consummate the marriage.

(3) Either party was mentally unbalanced at the time of the marriage.

(4) At the time of the marriage, unknown to the petitioner, the respondent was suffering from a contagious form of venereal disease.

(5) The respondent was pregnant at the time of the marriage, unknown to and not by the petitioner.

You can petition for nullity at any time – there is no 3-year rule.

Citizenship

If a woman marries a citizen of the United Kingdom and Colonies and later gets a decree of nullity, she may still register as a citizen of the UK. (◊ p. 169)

Maintenance

A wife may apply to a court for an order that her husband should maintain her; and she may do so without a divorce or judicial separation. In most cases she will have a choice of applying to a Divorce County Court or to a magistrates' court. Until now, most women have applied to the magistrates but the Divorce County Court has greater powers (e.g., to order secured payments or lump sums) and its procedure is more in keeping with modern law. If a wife applies to either court, she must show that her husband has *wilfully* neglected to provide reasonable maintenance for her or for a child of the family. A husband may also apply for a maintenance order against his wife, but only in limited circumstances (Matrimonial Proceedings and Property Act 1970).

When proceedings for divorce or judicial separation are contemplated a wife may obtain 'maintenance pending suit': this may consist of periodical payments only. When a divorce is granted, 'financial provisions' may be ordered by the court: these may consist of periodical payments, secured periodical payments, or a lump sum or sums which may be paid in instalments. The court must take the financial circumstances of both parties into account as well as their contributions to the welfare of the family, including those made by looking after the home and the family.

Secured periodical payments differ from unsecured payments because they are derived from property or investments that one spouse has been ordered to transfer to trustees for the benefit of the other, for a certain length of time. While an order for unsecured payments cannot last beyond the death of one spouse, secured payments may continue during the lifetime of the recipient. Secured payments may be 'assigned' by the recipient so that they are paid directly to a third party (e.g., to a shop).

When circumstances change, either party may go back to court to ask for the payments to be altered. For example, if the former husband should remarry, his obligation towards his second wife will be taken into account and may lead to the reduction of his payments to his first wife. But if the transfer of property or lump sums has been ordered, these cannot be reduced or increased. An order for secured or unsecured periodical payments will always cease when the recipient remarries, unless the payments are in arrears.

Arrears

Arrears of maintenance are not enforceable as of right, nor do they constitute a 'debt', recoverable by appropriate court action. Payment of up to 12 months' arrears may be enforced, either in the High Court or in the magistrates' court; but the person to whom they are due should inform her (or his) solicitor in good time if the payments are not made punctually. One way of enforcing payment of arrears is by attachment of earnings (i.e. to have the amount deducted at source from the person's wages). This can only be done if the amount due is equal to 4 weekly payments, or (where payments are ordered at longer intervals) to 2 payments.

Widows and Widowers

A widow is entitled to a £30 death grant; a widow's grant for 26 weeks after the death of her husband; and a widow's pension if she is over 50.

A widower is entitled to a £30 death grant and, if his income is below a certain level, an allowance to pay for a housekeeper.

Further Information and Advice

Association of British Adoption Agencies
Family Planning Association
Independent Adoption Society
National Council for the Unmarried Mother and her Child
National Marriage Guidance Council
Rayden on Divorce, Butterworth, 1971

19. Landlord and Tenant

Introduction

This chapter sets out some of your rights, but you should re-member that if you try to put them into effect, you *may* risk legal reprisals from your landlord (e.g., he may give you notice to quit). The situation is deplorable but there is nothing in law to prevent this happening. So it is important to weigh up the pros and cons of the situation before you take action, especially when your landlord lives on the premises.

Written Agreements

Do not sign a tenancy agreement without reading it carefully and making sure you understand it. In particular, you should not sign it before you appreciate and accept the points in the landlord's favour. If in any doubt, get advice from a lawyer or a Citizens' Advice Bureau. In many cases, there is no written agreement, but once terms have been agreed between you and the landlord, you have the right to enforce them, although it may be difficult to prove the exact terms of the agreement in court.

Rent Book

If you have a weekly tenancy your landlord must provide you with a rent book. You should insist on having one and enter every payment into it. Do not let the landlord take it away. The rent book must contain the name and address of the landlord. It is a criminal offence to fail to provide a rent book or to fail to see that the information is accurate. The landlord's agent is liable to prosecution as well as the landlord.

Deposits

If you pay a deposit to reserve accommodation, it is almost impossible to get it back if you decide not to take the tenancy. In law, however, your deposit is recoverable provided you did not make a definite agreement to take the accommodation. It is best not to pay a deposit unless you are absolutely sure that you want to live there, and you know all the terms and conditions of the tenancy.

Premiums

It is now illegal to pay or receive premiums ('key money') for the privilege of being allowed the grant, transfer or renewal of a lease or tenancy: this applies to almost all residential premises. The same is true of excessive prices asked for furniture or fixtures, which are simply premiums in disguise.

If you are asked to pay a premium, the landlord is committing a criminal offence and you should report him to the local authority. If you have already paid a premium, you may be able to recover it by suing the landlord, but you are not allowed to recover it from someone who takes over the tenancy from you.

Deposits as Security

Landlords frequently ask for a deposit as security against non-payment of rent or damage done by the tenant. If you are asked to pay a deposit, make sure that you get a receipt and that it states clearly under what circumstances the landlord is entitled not to pay it back; get an inventory of everything contained in the flat, signed by you and the landlord. This type of deposit is sometimes a premium in disguise, as the landlord has no intention of paying it back.

Repairs and Decorations

Your responsibility for these will depend on the terms of the agreement between you and your landlord. If you have a short lease or tenancy agreement (for 7 years or less) your landlord is compelled by law to be responsible for the repair of the structure and exterior of the premises, including drains, gutters, and external pipes. He must also keep in proper working order the water supply, gas, electricity, sanitation, and the fuel supply for heating water (though not the appliances themselves). If you sign an agreement to be responsible for the repairs to any of these facilities, it will not be binding, as the landlord has a legal obligation to carry out the repairs despite the terms of the agreement.

If there is no agreement then the landlord is under no duty to carry out repairs other than those previously mentioned. It is your duty to take care of the premises and to use them properly. You must not alter the structure, for example by knocking down walls or removing partitions. You must repair damage or breakages done by you or your family, and if you have a yearly tenancy there is an additional duty to keep the premises wind- and watertight.

If an agreement requires you to be responsible for keeping the premises in a good state of repair, you should insist on the phrase 'fair wear and tear excepted' being included in the agreement.

Local authorities have wide-ranging powers to compel landlords to carry out repairs and improvements, particularly in multi-occupied properties. If you have any complaints, contact the public health inspector at your local town hall.

Assigning and Sub-Letting

Many agreements have clauses forbidding assigning or sub-letting. *To assign* means to transfer or dispose of your interest in the premises so that you have no further rights or obligations, although if you are the original tenant you will still be liable for the rent if a future tenant fails to pay. *Sub-letting* (or under-letting) means remaining a tenant to your own landlord but allowing someone else into the premises who becomes your tenant.

You should be careful before signing a lease which forbids assigning or sub-letting, because your landlord can refuse to accept any other person to take over from you throughout the length of the agreement.

You should try to add a clause to the agreement which will allow you to assign or sub-let with the consent of the landlord, 'such consent not to be unreasonably withheld'. But if these particular words are not included, the landlord will still not be allowed by the courts to refuse unreasonably.

If you feel that your landlord is acting unreasonably, it may be advisable to consult a solicitor.

Notice to Quit

Notice to quit must be in writing and must expire on a rent day, otherwise it is not valid. The minimum period of notice is now 4 weeks, even if the tenancy is on a weekly basis. If the tenancy is monthly, a landlord must give a full month's notice and if it is a longer tenancy the terms of notice are usually dealt with in a written tenancy agreement. Landlords frequently serve notices which are not valid (e.g., less than 4 weeks) and it is worth getting advice about this.

Court Order

If a summons has been taken out against you for possession of the premises and you want to stay, always seek advice. You may make an application to the court for an adjournment if you do not have enough time to get proper advice before the hearing. An application form can be obtained from the County Court offices. Do not leave matters until the last minute.

Even if an order for possession is made against you, it will not take effect the same day. The court has power to prevent the order becoming operative immediately. (◊ pp. 188, 190)

Rent Acts

If your tenancy is protected by the Rent Act 1968 you may be protected from paying a high rent and you have security. If the tenancy is outside the Act you are not protected. It is therefore important to find out if your tenancy is within the Act before you move in or sign an agreement. This will depend on the rateable value of your property. Many furnished and unfurnished tenancies, with the exception of luxury accommodation, will be within the Act.

The following paragraphs deal mainly with tenancies covered by the Act. It is important to know whether your house or flat is officially 'furnished' or 'unfurnished' because your rights under the Act differ according to the type of accommodation.

Furnished or Unfurnished

The distinction between furnished and unfurnished property is important because it affects security of tenure. Tenants of unfurnished property usually have an almost unlimited right to go on living there, but those living in furnished property have not. The question of distinguishing between the two is by no means obvious: flats which contain a few basic pieces of furniture are sometimes held to be unfurnished.

If you have been given notice to quit and you are uncertain which definition applies to your case, it is essential to get expert legal advice.

Rent

Furnished

If you live in furnished accommodation and want your rent reduced, you can usually appeal to your nearest Rent Tribunal, but remember that this may lead to your landlord giving you notice to quit.

You do not have to tell your landlord that you are making an appeal. The tribunal will probably want to inspect the property before the hearing is fixed. Unfortunately you cannot get Legal Aid for a Rent Tribunal hearing, and if you want to employ a solicitor, you will have to pay the costs yourself. (▷ pp. 97, 103)

Once the rent has been fixed, the landlord cannot legally charge a higher rent either to you or to a new tenant without making a fresh application to the tribunal. Generally, it will not accept such an application unless there has been a change in circumstances, e.g. the landlord has added new furniture or provided extra services. This does not stop many landlords from charging new tenants higher rents, so it is worth checking the register before you take over a tenancy. If you have paid more than the registered rent you should be able to recover the extra money by suing the landlord in the County Court.

Unfurnished

If your tenancy is covered by the 1968 Rent Act, you can apply to the Rent Officer (not to be confused with the Rent Tribunal) to get a 'fair rent' fixed (▷ p. 104). At present, you cannot apply if you are a council tenant or a member of a housing association or trust. Your Citizens' Advice Bureau or local authority will tell you where to contact the Rent Officer. You can do so even if you have agreed to your present rent, but you will have to propose a fair rent. 'Fair rent' is determined by a number of factors, including the age, character, and locality of the accommodation, and its state of repair. In theory, the fact that there is a scarcity of accommodation should not be taken into consideration, but it quite often is.

The Rent Officer will want to see your accommodation. He will then ask you and the landlord to discuss the rent with him. If an agreement is reached at this stage, the Rent Officer will register the rent: and this will include all payments you make to the landlord except rates.

If you or your landlord do not accept what the Rent Officer considers to be a fair rent, he will refer the question to the Rent Assessment Committee (◊ p. 105). Until the Committee considers the matter, you will have to pay the rent fixed by the Rent Officer. If the rent has been increased, the extra payment can be phased over a period of time.

The Committee may ask you for additional information and you may, if you wish, put your views in writing; a hearing date will be fixed and you may attend. Unfortunately, you cannot get Legal Aid for this, but you are entitled to be represented by a friend or by a solicitor if you are willing to pay him. You cannot appeal against the Committee's decision except on legal grounds: in such a case you may be able to go to the High Court to have the decision set aside, and you can apply for Legal Aid.

If you do not dispute your rent and it is not registered, the landlord may increase it to cover an increase in his own costs, such as services and improvements. Always get advice if he does this. In some cases, he must give you notice of the increase on a special form. If costs go down, the rent should be reduced. Disputes about this can be dealt with by the County Court, and Legal Aid can be obtained.

If you are thinking of taking unfurnished accommodation, it is important first to check whether or not it is registered: the register is kept by the Rent Officer. If it is, you cannot be asked to pay more than that amount, except rates, for the following 3 years.

If the property has been let in the past 5 years, the landlord will, in most cases, be unable to charge you more than the previous tenants, even if the rent has not been registered. If, however, the property is being let for the first time, you must try to get the best terms possible. You cannot ask the Rent Officer to fix a fair rent until you have actually become a tenant.

If your tenancy began before July 1957 and was not de-controlled by the Rent Act 1957, your rent cannot be increased except in certain circumstances, the most important of which are determined by the Housing Act 1969. Your landlord can apply for an increased rent if your home is improved to reach a specified standard or if it has already reached that standard.

The specified standard is defined as follows: the property must have all standard amenities (bath, hand wash-basin, sink, hot water supply to these, and WC of an approved standard); it must be in good repair (excluding internal decorative repair) with regard to its age, character and locality; it must be fit for human habitation, i.e. reasonably suitable for occupation with regard to repairs, stability, freedom from damp, internal ar-rangement, natural light, ventilation, water supply, drainage and sanitary conveniences, and facilities for preparing and cooking food and disposing of waste water.

If the property reaches this standard, the landlord can apply to the Rent Officer for a certificate of fair rent (▷ p. 186). Any in-crease will be phased over 5 years. No improvements can be made without your consent, although the landlord may be able to ob-tain an order from the County Court.

Security
Furnished

A tenancy for a fixed period, e.g. 3 months, requires no notice to quit and therefore the Rent Tribunal cannot give security of tenure. If your tenancy is weekly, monthly, or yearly, your landlord must give you notice to quit if he wants you to leave. (⟡ p. 183)

If you are given notice to quit and you wish to stay, contact the Rent Tribunal, but make sure you do this before the notice to quit expires: if you leave it until after the expiry date, the tribunal cannot help you. You do not have to inform the landlord.

You will be asked to complete a number of forms. The tribunal will then notify the landlord that you have applied for an extension of time; a hearing date will be fixed and you will be informed of the date. The landlord is entitled to object to any extension, but the tribunal has the power to override this and extend the notice for a maximum of 6 months.

If you want another extension after this, you can make another application to the tribunal, but you must do so before the first 6 months expire. You can keep going back in this way to apply for extensions. In theory, however, you cannot ask for a further extension if the first extension is for less than 6 months.

Your landlord can apply to the Rent Tribunal to reduce the existing period of security and this can be granted where (1) you have not complied with the terms of your agreement, or (2) you have been guilty of nuisance or annoyance to the occupiers of adjoining property, or (3) the condition of the premises has deteriorated because you have damaged or neglected it.

There are a few cases where the tribunal cannot give you any security. If your tenancy is fixed (e.g. for 6 months or for one year), this cannot be lengthened.

Whatever the circumstances, the landlord cannot evict you without first getting a *court order*. The court can usually make an order if a valid notice to quit has been served and has expired; and if any extension period given by the Rent Tribunal has expired. The court has power to prevent an order becoming operative for up to 28 days, so even if you have no grounds for objecting to a court order, it is worth applying for this extension.

Unfurnished

You will have security from a private landlord under the Rent Act 1968 if the rateable value of your accommodation is within the limits mentioned earlier. You will not be protected if you have a tenancy for more than 21 years or if your rent is less than two-thirds of the rateable value.

If you are protected it is very difficult to be evicted legally from unfurnished accommodation. The landlord cannot usually get you out by serving a notice to quit; even if you take a lease for a fixed number of years, you do not have to go when it expires. He can only make you leave by obtaining a *court order*. The court may grant an order in a few limited circumstances:

(1) The landlord can provide suitable alternative accommodation: this means that the accommodation must be reasonably suited to the needs of the tenant and his family, considering its rent, size and proximity to work.

(2) The tenant is in arrears with the rent or has committed other breaches of the tenancy agreement.

(3) The tenant is convicted of using the property for immoral or illegal purposes, has caused nuisance or annoyance to neighbours, or has damaged property.

(4) The condition of the premises has deteriorated because the tenant damaged or neglected it.

(5) The tenant has given notice to quit and as a result the landlord has contracted to sell or re-let the property.

(6) The tenant has sub-let the whole property without the landlord's consent.

(7) The landlord needs the accommodation for himself or his family. This will apply in cases where the landlord purchased the property before 1965 (and in some cases before 1956), and even then only if the court decides that greater hardship would be caused to the landlord and his family if an order for possession was not made.

(8) The accommodation went with a job which the tenant no

189

longer holds and the former employer requires it for another full-time employee.

Even if the landlord can show that any of these conditions apply, the court may still not grant an order. He must also show that it is *reasonable* to make an order. The court may suspend an order if the tenant undertakes to pay arrears in rent or to stop causing a nuisance.

The court *must* make an order for possession in one important set of circumstances. This is where the landlord was originally the owner-occupier of the premises and, when he made the tenancy agreement, gave written notice to the tenant that he might want to re-occupy the premises. The landlord must have lived elsewhere throughout the tenancy and must also require the premises for himself or for a member of his family who lived with him when he last lived in the house.

Eviction

If your landlord harasses or evicts you, or attempts to do so, you may have grounds for suing him in the County Court. The court also has the power to make an order preventing him from taking action which will harm or inconvenience you: this is known as an injunction. In emergencies you can obtain an injunction very quickly, long before the case itself is heard. You should therefore seek legal advice at the earliest possible opportunity. In an emergency, you can get legal aid within 24 hours. (⋄ p. 16)

It is also a criminal offence for anyone to evict a tenant without a court order. It is also a criminal offence to drive out or attempt to drive out a tenant by threats, violence, or any other means. A landlord can be fined up to £100 or given 6 months' imprisonment for a first offence, and £500 or 6 months for a subsequent conviction. These offences apply to all tenancies of whatever length, and not merely those within the Rent Act.

It is also an offence to interfere with the peace of a tenant, to cut off gas, water, or electricity, or to harass him in any way in order to make him leave. If this happens to you, and if there is any possibility of danger to you or your family, you should first inform the police. It has been found in many cases that the police are reluctant to interfere in what they describe as 'private disputes' and they will often say that they cannot interfere unless there is likely to be a breach of the peace. But most evictions or harassments are in fact 'public disputes' and the help of the police should be sought.

The police officer can only tell the landlord that he may be committing a criminal offence: he has no power to arrest him, even if he suspects him of committing this offence. The only way your landlord can be prosecuted is by the local authority, so if you want to complain about your landlord's behaviour, you must go to the Town Clerk's office and make a formal complaint.

A letter will be sent to your landlord explaining the law to him and warning him that he can be prosecuted. Most local authorities are reluctant to start prosecutions and in any case the procedure is slow and will not always help you to exercise your rights. When convictions occur, fines are usually quite light.

However, the landlord can be prosecuted by the police if he has committed other offences, such as assault. You can take civil proceedings against him for wrongful eviction, or if he keeps or disposes of any of your belongings; and you can apply for Legal Aid. If the landlord has shown racial discrimination, he may be reported to the Race Relations Board. (◊ p. 263)

Further Information

Citizens' Advice Bureaux
Citizens' Rights Office
Surveyors' Aid Scheme

20. Mental Health

There are four categories of mental disorder which may result in a person being detained in hospital or under special care:

(1) *Mental illness:* this means any mental disorder not included in the three categories below. It will include illnesses such as schizophrenia; or paranoia which may be of relatively short duration; or lasting brain damage resulting from an accident.

(2) *Severe subnormality:* when a person suffers from arrested or incomplete mental development, which includes subnormal intelligence, and is therefore incapable of leading an independent life, or is in danger of serious exploitation.

(3) *Subnormality:* a state of arrested or incomplete development which requires or responds to medical treatment or other special care or training (but which does not amount to severe subnormality).

(4) *Psychopathic disorder:* a persistent mental disorder, which may or may not include subnormal intelligence, which results in abnormally aggressive or seriously irresponsible behaviour, and which requires or responds to medical treatment.

Promiscuity or other 'immoral' behaviour may not by itself be considered as a form of mental disorder. A person who behaves in this way must not be detained in hospital unless his illness is so severe that it warrants observation or treatment, and it is in the interest of the patient's own health or safety or the protection of others.

Detention by Application

Anyone can make a voluntary application for treatment and may be admitted to hospital informally. Most patients are admitted to hospital this way. What follows concerns applications for compulsory detention.

A person may be compulsorily detained in hospital as a mental patient on application by a mental welfare officer, or by his nearest relative. Except in an emergency the application must be supported by the recommendation of two doctors, one of whom should be his G.P. These two must not have family or business connections with the patient, and one of them must be approved by the local authority as having experience in dealing with mental disorder. There are three kinds of application: observation, emergency and treatment.

(1) Admission for Observation

This is for cases where the medical officer needs time to decide whether the patient satisfies the conditions of mental illness and need for treatment, as described above. A patient may not be detained for observation for more than 28 days, and after that the application cannot be repeated immediately (Mental Health Act 1959, s.25).

(2) Emergency Admission

In an extreme emergency any relative or mental welfare officer can apply for admission with only one medical recommendation. The patient cannot be detained on this basis for more than 72 hours unless within that time a second doctor makes a recommendation, in which case the admission becomes an ordinary admission for observation. A patient who is already in hospital informally can be detained for 72 hours for observation on a

193

recommendation by the doctor in charge of the patient's treatment, and the same consequences may follow (s.29).

(3) Admission for Treatment

An application may be made for a patient already admitted for observation, or for a person outside hospital. A mental welfare officer may not apply for admission for treatment until he has consulted the nearest relative (◊ p. 198) (if easily available). If the nearest relative notifies him or the local health authority that he objects, then he has no power to make the application. In an extreme case, he can challenge the nearest relative in a court of law (s.26). An application for treatment cannot be made for a Subnormal or Psychopath over 21.

If a policeman finds a person in a public place who appears to be in need of immediate care or control, he can take him away to a safe place. He may not detain him compulsorily for more than 72 hours: during that time an application for admission for observation or treatment should be made.

An application for treatment is valid for one year. The responsible medical officer may then renew it for another year and after that for periods of 2 years at a time. Subnormals and Psychopaths must be released from hospital when they reach the age of 25 unless they are recorded as being dangerous.

Leave of absence may be granted indefinitely or for a specific period. If a patient is continuously on leave for 6 months and if at the end of that time he has not run away or been transferred to guardianship (◊ p. 197) he is automatically discharged.

A patient absent without leave may be detained and forcibly returned to hospital. A Subnormal or Psychopath over 21 may not be forced to return after an absence of 6 months and no other patient can be returned after 28 days: in both cases, the patient will be automatically discharged.

The responsible medical officer or the patient's nearest relative can discharge a patient at any time, but the medical officer can forbid discharge by the relative on the grounds that the patient is potentially dangerous to himself or to others.

Appeals

No appeals may be made against admission for observation. In other cases, the patient or the nearest relative has the right to appeal to a Mental Health Review Tribunal (◊ p. 113). A patient over 16 can appeal:

(a) At any time within 6 months of admission to hospital or of reaching the age of 16.

(b) Within 28 days when not released at the age of 25 (Subnormals and Psychopaths only).

(c) Within 28 days when reclassified from one of the four categories of mental disorder to another.

(d) At any time when the order for detention has been officially renewed.

A patient's nearest relative has the right to appeal:

(a) Within 28 days when his order for discharge is cancelled by the responsible medical authority.

(b) Within 28 days when a Subnormal or Psychopath is not released at the age of 25.

(c) Within 28 days if the patient is reclassified.

If a tribunal rejects an appeal, a further appeal cannot be heard for 12 months, except when appeals have to be made within 28 days, and in a few other special cases.

Detention by Court Order

When a person is tried for any offence punishable by imprisonment, the court or magistrate may make a hospital order on the recommendation of two doctors, if it is established that he committed the offence and suffers from mental disorder needing treatment (as above). In that event, the court may not impose any sentence of imprisonment or fine, or make a probation order. Hospital orders have no time limit.

This procedure is subject to the same conditions as an admission for treatment, with the following exceptions:

(a) The nearest relative need not be consulted.

(b) Subnormals and Psychopaths can be subject to such orders above the age of 21 and will not automatically be released at the age of 25.

(c) The nearest relative has no right of discharge, but he may appeal to a Mental Health Review Tribunal once every 12 months.

Restriction Orders

When a Court of Assize or Quarter Sessions makes a hospital order, it may also make an 'order restricting discharge'. If this happens, neither the patient nor the nearest relative may apply to a tribunal for discharge; the order does not have to be renewed at the normal times; leave of absence can only be given with the consent of the Home Secretary; patients absent without leave can be forced to return at any time. The Home Secretary becomes the only person who can release the patient.

The only right which remains to the patient is to ask the Home Secretary to refer his case to a tribunal for advice. The patient may do this whenever the order would have come up for renewal in the absence of a restriction. The Home Secretary must accept this request, but he is not obliged to take what advice the tribunal gives him.

A magistrates' court may not make a restriction order, but may refer a case to a higher court for the purpose. When a restriction order ceases to have effect, the patient is treated as coming under a hospital order only.

Detention by Direction of the Home Secretary

Any person serving a term of imprisonment may, on the recommendation of two doctors, be transferred to hospital by direction of the Home Secretary. Such a 'transfer direction' may also be made on anybody detained in a Children's Home, Borstal, Remand Home, or Approved School. It has the same effect as a hospital order made by a court and has no time limit.

When making a transfer direction, the Home Secretary may also make a 'restriction direction', with or without time limit. This has the same effect as a restriction order made by a court, with one exception: it must lapse when the period of imprisonment comes to an end. After that, the patient can appeal to a tribunal for release from hospital.

Guardianship

If a patient is suffering from mental disorder and requires treatment or care but is not likely to be a danger to himself or to others, he can be put into the care of a guardian instead of being detained in hospital. The guardian may be a close relative or appointed by the local health authority. This procedure is subject to the same conditions as admission for treatment, with the following important exceptions:

(a) Subnormals and Psychopaths must always be discharged at the age of 25.

(b) The patient's nearest relative has an absolute right of discharge; it cannot be cancelled by the medical officer.

An application for guardianship should be made to the local health authority, which is responsible for making the necessary arrangements. A court can pass a guardianship order instead of a hospital order, under the same conditions. It cannot, of course, pass a restriction order, as no potentially dangerous patient would be admitted to guardianship. The Home Secretary can make a guardianship direction on children at Community Homes, under the same conditions as a transfer direction.

Patients can be transferred from hospital to guardianship and vice versa. But a transfer from guardianship to hospital requires two medical recommendations. The patient can appeal to a tribunal at any time within 6 months of the transfer.

Mental Health Review Tribunals
(⇨ p. 113)

Who Is the 'Nearest Relative'?

The nearest relative is the first of the following who is over 18 and resident in the UK: husband or wife; child; father; mother; brother or sister; grandparent; grandchild; uncle or aunt; nephew or niece. When there is more than one person in any category, they are taken in order of age. There are a number of exceptions and the major ones are:

(a) Husband, wife or parent may be under 18.

(b) If a married couple are separated, the spouse will not be considered as nearest relative; any person who has been living as spouse with the patient for 6 months will be regarded as spouse.

(c) If a child or adolescent patient has at any time been taken away from its parents under the Children and Young Persons Act, the local authority or guardian will act as nearest relative, unless the patient is married. The same applies when there is a legally appointed guardian, except when the guardian has been appointed under the Mental Health Act.

(d) An illegitimate child is considered as the child of the mother only.

Anyone who is a relative or 'spouse' of the patient, or a mental welfare officer, may apply to the County Court for an order depriving the nearest relative of all his rights concerning the patient and appointing somebody else. This can be done on a number of grounds, the most important of which is that the nearest relative objects unreasonably to the patient being admitted to hospital, or misuses his power of discharge. In this case, the nearest relative (now the 'displaced relative') may still appeal to a tribunal once a year on the patient's behalf.

If such an order has been made and somebody else becomes nearest relative (e.g. by returning from abroad or becoming 18) he may apply to the court to have the order discharged. He must do so if he wishes to act as nearest relative. On the other hand, the nearest relative may renounce his rights in favour of anybody over 18 and resident in the UK; he may resume his rights at any time by a similar procedure.

The Patient's Rights within Hospital

(1) Letters

A postal packet addressed to the patient may only be withheld if the medical authorities consider that the contents may be harmful to the patient. If so, it must be returned to the sender. A postal packet sent by the patient may only be withheld if: (a) the addressee requests it; or (b) the contents are unreasonably offensive to the addressee, or defamatory to other people (not including the hospital staff); or (c) would prejudice the patient's interests.

No letters to the following people can be withheld under any circumstances: an M.P.; an officer of the Court of Protection; a manager of the hospital; the nearest relative or someone else acting in that capacity; a Mental Health Review Tribunal to which the patient can appeal; a solicitor nominated by the patient (unless he is unwilling to receive such letters).

(2) Visitors

The medical superintendent can refuse to admit any visitor if he considers it would interfere with the patient's treatment.

If the patient wants to be examined by an independent psychiatrist, this must be allowed, but the patient or nearest relative must pay the bill.

(3) Property

A patient's property remains his property and nobody is allowed to interfere with it without the patient's consent, unless authorized to do so by the Court of Protection (which can protect and manage property of mentally disordered people).

(4) Maltreatment

It is a criminal offence to ill-treat or neglect a patient who is undergoing treatment for mental disorder. Unfortunately it is extremely hard for a patient to convince the appropriate authority that an offence has been committed, but hospital staff managers and visitors who are alert and careful can do much to protect patients.

Further Information

Mental Aftercare Association
National Association for Mental Health
The Mental Health Act, 1959; *The Mental Health Review Tribunal Rules* (Statutory Instrument (1960) No. 1139); *The Court of Protection Rules* S.I. (1960) No. 1146, as amended by S.I. (1962) No. 553 and S.I. (1970) No. 1783: from HMSO and to order from most bookshops

21. Education

The Right to Education

Every child aged from 5 to 15 must receive full-time education. Local educational authorities (LEAs) are obliged to provide schools for secondary and primary education which are 'sufficient in number, character and equipment to afford for all pupils opportunities for education offering such variety of instruction and training as may be desirable in view of their different ages, abilities and aptitudes, and of the different periods for which they may be expected to remain at school, including practical instruction and training appropriate to their respective needs' (Education Act 1944, s.8. The wording of the section is ambiguous and it is difficult to know when an LEA is carrying out its obligations and when it is not.

It is the duty of parents to ensure that their children receive education. LEAs should see that they fulfil this duty and must serve a school attendance order on parents who fail to do so. The parents are first given the chance to prove to the LEA that their children *are* receiving full-time, efficient education and in theory they may be able to prove this even when their children are not attending school regularly. An attendance order will only be served if the LEA is not satisfied that the children are receiving adequate education.

If the parents object to the school named in the attendance order, they may ask the LEA to substitute another. They may also ask for the order to be revoked on the grounds that they have made arrangements for the child to be educated outside school. If the LEA refuses either request, the parents may refer the matter to the Secretary of State for Education who then has the final decision. If the LEA considers that the school proposed by the parents is unsuitable, it may decide to refer the matter to the Secretary of State for a final decision. If the parents still refuse to send the child to school, they may be prosecuted.

If the LEA fails to fulfil its duty to provide suitable facilities for a child's education, the parents may complain to the Secretary of State who, if satisfied that the parents' complaint is justified, may order the LEA to fulfil its duty. If the necessary facilities are not available within its area, the LEA should find a place for the child in another area.

Choice of Schools

Parents do not have an absolute right to choose which school their child attends. If more than one school offering the right type of education and within their area has places available, LEAs are supposed to meet parents' wishes where possible. The law is very vague on this point:

> 'The Minister and local authorities shall have regard to the general principle that, so far as is compatible with the provision of efficient instruction and training and the avoidance of unreasonable public expenditure, pupils are to be educated in accordance with their parents' wishes' (Education Act 1944, s.76).

The fact that the LEAs must merely 'have regard to the general principle' does not leave parents in a very strong position. In any case, there is little real choice because school places are usually so limited.

If parents want to apply to send their child to an alternative school, their case will be strongest if backed up with one or more of the following reasons:

(1) The school's religion is appropriate.
(2) The journey to the school is safe and convenient.

(3) There are special facilities, such as a midday meal if both parents are working.

(4) A single-sex or co-educational school is preferred.

(5) The child has brothers or sisters at the same school.

(6) Medical reasons.

(7) In Wales, there is a special consideration as to whether the school holds its lessons in Welsh.

However, there are equally strong reasons why the parents' application may be turned down:

(1) Distance: as a rule, children should not be allowed to attend a school where the journey is over 5 or 6 miles or takes more than 45 minutes, at primary school level; or over 10 miles or $1\frac{1}{4}$ hours at secondary school level.

(2) Overcrowding of the school of their choice: obviously the whole system would break down if all children could desert the 'bad' schools in favour of the 'good' schools.

If the parents' application is refused, they may appeal to the Secretary of State for Education and Science.

Many parents can only exercise freedom of choice by moving house to be near a school which they feel is suitable or, if they can afford it, by sending their child to a private school.

Regular Attendance

Parents have a duty to see that their children regularly attend the schools where they are registered. The proprietor of every school must keep a record of attendance and if any child of compulsory school age fails to attend regularly, the parents may be guilty of an offence. There are three defences available to them:

(1) The child was prevented from attending by sickness or another unavoidable cause – this must have affected the child, not the parent.

(2) The child was absent on days exclusively set apart for religious observance by the religious body to which his parents belong.

(3) The parent can prove that the school is not within walking distance of the child's home and that the LEA has made no suitable arrangements for his transport to school, for boarding him at or near the school, or for transferring him to another school nearer his home. 'Walking distance' is 2 miles for a child under 8 and 3 miles for a child over 8, measured by 'the nearest available route'. The determining factor is distance, not safety, so the parents cannot claim that the existing route is not safe; the 'route' does not have to be suitable for wheeled transport.

Transport

An LEA must provide free transport to enable pupils to attend its schools. If it fails to do so, it must give the children reasonable expenses to enable them to travel by other means of transport.

Private Schools

A private or independent school has no obligations to its pupils beyond what is stated in the contract made between the school and the parent. This may be incorporated in a formal document, or simply in an exchange of letters. The terms are laid down in the prospectus and the school rules, and they are usually the only terms on which the school is prepared to accept a child. The parents have very little bargaining power. They do, however, have the right to appeal to the Secretary of State on the following grounds:

   (i) the school has committed a serious injustice;
  (ii) unsuitable school premises;
 (iii) inadequate or unsuitable accommodation;
 (iv) insufficient or unsuitable instruction;
  (v) the proprietor or any teacher is unfit for the post.

What is said in the rest of this chapter applies mainly to schools maintained by the state, not to private or independent schools.

Authority over the Child

While a child is at school, within school hours, the teachers exercise the normal rights and obligations of parents towards children. They are therefore said to act '*in loco parentis*' and accordingly have the right to exercise reasonable discipline over the child. The LEA bears legal responsibility for any harm the child might suffer. If a child is sent home early for any reason, the school is responsible for his safe passage home.

In a strictly legal sense, the head teacher can exercise no control over what a child does or wears after school hours, but he can often exert pressure in other ways, e.g. by expressing displeasure.

Course Content

If a parent and teacher disagree about the subjects a child is to study, the parents may have strong grounds for pursuing their complaint if they can show that the subjects proposed by the school do not suit the *age, ability and aptitude* of the child. This constitutes a breach of the LEA's statutory duty and must therefore be put right.

Expulsion

A child under 15 (under 16 from September 1972) cannot be expelled from a maintained school. He can be suspended for a limited period, or transferred to another school, but the local authority must continue to provide facilities for his education. If a child of 15 or over is suspended for more than 2 weeks, he can then be expelled, but there must be a valid reason for expulsion, such as serious misbehaviour, prolonged absence, or failure to work.

Corporal Punishment

Each LEA makes its own rules about corporal punishment. Schools are supposed to keep a book which records corporal punishments, to be submitted to the school inspector. In practice, these books seldom record all the corporal punishments, and parents often do not know of their existence.

If a teacher contravenes the punishment rules of the LEA, or gives punishment which is not in line with the practice of the school, he should be reported to the LEA or to the headmaster. If a child receives punishment which causes bodily harm the teacher should be prosecuted for criminal assault. An LEA cannot be held responsible for the criminal act of a teacher if it can prove that the teacher acted contrary to express instructions.

Other School Rules

A school has no legal right to insist that a child does homework outside school hours. Unfortunately, if a parent objects, the school may retaliate by putting the child into a lower, less academic class which does less homework and thus limit his chances of academic success. There is no statutory power to compel children to wear school uniform, but the school can bring pressure to bear in other ways, in order to encourage the child to conform. A head teacher can make uniform a matter of school discipline and so can lawfully insist that it is worn.

Some schools, usually grammar schools, ask parents to sign a copy of the rules before their child is admitted. The parent is not obliged to sign them and has the right to object, within reason, to any of the rules.

Employment of School Children

(1) *Children under school-leaving age:* If an LEA thinks that a child at one of its schools is employed outside school hours in a way which is prejudicial to his health or which makes him unfit to obtain full benefit from his education, it may prohibit the employer from employing the child, or restrict the hours or type of the employment. The LEA may ask for information about the employment from the child's parents or employer. It is an offence to contravene the instructions of the LEA in this matter, or to refuse to provide the necessary information.

(2) *Children over school-leaving age:* An LEA cannot restrict or prohibit the employment of children over school-leaving age, but it can impose conditions on the child's continued attendance at school; in addition, a head teacher may make it a matter of school discipline. In one case the headmistress of a girl's grammar school threatened to refuse a testimonial for university or college entrance to any girl in the sixth form who took a 'Saturday job'. (▷ pp. 151–2)

Religion

Maintained and voluntary schools must begin every school day with 'collective worship' and must provide religious instruction according to the 'Agreed Syllabus'. This syllabus is agreed by representatives of the various churches in each area. In practice, many areas use the Cambridgeshire Agreed Syllabus. Any parent has the right to withdraw his child, both from religious instruction classes and from prayers. There must be a short break between morning prayers and announcements so that these children can be present for the announcements only.

If parents want their child to receive religious instruction of a kind not provided by the school, the child may be withdrawn from the school when necessary to receive religious instruction elsewhere. Certain conditions must be met:

(1) It must be impossible for the child to be sent to another school to receive the necessary instruction.

(2) Arrangements must have been made for instruction.

(3) Arrangements must not interfere with the child's attendance at school, except at the beginning or end of the school day.

Medical Inspection

An LEA must arrange for the pupils at its schools to be given a medical inspection at 'appropriate intervals'. This includes dental inspection. It is an offence for a parent to refuse to allow this without a reasonable excuse.

Special Education

If the LEA assesses a child to be in need of special education (e.g., if the child is handicapped, deaf, or educationally subnormal) and decides to send him to a special school, parents must be notified. They have the right to appeal against the decision. No single test should determine the issue – the assessment should be made on the combined evidence of the educational psychologist's report, teachers' opinions, doctor's opinion, etc. If there is a shortage of places at special schools, LEA's should try to provide special educational treatment in normal schools, although they are not obliged to do so.

Educational Welfare Benefits

These vary considerably from one area to another. Some LEAs will pay for a child to be sent to boarding school if the schools in the area are not suitable. Parents whose incomes are below a certain level can obtain grants to help buy school uniform or ordinary clothing for school wear, school maintenance grants to help support children over 16 who are still at school, free school meals, and free milk. Such benefits are usually badly publicized and many parents do not know that they are available. They can obtain information from the local divisional office of the Department of Education and Science, or from a Citizens' Advice Bureau.

Where to Lodge Complaints

Parents have few legal rights where their children's education is concerned, but a complaint to the headmaster can often have a considerable effect within the school although parents and children will not immediately be aware of it.

Complain first to the headmaster; if that fails, to the Divisional Officer for Education (the address can be obtained from your Citizens' Advice Bureau) and then to the Director of Education in your area. Ultimately, there is the right of appeal to the Secretary of State for Education and Science, who has powers to intervene if LEAs, school governors, or managers have failed to fulfil their duties, or are proposing to use their powers unreasonably (Education Act 1944, ss.68, 99).

Further Information and Advice

The Advisory Centre for Education

The Department of Education and Science, Curzon Street House, Curzon Street, London w1

Public libraries normally have copies of the Education Act 1944.

For information on special education: The Association for Special Education; The National Society for Mentally Handicapped Children

22. Law and the Consumer

Every time you pay for goods or services, you enter into a contract. The rights of the tradesman and the consumer are affected by the terms of such contracts. They vary a great deal: some are written and some are spoken, or simply understood by the nature of the transaction, but all are legally binding. Both parties are usually free to make whatever kind of agreement they like, but in some fields the law lays down special requirements to protect the consumer (e.g. hire purchase contracts are regulated by law and must be in writing; some unfair selling methods and the sale of unsafe products are illegal).

Food

Quality

Food sold for human consumption must be of sound quality. The places where food is prepared and sold must conform to certain standards of hygiene. If you buy unfit food and fall ill as a result, you can sue the retailer for compensation. Sometimes the manufacturer is responsible and can be sued, e.g. when food is in tins and reaches the consumer in the same state as it left the factory. Other complaints about the purity and fitness of food should be made to the local Public Health Inspector.

Quantity

If food is pre-packed, the net weight must be shown on the container. Certain types of goods can only be packaged in specified amounts (e.g. flour and rice can only be sold in packages of 1 oz, 2 oz, 4 oz, 8 oz, 12 oz, 1 lb, 1½ lb, or multiples of 1 lb). Pre-packed apples, oranges, etc. need not have the weight marked if the wrapping is transparent and there are not more than 8 in the pack.

When food is not pre-packed, its weight must be made known to the buyer before he pays for it. The seller can make the weight known in several ways:

(a) By measuring or counting the food in front of the customer, in which case the scales must be well in view.

(b) By writing the weight on the invoice when goods are delivered.

(c) By providing scales for the customer to weigh pre-packed fruit and vegetables.

Complaints about short weight, faulty scales, etc. should be made to the Weights and Measures Department at the local Town Hall.

Shopping Generally

Examine every article carefully before buying it; find out how it works and whether it will be suitable for the purpose for which you intend it. If you do not do this, and you later find some defect, you may have no legal remedy. Of course this does not apply if the article is wrapped up and it is difficult to open the package in the store.

If goods are faulty, complain first to the seller. You have the right to compensation under the Sale of Goods Act 1893, except in the following circumstances:

211

(a) When the seller indicated in the first place that the goods were sub-standard.

(b) When the seller has opted out by stating beforehand (and in theory letting his customers know) that transactions made by him will not be affected by the Act. The Act allows him to do this.

(c) When the goods are covered by a manufacturer's guarantee which frees the seller from his obligations.

When the seller is obliged to put matters right, he may do so in one of five ways:

(a) By repair which corrects the fault without materially altering the value, appearance or usefulness of the article.

(b) By replacement.

(c) By refunding part of the purchase price, according to the nature of the defect.

(d) By refunding the whole sum if the article is entirely unfit for its intended purpose.

(e) By giving a credit note.

A different article can be substituted, but you do not have to agree to this. If part refund is offered, you do not have to accept if you think it is inadequate.

If the matter cannot be settled voluntarily, you can sue the seller for compensation. But first consult your Citizens' Advice Bureau, who may be able to help settle the matter out of court, or otherwise help you to apply for Legal Aid (◇ pp. 15 ff.).

Sometimes it is possible to sue the manufacturer, but only if he has made himself responsible, e.g. by a guarantee.

Manufacturer's Guarantee

An enormous range of goods is now covered by guarantees. The wording is not standardized and should be read carefully. Some must be signed and sent back before they have any effect; others apply immediately. By accepting some guarantees, you forfeit your right to complain against the seller, but the law may soon be changed to make this illegal.

A guarantee can be useful if it preserves the rights the buyer would ordinarily have under the law; if it provides repair and replacement free of charge; and if it provides compensation for loss or damage caused by defects.

Credit Notes

Shops frequently offer credit notes when goods are returned by dissatisfied customers. They should be read carefully: some are only valid if used before a certain date; but if no date is mentioned, they are valid for 6 years.

You have the right to refuse a credit note if the goods you have returned were defective when you bought them; but not if there was nothing wrong with them and you simply changed your mind.

Credit Sale and Hire Purchase

The law protects people who buy goods on credit, and particularly those who buy on hire purchase, because the owner (usually a finance company) has the right to reclaim possession of the goods if instalments are not paid.

Difference between Hire Purchase and Credit Sale

(1) Under a hire purchase agreement, the goods do not belong to the buyer until he has paid the last instalment. Therefore the buyer is not allowed to re-sell or give away the goods without the owner's consent; he must take good care of them; if goods are lost or damaged, he is still liable to pay any outstanding balance.

(2) Under a credit sale agreement, the buyer becomes the owner as soon as he takes possession of the goods.

Agreements Protected by the Hire Purchase Act 1965

(1) All hire purchase agreements for any sum up to £2,000.

(2) Credit sale agreements between £30 and £2,000 where repayment is to be made in 5 or more instalments.

Rights under Hire Purchase and Credit Sale Agreements

(1) If you sign the agreement at home, a copy of the agreement must be sent to you within 7 days. For 3 days after receiving this copy, you may notify the seller that you want to cancel the agreement altogether. If so, you must return in good condition any goods you have already received and refuse delivery of any that are yet to arrive. You have the right to receive back any deposit you have paid.

(2) After one third of the purchase price has been paid, goods can only be re-possessed if the owner gets an order from the County Court.

Additional Rights under Hire Purchase Only

(1) If goods are defective, the owner (i.e. the finance company) is responsible for putting them right.

(2) The owner is liable for the quality of the goods he sells unless they are sold as second-hand or defective goods. But the clause of the agreement which releases an owner from responsibility must be shown and explained to the buyer. Otherwise the owner will still be liable.

If You Cannot Keep up with Instalments

If the goods were bought on *credit sale*, you can sell them and use the money to pay the remainder of what you owe. If the goods were bought on *hire purchase*, you can give them up at any time. You must notify the owner in writing that you are discontinuing payments. You must also pay all the instalments owing up to the date when you return the goods. *In addition*, you must, if necessary, make up the amount you pay to half the total sum in the original agreement (although if you feel that the owner has not lost this amount on the transaction you can allow the matter to go to court and the court *may* decide that you should pay less).

When you return the goods you may be liable for any damage done to them over and above what is fair wear and tear. Some hire purchase companies make excessive claims for damage. If this happens it may be worth withholding payment and letting the matter go to court.

Safety

Some goods are controlled by the Consumer Protection Acts 1961 and 1971, and have to meet certain standards of safety:

(a) Paraffin heaters.

(b) Inflammable nightdress material.

(c) Children's cots.

(d) Toys: the use of celluloid is prohibited except in ping-pong balls, and the amount of lead, arsenic and other poisons is restricted in paint used for toys.

(e) Electric blankets.

Complaints should be made to the Weights and Measures Department at your local Town Hall, or to the Public Health Inspector.

Unsolicited Goods

If you receive goods at your home that you have not ordered and do not want, the sender has 6 months in which to take them back. If he does not, they become your property. This 6-month period can be reduced if you write to him saying you do not want the goods. He will then have 30 days in which to arrange to take the goods back. You can write any time after you have received the goods provided there are not less than 30 days remaining of the 6-month period.

In your letter – which may be delivered by hand or sent through the post – you must give your name, your address (or the address from which the goods may be collected) and you must also say that you had not ordered the goods (Unsolicited Goods and Services Act 1971).

Pricing

A price tag is not legally binding. The buyer has the right to offer the seller a different price for his goods from the one stated, and it is then up to the seller to accept or not.

If the seller claims that there has been a mistake and the price is in fact higher than the one marked, he is within his rights to refuse to sell for less. But he is in danger of breaking the law. It is an offence under the Trade Descriptions Act 1968 to indicate that goods are actually cheaper than the price at which they are meant to be sold. If he claims a price reduction, the goods must have been sold at the higher price for 28 consecutive days during the last 6 months. On the other hand, there is nothing to stop him claiming that his goods are cheaper than his competitors', or that they are a special cheap line.

Misleading Information

It is an offence to make a false description of goods – about their quantity, purpose, previous history, date and place of manufacture, etc. It is also an offence to make a false description about services, e.g. holiday brochures which inaccurately describe accommodation and facilities. But a seller is not obliged to give any description at all.

Part-Payments and Deposits

These should not be confused.

A *part-payment* is part of the agreed price and the buyer is entitled to claim some or all of it back if the sale falls through.

A *deposit* is a separate agreement, a sign of the buyer's serious intention to enter into negotiations. Unless it is previously agreed that the deposit is in part-payment and recoverable, it may be impossible to claim it back.

Repairs and Services

A person who repairs or cleans other people's belongings has the right to keep them until his charge has been paid. He can sell uncollected goods provided he prominently displays a notice to say that goods are accepted for treatment under the provision of the Disposal of Uncollected Goods Act 1952. He must follow certain steps before the goods can be sold:

(a) Notify the customer that the goods are ready and tell him how much the service has cost.

(b) Tell the customer that his goods will be sold if payment is not made within 12 months.

(c) 14 days before the sale is due, send notice by registered letter that the goods are to be sold.

If he indicates the lowest price that he is prepared to sell for, he can then sell to anyone; if not, the goods must be sold by public auction. After he has deducted his charges, the previous owner may recover any surplus.

Sale by Agreement

The above conditions will not apply if the repairer or cleaner makes a separate arrangement which is not bound by the Act, e.g. if he puts a notice on the wall and on the collecting slip, stating when goods are to be sold (sometimes as soon as 3 months). This constitutes an agreement, and the repairer can sell the goods if they are not paid for within that time.

Powers of Entry by Gas and Electricity Board Officials

Gas and Electricity Board officials may seek entry into private homes to carry out inspections, repairs, maintenance, or to cut off the supply if bills have not been paid. In some cases, no notice need be given.

(a) Electricity Board officials need not give notice to inspect lines, meters, accumulators, fittings, works, and other apparatus belonging to the Board; to read meters; or to discontinue a supply.

(b) Gas Board officials need not give notice to read meters or to inspect fittings and works; the Board must give 24 hours' notice if it intends to remove pipes to discontinue the supply.

An authorized official must arrive at a reasonable time (this is not defined, but presumably a visit made during daylight would satisfy the requirement), and must produce evidence of his authority.

When notice is required, it can be delivered to the person, sent by registered post or left at his usual address, or addressed to the occupier and left in a conspicuous place not less than 48 hours before the premises are entered.

Cutting off Power

The Gas Board can cut off supplies if a bill is not paid within 28 days, but must give written notice 7 days beforehand.

The Electricity Board must allow 21 days' notice, then after a further 7 days a final notice must be sent, saying that if the bill is not paid, the Board may cut off supply. Next, an authorized officer calls and if he cannot get in, further steps are taken. The Boards must either have the owner's consent or obtain a warrant from a magistrates' court. To obtain the warrant, they must satisfy the magistrate that 24 hours' notice has been given. (In practice, more than 24 hours is given.) They must give sworn information as to why admission is required and show that they have a statutory right to enter for that purpose. They must also show that preliminary proceedings have been carried out as required by law.

In the case of emergency (i.e. when life or property is endangered), the above conditions do not apply. The Boards must satisfy the magistrate that there is an emergency; that admission is refused or that the premises are unoccupied; and that it would be inappropriate to go through the normal procedure.

When a warrant is issued, it remains in force until entry has been successfully completed. The Boards must repair all damage caused by entry, or pay compensation. If the occupier is absent, premises must be left as secure against trespassers as they were found.

Complaints

Gas

If you have a complaint about supply, services, or appliances from the Gas Board, first complain to the local showroom. If your complaint cannot be settled at this level, refer it to the nearest Gas Consultative Council (the address can be obtained from your Citizens' Advice Bureau) and if that fails, to the Minister for Industry at the Department of Trade and Industry.

Electricity

Complain first to your local showroom; then to the nearest Electricity Consultative Council; failing that, to the Electricity Council, and finally to the Minister for Industry.

Solid Fuel

First approach your coal merchant; if he does not help, complain to the producer of the fuel, e.g. the National Coal Board. Complaints about service should go to the regional panel of the Approved Coal Merchants' Scheme (address from merchants who are members of the scheme). Finally, you can complain to the Secretary of the Domestic Coal Consumers' Council, Thames House South, Millbank, London sw1.

Railways

Complain first to the regional railway board and if that fails, to the local area Transport Users Consultative Committee (address from main post offices, railway booking and inquiry offices, and telephone directories).

Plumbing

Most established plumbing firms are members of the National Federation of Plumbers and Domestic Heating Engineers – if the plumbing firm does not deal with your complaint, write to the Federation at 6 Gate Street, London wc2.

Building

If you want to complain about building that was done within the last 5 years, it may have been certified by the National House-builders Registration Council, 58 Portland Place, London w1. If so, you can complain to them.

Complaints to Local Authorities

The Weights and Measures Departments of local authorities enforce the Trade Descriptions Act, the Weights and Measures Act, and other Acts which affect consumer interests. The Public Health Inspector deals with complaints about bad food, unhygienic shops, eating places, and lavatories, rubbish dumps, etc. Complaints about education, school meals, etc. are dealt with by the local education authority; street lighting, parks, playgrounds, etc. by the borough engineer and surveyor; housing and planning permission by the borough architect and planner; and any other complaints should be addressed to the Town Clerk.

Citizens' Advice Bureaux can often help with a wide range of complaints.

Further Information and Advice

Citizens' Advice Bureaux
Consumers' Association
National Federation of Consumer Groups

23. Drugs

Classification of Drugs

Controlled drugs are divided into three classes:

CLASS A: includes heroin, opium, morphine, and other narcotics; it also covers LSD, injectible amphetamines, STP, and cannabinol.

CLASS B: controls 6 narcotics and 5 stimulant drugs of the amphetamine type, such as Drinamyl (purple hearts), Benzedrine and Dexedrine; it also covers cannabis and cannabis resin.

CLASS C: includes 9 named amphetamine-type drugs which are considered to be less dangerous.

For all offences, penalties for class C drugs are lower; class B drugs carry lower penalties than class A for possession, but for all other offences, classes A and B carry the same penalties (Misuse of Drugs Act 1971).

Possession

Some of these drugs, in certain circumstances, can be obtained legally on a doctor's prescription. Amphetamines and morphine, for example, are used for medicinal purposes. Registered addicts can obtain heroin on prescription, but only from doctors at treatment centres, who hold special licences. Cannabis cannot be obtained legally, except in very limited circumstances for research.

It is an offence to possess a controlled drug except on prescription. It may be a defence to say that you thought you were entitled to have it – i.e. on prescription. It may also be a defence if you can show that you did not know that the drug was in your possession, but that is not easy because the burden of proof lies with the defence.

You may be found guilty of possession even when the amount is too small to be of any use to you – such as traces found in a pocket or ashtray which are visible only under a microscope.

If the drug is one that can be detected by means of a blood or urine test, you may be convicted on the basis of this evidence. Amphetamines and hard drugs can be detected this way, but cannabis cannot as yet.

Penalties for Possession

The maximum penalties are: class A – 12 months and/or £400 fine on a summary conviction, or 7 years and/or an unlimited fine on indictment; class B – 6 months and/or £400 fine on a summary conviction, or 5 years and/or an unlimited fine on indictment; class C – 6 months and/or £200 on a summary conviction, or 2 years and/or an unlimited fine on indictment. ('Summary conviction' means conviction by a magistrate; 'indictment' means trial before a judge and jury.)

Production and Supply

It is an offence to produce or supply controlled drugs, to have possession with intent to supply, or to attempt any of these things. There is no definition of what constitutes 'intent to supply' but no doubt anyone found in possession of more than a very small quantity could be accused of 'intent to supply'. It is also an offence to grow, or try to grow, cannabis.

Penalties for Production and Supply

The maximum penalties for these offences are much higher than those for possession: classes A and B – 12 months and/or £400 fine on a summary conviction, or 14 years and/or an unlimited fine on indictment; class C – 6 months and/or £200 fine on a summary conviction, or 5 years and/or an unlimited fine on indictment.

Although it is logical to impose heavier penalties on the supplier than on the user, there is a danger that the police may find it too easy to add this charge to the charge of possession, merely to encourage the accused to plead guilty to the lesser charge.

Liability of Occupiers and Managers

An occupier or manager of premises where people are found taking or supplying drugs may be guilty of an offence – but only if the prosecution can prove that he knew what was going on. Penalties for this offence are the same as those for production and supply.

Analysis

In all cases involving drugs, the substance must be analysed and this can take up to three weeks. Meanwhile, the accused may be released on bail, either by the police or by the magistrate (◊ p. 4). In some cases, a suspect tends to be formally charged in a magistrates' court before the analysis has been completed, but it is now more common to wait until after the substance is known to be illegal before a charge is made – a far more reasonable procedure.

Defence solicitors may arrange for a separate analysis to be made, but this must be done in the presence of the forensic scientist who carried out the analysis for the prosecution.

If the drug, on analysis, is found to be harmless, it is still possible to be convicted for attempting to procure a controlled drug.

Police Powers

Search of Person

Police have powers to search and detain anyone whom they reasonably suspect of illegal possession of drugs (◊ p. 47). But what amounts to 'reasonable suspicion' cannot adequately be defined:

> 'The police seem to have interpreted this law to mean that they have the right to make random searches. Long hair, unconventional dress, youthful appearance and being out on the streets after midnight are all considered by the police to be reasonable grounds. Any young person can be stopped and searched for no other reason than that they are perceived as part of a suspect generation. Their pockets will be gone through and, if the police are not convinced of their innocence, they will be taken to the police station for a more thorough search.' Michael Schofield, *The Strange Case of Pot*.

The Home Office Advisory Committee on Drug Dependence (Deedes Report) recommended that the police should accept that modes of dress and hairstyle do not by themselves constitute reasonable grounds to stop and search a suspected drugs offender – but this has had no noticeable effect on police behaviour.

If a policeman asks to search you, it is usually advisable to let him, even if you believe that he has no reasonable grounds for suspicion. If you refuse, you may be accused of obstructing the policeman in the course of his duty – and the court is more likely to be sympathetic to a policeman's view of what is 'reasonable suspicion' than to the view of an ordinary citizen. If you object to the way the policeman has treated you, you will have the opportunity to complain later. (◊ pp. 88 ff.)

If you are taken to a police station, you may be made to strip for a more thorough search; if you are a woman, you may be searched only by a female officer.

Search of Premises

The police have powers to search any vehicle or vessel suspected of containing controlled drugs and to seize and detain anything that may be evidence of a drugs offence. They may search private premises only with a warrant from a magistrate. In order to obtain a warrant, they should satisfy the magistrate, with sworn evidence, that there is reason to suspect that drugs, or documents concerning drugs offences, may be on the premises. Once the warrant has been issued, it lasts for one month and may be used by any policeman operating in the area of the premises named in the warrant.

There seems to be no limit to what a policeman may seize during a search. Address books, for instance, are often retained on the grounds that they are needed as exhibits.

Arrest

The Misuse of Drugs Act gives a police officer power to arrest without a warrant if:

(a) He reasonably suspects that the person will abscond if he is not arrested.

(b) He cannot find out the person's name and address.

(c) He is given the name and address, but is not satisfied that they are genuine.

Cannabis and the 1971 Act

The main drawback of the present law is its treatment of cannabis offences. The Wootton Report has been almost totally ignored: it suggested in 1969 that the use of cannabis should not be associated in legislation with hard drugs, but should be treated separately as a less serious offence; for all cannabis offences, it suggested a maximum fine of £100 and/or 4 months' imprisonment on a summary conviction, or up to 2 years' imprisonment and/or an unlimited fine on indictment.

For all offences except possession, the 1971 Act treats cannabis and heroin offences with equal severity and imposes penalties which are even higher than those imposed by the courts before the Act was passed.

Barbiturates are not on the list of controlled drugs, although when taken habitually in large quantities they produce all the characteristics of addiction. They are most frequently prescribed for middle-aged people as sleeping pills and sedatives – and, like alcohol, they have become socially acceptable. On the other hand, while theories about cannabis leading to crime, violence, promiscuity, addiction, and escalation to 'hard' drugs have been thoroughly discredited, the drug and its advocates are still the subject of irrational prejudice.

Further Information and Advice

Association for the Prevention of Addiction
Release
Michael Schofield, *The Strange Case of Pot*, Penguin Books, 1971
The Non-Medical Use of Drugs, Interim Report of the Canadian Commission of Inquiry, Penguin Books, 1971

24. Law and the Motorist

The Driver

If you are over 17 and you hold a valid, signed driving licence, you have the right to drive a motor car. At 16, you may drive a 3-wheeled vehicle and a motor cycle under 250 cc.; and at 15 you may drive a pedal cycle with a motor under 50 cc.

Certain people are barred from holding a licence, including those suffering from blindness and those unable to read (even with spectacles) a number plate at 25 yards. Epileptics can now obtain a licence under certain conditions.

Learner drivers must hold a provisional driving licence and carry 'L' plates at the front and back of the car or motor cycle. Car drivers must be accompanied by a qualified driver. A provisional licence lasts for one year. A third licence may be refused if the learner has not yet attempted the test.

If you drive a motor cycle, you do not have to take a test as long as you carry 'L' plates. But you must hold a full licence before you can carry a pillion passenger who is not qualified. You do not need to be accompanied by a qualified driver.

The Vehicle

A vehicle must come up to certain standards laid down by law. If it is in use, or parked in the road, it must be taxed and insured.

There are certain compulsory features which most vehicles must have: a working speedometer (this does not apply to tractors, motor cycles under 50 cc. or invalid carriages); brakes,

228

rear-view mirror, windscreen wiper, horn, silencer, safety belts; headlights which can be dipped, white side lights, red rear lights, reflectors (all must be of a certain intensity, and must work in daylight and at night). Direction indicators are not compulsory, but if fitted they must meet certain standards.

Tyres must have a good tread. Police now make spot checks on tyres and will prosecute if they are below standard. They can also check other features on the vehicle, such as steering and brakes.

MOT Testing

All vehicles over 3 years old are subject to an annual test. It is illegal to drive such a car without a current test certificate, except to and from the test. If a vehicle fails the test, the owner may appeal to the Ministry of Transport, but it would probably be easier to have the vehicle repaired and brought up to the required standard.

A uniformed policeman has the power to stop any vehicle and test it. The policeman must be a qualified mechanic registered with the Chief Road Traffic Officer and he must, if asked, produce evidence of his authority. You may postpone the test if it is inconvenient to have it done on the spot. If you are not the owner, you must say who is; the owner will then have the opportunity to say when the vehicle can be tested. It is an offence to obstruct an examiner from carrying out a test.

Laws Affecting the Motorist

A motorist can break the law in three ways: (1) when driving; (2) when using but not driving his car, e.g. when his employee is driving it for him; (3) when in charge of a vehicle but unable to drive it, e.g. when drunk.

Driving Offences

(1) *Causing Death by Dangerous Driving:* This is the most serious offence (apart from manslaughter which is rarely brought), and carries a maximum penalty of 5 years' imprisonment.

(2) *Dangerous Driving:* Your action is judged objectively and you need not have caused actual harm. Maximum penalty is 4 months and/or £100 if tried at a magistrates' court, or 2 years and/or an unlimited fine if tried at Quarter Sessions.

(3) *Careless Driving:* This is also judged objectively; the charge is summary, i.e. tried in a magistrates' court, with a maximum penalty of £100 on the first offence, and 3 months' imprisonment and/or £100 fine on a subsequent offence. The difference between dangerous driving and careless driving is not defined in law – it is simply a matter of how the court sees it. There is a tendency for the police to charge people with both offences in an attempt to encourage them to plead guilty to the lesser charge of careless driving.

(4) *Speeding:* It is an offence to exceed a speed limit, even when no harm results from it. The opinion of a single policeman can be sufficient if supported by the evidence of a mechanical device such as a radar unit; if not, it must be backed up by a second opinion. Certain vehicles, such as vans, lorries, buses, and cars pulling caravans, may not exceed 40 m.p.h. except on motorways.

(5) *Traffic Signs:* It is an offence to disobey a traffic sign, road sign, or a policeman on point duty; to fail to give a pedestrian right of way on a pedestrian crossing; and to fail to stop when ordered to by a uniformed policeman.

(6) *Miscellaneous:* It is illegal to take part in a race on a public road; to carry passengers in a dangerous manner; to sound a horn when a vehicle is stationary or between 11.30 p.m. and 7.00 a.m. within a built-up area.

Driving under the Influence

It is an offence to drive, or try to drive, when unfit due to the effects of drink or drugs. The maximum penalty is 2 years' imprisonment and/or an unlimited fine if tried at Quarter Sessions, or £100 fine and/or 4 months' imprisonment (6 months for a second or subsequent offence) if tried at a magistrates' court (Road Traffic Act 1962).

It is a less serious offence to be found in charge of a vehicle when unfit to drive. It is a valid defence if you can show that there was no likelihood of your driving the car while you were in that state.

The Breathalyser

It is an offence to drive, or try to drive, with more than 80 milligrams of alcohol in 100 millilitres of blood. The Breathalyser test can be administered by a *uniformed* policeman if: (1) there has been an accident; (2) he suspects you of committing a moving traffic offence; or (3) he simply suspects you of being drunk (Road Safety Act 1967).

If you refuse to take the test, you may be fined up to £50. But it is *not* an offence to fail the test. The policeman will have to arrest you, take you to a police station and administer further tests. You will have to give a blood or urine sample and you will be found guilty only if one of these tests proves positive. You may refuse to take a blood test, but if you also refuse a urine test, you will be found guilty, as if you had taken the test and failed. You may insist that the blood test be administered by your own G.P.

You are not entitled to know the results of the police analysis, but you may ask for an extra sample of your blood or urine for a separate examination. After the tests, you may leave the police station, unless you are intending to drive.

If the tests prove positive, there is unlikely to be a defence, except to prove that your drinks were doctored or that the police did not follow the correct procedure when administering the tests. Your ability to drive with that level of alcohol in your blood is irrelevant to the charge. If you are found guilty, the maximum penalty is 12 months' imprisonment and/or an unlimited fine if tried at Quarter Sessions, or £100 and/or 4 months' imprisonment if tried at a magistrates' court. You will also be disqualified from driving for at least one year unless you can show special circumstances relating to the offence.

You do not necessarily have to take and fail these tests in order to be found guilty of driving, trying to drive, or being in charge of a vehicle while unfit due to the effects of drink or drugs. All that need be proved, if you are charged under the Road Traffic

Act 1962, is that your ability to drive properly was for the time being impaired.

Endorsements

Your licence will usually be endorsed if you are found guilty of any of the offences listed above. The more serious offences result in disqualification. As a general rule, you will be disqualified if your licence is endorsed 3 times within 3 years. If you have been given more than one endorsement for offences arising out of the same incident (e.g., 2 endorsements for 2 faulty tyres discovered at the same time, or 2 endorsements for driving without due care and attention and failing to comply with a traffic signal because you went through a red light) they will be counted as one when calculating the number of endorsements for disqualification. Endorsements for minor offences remain on your licence for 3 years until they lose effect; endorsements for major offences remain for 10 years. Records of old endorsements will exist on court and criminal records.

Parking

(1) *Dangerous Parking:* The penalty for this can be a fine and disqualification.

(2) *Obstruction:* The police need not show that you actually obstructed someone. The penalty is usually a fine, but the police have the power to move your vehicle from one place to another, or to tow it away to a car pound. The fixed charge for this is £4 plus 50p a day until the car is recovered.

(3) Yellow lines at the side of a road mean that there is a restriction on parking. Details can be found on a nearby lamp post.

(4) 'No parking' signs put up by a private citizen on public property have no effect in law.

(5) *Meters:* In a meter zone, parking is only allowed in a meter bay. You are not allowed to 'feed' meters after the maximum time

has been allowed, nor to move your car to another meter in the same group. (Groups of meters are marked either by their obvious location or by two white lines on the pavement between two groups.) The fine for the first 30 minutes' excess time is 50p, payable to the Council; after that, a fine of up to £5 may be levied. In most areas, meters operate from 8.30 a.m. to 6.30 p.m. on weekdays and from 8.30 a.m. to 1.30 p.m. on Saturdays. Cars, vans, lorries, and motor cycles may park at meters.

(6) Once parked, it is an offence to open the car door in a way which causes injury.

Traffic wardens are employed under the direction of the police. Their powers are mainly confined to dealing with parking offences, but are gradually being extended to take over other traffic duties. Outside this sphere, they do not have the same powers as policemen.

Police Powers

A policeman in uniform may request the name and address of anyone driving or in charge of a motor vehicle on the road – even when there is no suspected offence. He may ask the driver to produce his licence, certificate of insurance, MOT test certificate and date of birth. If this happens to you and you do not have the documents with you, you may produce them within 5 days at any police station. You must produce your licence in person, but someone else may produce the other documents on your behalf.

A policeman may inspect your licence to find out your name and address and the Council where it was issued, but not to see whether you have any endorsements.

A policeman has the power to stop and search any vehicle if he reasonably suspects it to contain dangerous drugs (illegally), or to be involved in any other crime. (◊ pp. 47, 226)

In the Case of an Accident

If you are involved in an accident in which a person or vehicle is harmed, you must stop and give your name, address, and car number to the driver or passenger of the other vehicle or, if asked, to any interested party. If the car is not yours, you must give the owner's name and address. It is an offence not to stop. If a person is injured, you must produce your insurance certificate to any interested party (e.g. the driver, passenger, or injured person). If you do not produce your name, address, or insurance certificate at the time, you must report the accident to the police within 24 hours and produce the insurance certificate within 5 days.

A motorist has no duty to report an accident in which he was not involved, but it is often helpful to do so.

Procedure in Prosecutions

In cases of dangerous driving, speeding, and disobeying a road sign, the police must either (1) give warning at the time that prosecution is intended – and this may be very informal; (2) serve a summons within 14 days; or (3) send notice of intended prosecution within 14 days.

You have a right to know within 14 days whether you face prosecution, although the actual time limit for prosecution is 6 months.

Legal Aid in criminal cases is available 'if it is desirable in the interests of justice' (◇ p. 18). In practice, it is rare for Legal Aid to be granted for minor driving offences. The RAC and AA will provide free legal advice to their members and, in some cases, free legal representation. It is often possible to obtain legal representation under the terms of a motor insurance policy.

It is possible to plead guilty by post to certain minor charges, but do not confuse this with paying parking fines by post: the first is a conviction, the second is not.

Compensation

The Motor Insurers' Bureau can give compensation for death or personal injury caused by an uninsured or 'hit-and-run' driver. Compensation will be for personal injury to third parties only and it is not possible to claim for damage to a vehicle. Otherwise civil action in a County Court or the High Court is the only way of getting any compensation which is not provided automatically by an insurance policy.

Further Information and Advice

The Automobile Association
Motor Insurers' Bureau
The Royal Automobile Club
The Law for Motorists, a Consumers' Association publication, 1971

25. Immigration and Citizenship

(*At the time of writing the Immigration Bill has received its final reading in the House of Commons and is being debated in the House of Lords. This chapter is written on the assumption that the Bill will have become law without any amendments in the Lords other than those promised by the Government, and will be referred to as the Immigration Act 1971. If you are in doubt about any aspect of the Act, you can always check with one of the organizations mentioned at the end of the chapter.*)

Introduction

Until the Immigration Act 1971 there were two separate codes governing entry into the United Kingdom: one for aliens and the other for Commonwealth citizens. The Act introduces a new unified system and creates a distinction between those who have the 'right of abode' and those who have not. Those who have the 'right of abode' (i.e. the right to remain here permanently) have 'patrial' status. *Non-patrials are subject to the controls and restrictions referred to in this chapter*, with the exception of certain Commonwealth citizens already resident in Britain and citizens of the Republic of Ireland. (◊ p. 256)

Patrials

Patrials are not subject to any controls. Patrial status is given to only 4 groups of people:

(1) Citizens of the United Kingdom and Colonies who were born, adopted, naturalized, or registered as such in the United Kingdom.

(2) Citizens of the United Kingdom and Colonies who at birth have at least one parent or grandparent (including an adoptive parent or grandparent) who is a citizen of the United Kingdom and Colonies.

(3) Citizens of the United Kingdom and Colonies who have been resident in the United Kingdom at any time for a continuous period of 5 years.

(4) Any Commonwealth citizen who at birth was a child of a United Kingdom citizen born in the United Kingdom.

It can be seen that not all citizens of the United Kingdom and Colonies qualify for patrial status. East African Asians are one group who do not, as they are unlikely to have parents or grandparents who are UK citizens. Yet certain Commonwealth citizens, most of them white (including many Australians and Canadians), do qualify. A United Kingdom citizen with a passport issued here or in Ireland will not normally be challenged on entry unless his passport has some endorsement showing that he is subject to control. A Commonwealth citizen who qualifies as a patrial can obtain a certificate of patriality from the Home Office or British High Commission in his own country. Patrial status can be acquired by becoming a United Kingdom citizen, by registration or naturalization. (◊ pp. 258–9)

Entry into the UK

If you are a non-patrial you have no automatic right of entry into the United Kingdom. Even if you satisfy all the formal requirements, you can only enter if you are given leave, which may be for an indefinite or limited period. If leave is granted for a limited period, it can be made subject to conditions restricting your employment or occupation (◊ p. 240), or you may be required to report to the police. (◊ pp. 247–8)

If you are coming for any purpose other than as a visitor, and particularly if you are coming to settle here permanently, you will need an *entry clearance*. This document will be a *visa* if you are a foreign national of a country from which a visa is required (for example, all Eastern European and most Asian countries); or a *Home Office letter of consent* if you are a foreign national from any other country; or an *entry certificate or voucher* if you are a Commonwealth citizen. You will always need a passport or similar identity document whatever your reason for coming here.

Under the Act, immigration officers and medical inspectors have wide powers to question and examine people wanting to come into the country, and to refuse them entry. You can be refused entry if you have a criminal record, if you are already subject to a deportation order, or if an immigration officer considers that it is 'conducive to the public good' to keep you out of the country. If an immigration officer decides that you are not in good health, you can be examined by a medical inspector and may be refused entry.

You should remember that an immigration officer has a general discretionary power and can refuse entry even if you do not come within one of the categories mentioned. But an immigration officer cannot exercise this power without first obtaining the authority of a Chief Immigration Officer or an Immigration Inspector. An immigration officer also has the power to admit you temporarily while the Home Office decides whether or not to admit you formally. You can make an appeal to the adjudicator against refusal of entry, or against any entry condition which the immigration officer has imposed, under the appeal machinery originally set up under the Immigration Appeals Act 1969 (◊ p. 253). But unless you hold a current entry clearance (see above) or work permit, you must leave the country before you can appeal against refusal of admission.

If you are told to leave or are in a dispute with an immigration officer, ask to telephone a friend or relative, your High Commission or Consulate for additional help or advice.

If you are allowed into the United Kingdom (including the Channel Islands and the Isle of Man), you will be free to travel to the Republic of Ireland. If you are refused entry to the United Kingdom, you will not be allowed to go to Ireland. Similarly if you are not acceptable to the Irish immigration authorities you will not be allowed into the UK.

Temporary Residents

Visitors

You will generally be admitted if you can show you are a genuine visitor, that you intend to leave at the end of your visit, and that you can support yourself and your family and afford the return journey. Time limits are imposed on the length of visits, and although immigration officers can give admission for as much as 6 months, many people are admitted for a shorter period. At the end of your stay you can apply for a renewal, but you will have to satisfy the same entry conditions as those on entering. You cannot stay indefinitely as a visitor.

Students

Students who have obtained an entry clearance certificate in their country of origin should have no difficulty in gaining entry. If you do not have one, you must satisfy the immigration officer that you have been accepted for a course of study at a *bona fide* educational institution, that the course will occupy the whole or a substantial part of your time (usually at least 15 hours per week day-time study); that you can meet the cost of the course, and that you can maintain yourself. Your dependants can also come to Britain provided that you can show proof that they can be maintained by you.

Immigration officers and the Home Office have wide powers to refuse admission if they are not satisfied that you meet the necessary requirements, and they have considerable discretion in the matter. For example, they have power to decide whether your qualifications are adequate for the course you intend to study,

239

and they can refuse you admission if they are not satisfied. Their assessment can be most subjective, so it is advisable to have a letter from a reputable educational institution or authority confirming that your qualifications are adequate for the course. Admission is granted for a maximum of 12 months only. You must then renew your application. You will have to show that you have been accepted to continue your studies and can support yourself and (where appropriate) your family.

If you cannot satisfy all the requirements, immigration officers have power to admit you for a short period while the Home Office considers your case.

Workers

You cannot enter without a work permit issued by the Department of Employment to a specific employer for a definite period, normally 12 months. You will need to obtain a work permit from outside the United Kingdom. If you come here as a visitor, you cannot obtain a work permit in normal circumstances until you have left and made an application from another country.

You will also need an 'entry clearance' (⟡ p. 238), which must be obtained before leaving for the United Kingdom because without it you will not be admitted, even if you have a work permit.

If you are a doctor or dentist coming to take up an appointment, you will be allowed into the country without a work permit. You cannot stay for more than 12 months without making a further application and you must hold an entry clearance. This concession also applies to people in a number of other special categories, e.g., ministers of religion, Commonwealth citizens whose employment will be incidental to a holiday, and others coming to work for a government department.

If you have a work permit and wish to continue to work after the permit has expired, you should consult your employer and then apply to the Department of Employment for another permit, with a covering letter from him confirming that he wants you to continue in your job. This should be done before the original permit expires. You cannot appeal against a refusal to renew your work permit. You can however appeal against a refusal to vary the duration or conditions of your leave to enter (▷ p. 253), although your chances of success will be slim if you do not have a work permit.

Au Pair Girls

'*Au pair* is an arrangement in which a girl of 17 and above may come to the United Kingdom to learn English and to live for a time as a member of a resident English family.'

If you come for full-time domestic employment you require a work permit.

If you are admitted as an *au pair* girl, you have no claim to stay here in any other capacity. You cannot stay for more than 12 months without applying for a renewal and you will not be allowed to take other employment. You cannot be an *au pair* girl for more than 2 years, consecutive or otherwise.

Commonwealth girls can come to Britain on an *au pair* basis although in the past permission has rarely been given.

Businessmen

If you are a businessman and are admitted as a visitor, you are free to transact business.

If you come here to join a business, you must have an entry clearance and you must satisfy an immigration officer that you are contributing some of your own money to the business and sharing some of the liabilities. You will also have to show that the net profits will be sufficient to support you and your dependants. This last requirement can produce arbitrary decisions by the Home Office, who are often reluctant to accept that people can live on a relatively small income. You should also bear in mind that permission has often been refused where the proposed partnership looks like a disguised form of employment.

— Persons of Independent Means

If you can show that you can maintain yourself and your dependants indefinitely in the United Kingdom without working, you may qualify for this category. You have to give documentary proof of a strong financial position, showing that you can support yourself for several years, and initially you will be allowed to stay for up to 12 months.

Permanent Residents

If you have been admitted for a limited period, you have no right to remain in the United Kingdom permanently. After you have been here for 4 years in employment, or as a businessman or a person of independent means, you can apply to have the conditions of your stay (including any time limit) removed. As soon as they are removed you do not need to get permission to work from the Home Office or Department of Employment. You will not become a *patrial*, i.e. a person who has a right of abode *but*:

(1) All restrictions concerning employment will have been lifted.

(2) Under normal circumstances you should have no difficulty leaving or entering the United Kingdom, provided that you have not been repatriated or have been out of the country for more than 2 years. Even then, you may be readmitted in certain circumstances, e.g., if you have lived most of your life here.

(3) After you have been ordinarily resident here for 5 years you can apply for registration or naturalization (▷ p. 258). In most cases the 5 years will be completed the year after you have applied for your conditions to be removed.

(4) Patriality will be automatic on registration or naturalization.

When considering your application the Home Office has complete discretion in deciding whether to remove the conditions. The Immigration Rules concerning control set out the issues that the Home Office regard as important in reaching the decision. These include:

(1) Whether you have observed the conditions on which you were admitted.

(2) Whether in the light of your character, conduct or associations, it is undesirable to permit you to remain.

(3) Whether you represent a danger to national security.

(4) Whether you have been convicted of an offence while in the United Kingdom.

Your immediate family will also have all conditions lifted if they are already here or they will be allowed to join you without any conditions being imposed, provided they have an entry clearance. At the time of writing it would appear that you will have to satisfy an immigration officer that your family will not be a burden on public funds. The exact effect of this rule is not certain but it is possible that you may have some difficulty if you are unemployed or sick over a long period.

Not every member of your family can settle here permanently. You will be allowed to bring your *wife*, or in some circumstances a person with whom you have been 'living in permanent association'. Your *children* under 18 will be admitted if:

(1) You or your wife are already resident in Britain or you are both entering together.

(2) You are resident here or entering with the child and you are the only living parent of the child or you have the sole responsibility for the child's upbringing.

(3) The Home Secretary authorizes admission for your child to join one parent because family or other considerations make exclusion undesirable (for example, where the other parent is physically or mentally incapable of looking after the child), and suitable arrangements have been made for the child's care.

When considering whether you have sole responsibility, the factors the Home Office take into account include the length of time for which you have been separated from your child; the arrangements you made for the child before you came to the

United Kingdom; the existing arrangements, the proportion of costs of your child's maintenance that you have borne; whether you have taken the important decisions about the upbringing of the child, and the relationship between you and your child. Remember, the fact that somebody else has helped to bring up your child will not necessarily prevent you from proving that you have 'sole responsibility'.

If your children are over 18, they must normally qualify for admission in their own right, but they and their dependants may be admitted in some circumstances provided they are under 21, fully dependent on you and – in the case of a daughter – single. You will have to show that every other member of your family is already here or has been admitted for settlement, and you must undertake to accommodate and maintain the children and any dependants.

Parents

Your widowed mother, whatever her age, or your widowed father, if he is over 65 (or both parents if one is over 65), can come here permanently if either or both are wholly or mainly dependent on you and you can afford to keep them. You will not normally be allowed to bring in one parent if the other intends to remain in another country.

Other relatives will only be allowed in if you can show that they are:

(1) Over 65 and you can afford to support them and provide their keep; *and*

(2) Near relatives (this will certainly include grandparents, brothers, sisters, aunts and uncles); *and*

(3) 'Distressed relatives' (living alone with no relatives in their own country to turn to and with a standard of living substantially below that of their own country).

Fiancés

Only in very rare cases will a man be admitted to settle in the United Kingdom to join his future wife. You will need a current clearance issued for that purpose, and clearance will not be given unless you can show that refusal to let you into the country 'would be undesirable because of the degree of hardship which would be caused [to your fiancée] if she had to live outside the United Kingdom in order to be with [you] after marriage'.

If you are admitted for this reason it will normally be for 3 months. After you have married you can apply to the Home Office for an extension. If you want to come here temporarily to marry, you will be refused admission unless you can show the immigration officer that your marriage will take place within a reasonable time and you will leave with your wife shortly after the marriage. You will be admitted for up to 3 months with a prohibition on employment. It should be made clear to you that you will not be allowed to stay permanently.

If you have been admitted as a student or visitor and marry a person settled here your conditions of stay will not be removed to enable you to settle here unless 'refusal would be undesirable because of the degree of hardship, which, in the circumstances of the case, would be caused if [your wife] had to live outside the United Kingdom in order to be with [you]'. Hardship can be either 'physical' or 'psychological', but must be of a serious and lasting nature.

Fiancées

You will be allowed to enter to marry your future husband if you can satisfy an immigration officer that you will get married within a reasonable time. You will usually be admitted for up to 3 months, but this limitation will be removed on application to the Home Office, once you have married, to enable you to have the same immigration status as your husband (e.g., student, right of permanent residence). You may be able to get an extension

245

beyond the 3 months if there has been a delay in the marriage taking place. You must have a good reason for the delay and provide evidence of an early date for the marriage.

Variations of Conditions of Entry

During the course of your stay in the UK you may want to change the conditions on which you have been allowed to enter, e.g., you may want to obtain the removal of a condition restricting your taking employment.

You must make an application to the Home Office, preferably in sufficient time before your period of stay runs out. Your case will be considered, and you should give all the information you have available which will help to support your case. The Home Office has complete discretion and the fact that you satisfy the formal requirements of the immigration rules will not necessarily be sufficient to guarantee a variation of your conditions of stay. The Home Office will take the factors previously referred to (◊ p. 243) into consideration.

Visitors

If you want to work, you will usually have to leave the country first and apply for a work permit from outside Britain. If you apply while you are here you will almost certainly be refused without any reference to the Department of Employment. In special cases, you may obtain an extension of your stay if you can obtain Department of Employment approval for your proposed employment. This may be possible if your proposed employer can give evidence that you have, for example, special skills which are in very short supply.

If you have sufficient funds you may succeed in gaining permission to settle here as a person of independent means. (◊ p. 242)

If you want to stay here in some other capacity, e.g., *au pair* girl or student, you may do so if you can satisfy the Home Office that you fulfil all the appropriate requirements.

Students

The position is the same for students. You cannot work in your free time or vacation without obtaining approval from the Department of Employment. But you may find it essential to work to support yourself during your studies, and as your earnings can be taken into account by the Home Office or immigration officer when assessing the adequacy of your maintenance arrangements, you should ensure that there is no condition prohibiting employment while in the United Kingdom. If your passport contains a prohibition, you should apply for a variation at the earliest possible opportunity.

Returning Residents

If you have been admitted for permanent settlement and been away for less than 2 years, there will generally be no difficulties (◇ p. 242). But if there were conditions attached to your entry, you will have no claim to admission as a returning resident and your application to re-enter will be 'dealt with in the light of all the relevant circumstances'. You may find it safer to apply before you come here but in any case it will always be a help if you can produce documentary evidence of any special circumstances which led to your absence.

Registration with the Police

If you have been admitted for a limited period you will have to register with the police (as will your wife and children over 16) in the following circumstances:

(1) There is a condition prohibiting you taking employment.

(2) You are an alien (but not Commonwealth) visitor or student admitted for more than 6 months.

(3) You have been admitted for employment, unless you come within a permit-free category. (◊ p. 240)

(4) You are an *au pair*, a businessman, or self-employed, admitted for more than 6 months.

If you receive an extension to your stay which puts you into one of these categories, you will have to register with the police, unless you are a Commonwealth citizen on a working holiday or are staying as a person of independent means. (◊ p. 242)

The Home Secretary has the power to make regulations concerning registration but at the time of writing no regulations have yet been made. You will probably have to register with the police in the district where you live and give them details of your address, marital status, and occupation. You will be given a certificate of registration and you must inform the police within 7 days if you change your address, status, or occupation. Failure to do so will make you liable to prosecution and possibly deportation. It is advisable to have your certificate of registration with you at all times.

Deportation

You can be deported from the United Kingdom in a number of circumstances. These are:

(1) *You have broken a condition of stay or overstayed your permitted time.* You can appeal to the adjudicator (◊ p. 114) against a decision on this ground.

(2) *The Home Secretary deems your deportation to be conducive to the public good.* The meaning of this phrase is vague and is designed to give the Home Secretary extensive power. You will be able to appeal to the Immigration Appeal Tribunal (◊ p. 115) except where the Home Secretary considers your deportation to be in the interests of national security, or for other political reasons. For these cases there will be a body of advisers appointed by the Home Secretary. You can make representations to them but their advice will not be binding on the Home Secretary.

If you are an alien and you have received a deportation order on this ground, you may ask for a hearing by the Chief Metropolitan Magistrate at Bow Street. He will hear any representations from you or from a lawyer acting on your behalf. The proceedings will be in private and will be quite informal. You cannot call any witnesses but you may be cross-examined by the magistrate, who then makes recommendations to the Home Secretary as to whether or not the deportation order should be carried out. In a number of cases of this kind the magistrate has disagreed with the Home Secretary, and in some cases the Home Secretary has accepted his decision. You should however appreciate that the Home Secretary is under no obligation to do so. This procedure is not available in cases where the deportation order is made on the grounds of national security or illegal entry.

(3) *Someone else in your family is ordered to be deported.* If you are a Commonwealth citizen who has been settled here for 5 years you cannot be deported under this provision, but there is no time limit for aliens. 'Family' means wife (or wives) and children under 18. A husband whose wife is deported will be allowed to stay.

You may be allowed to appeal against a deportation order made under this provision. If more than 8 weeks have elapsed since the other person (your husband or parents) left the UK, you cannot be deported at all. You should remember that these provisions exist even if you are living apart from the person who has received the deportation order. You will not be allowed to dispute your relationship to the deported person if it involves challenging a statement made by him or anyone else on your behalf, with a view to getting you into the country.

(4) *You have been convicted of an offence (of any kind) for which a sentence of imprisonment can be imposed and the court recommends deportation.* You cannot be deported if you were under 17 when you were convicted or if you were a Commonwealth citizen ordinarily resident here for the previous 5 years.

You can be recommended for deportation even if you have not been sent to prison. You are liable once you have been found guilty of an offence which can be punishable by imprisonment. But you must however be given 7 days' written notice that you are liable for deportation, and no recommendation can be made until this notice has been given. You or your counsel are entitled, after you have been convicted, to address the court as to all the circumstances which should be considered and which might persuade the court not to make a recommendation.

The Immigration Rules state that deportation will normally be the proper course if a person has been convicted of breach of conditions or illegal entry where a person has 'persistently contravened or failed to comply with a condition or has remained without authorization'. The Rules also state that if a person is convicted of an offence (other than breach of conditions or unauthorized stay), every relevant factor will be taken into account including:

(1) Age.

(2) Length of residence in UK.

(3) Strength of connections with UK.

(4) Personal history, including character, conduct and employment record.

(5) Domestic circumstances.

(6) Compassionate circumstances.

(7) Any representations received on the person's behalf.

(8) The nature of the offence of which the person was convicted.

(9) Previous criminal record.

You cannot appeal under the immigration appeals machinery against a deportation order made following a court recommendation, but you can appeal to a higher court. (◊ pp. 34 ff.)

If you have not received an immediate prison sentence you will be detained in custody while the Home Secretary considers making a deportation order, but you can apply for bail to the magistrate or judge at the end of your case. If it is not granted, the Home Secretary has the power to release you and an application should be made to the Home Office. If you have received a suspended sentence, the court has no power to grant bail and you must therefore apply to the Home Office.

In some cases, you might not wish to wait for the Home Secretary's decision (which might take some weeks) and would like to leave the country immediately and within a short period after your case. The Home Office will usually be quite cooperative, and arrangements can be made for you to leave even if you are in prison (provided you are not serving a sentence). Representations may still be made to the Home Secretary asking him not to make the deportation, but it is clearly more difficult to do so effectively if you have left the country. In any event, your intention to leave will probably be taken into account. On occasions, where a person has left the country, the Home Office has taken no action (i.e. never confirmed or rejected the court's recommendation). In such circumstances you may have difficulty in coming back into the country.

A recommendation for deportation is often made where a person is in breach of conditions of entry, but it is not automatic in these circumstances. Magistrates who are reluctant to make an order are often told by prosecution counsel that they have no choice and that it is a matter for the Home Secretary. A recommendation should not be made unless it is appropriate as a part of the sentence. In deciding whether to make an order, the Home Office usually regards it as a significant factor that a recommendation was made.

Representations to the Home Office

If you have been recommended for deportation, you will have an opportunity to make representations to the Home Secretary asking him not to make an order. The following advice may be useful when you approach the Home Office on an issue concerning immigration or deportation:

(1) Always try to find out the grounds on which the Home Office has decided your case, so that you can then ensure that

your representations, where possible, include matters which are relevant.

(2) Where possible, enlist the support of M.P.s, trade unionists, and others who can also make representations on your behalf. Do not delay – speed is usually essential.

(3) Remember that organizations like the NCCL and JCWI may be able to advise you and sometimes give help in drafting or making representations.

(4) When setting out your representations in writing to the Home Office, ensure that they are clearly laid out and that the important points are properly emphasized. Avoid repetition. Whenever possible, support your assertions or statements with documentary evidence.

(5) If you see a Home Office representative, it is often useful to make a short note of your interview immediately afterwards. This may help at a later date if there is a dispute as to what has been said. Mistakes have been known to occur on both sides. If in doubt about the effect of any statement made to you, check again by writing to the Home Office asking for clarification or contact the NCCL or your M.P. who can make the appropriate inquiries.

If you are a Commonwealth citizen resident here at the end of July 1971, you and your family may be protected from deportation (◊ p. 256). In all cases where a deportation order has been made, you can appeal to the adjudicator against the removal directions on the grounds that you ought to be removed (if at all) to a different country from the one named in the directions.

After a deportation order has been made, you may apply to the Home Secretary to revoke it, and if he refuses to do so, you may appeal to the adjudicator (◊ p. 114) except if your case is based on the 'conducive to the public good' provision. You cannot appeal while you are in the UK. You must leave the country and then make your application. You will not be allowed to attend the hearing, although your representative can. The Home Office acts on the principle that at least 2 years must elapse before a revocation should be allowed, but the Immigration Appeals Tribunal has allowed at least one appeal where only 15 months had passed. If there is new evidence which was not available to the Home Office at the time of the decision, it should always be submitted when your application to revoke it is made.

Repatriation

The Home Secretary has been given power to meet the expenses of those who wish to leave the UK for a country where they intend to reside permanently, including travelling expenses for members of their family or households. This is a voluntary scheme. If you are considering using it, you should remember that you may have considerable difficulties should you and your family wish to return here. Before making any decision it will probably be worthwhile to consult all members of your family and friends both inside and outside the country.

Mental Patients

Any person receiving in-treatment for mental illness can be removed from the UK by order of the Home Secretary, although no Commonwealth citizen will be removed unless it can be shown on medical advice that it would be in his own interest. Removal is not restricted to the patient's country of origin provided some other country will accept him. The cost of removal of the patient and his family will be met by the Home Office.

Appeals

You have a right of appeal in most circumstances against:

(1) Refusal of leave to enter.
(2) Refusal of an entry clearance.
(3) Refusal to revoke a deportation order.

(provided that you appeal from outside the United Kingdom)

(4) Refusal of a certificate of patriality.

(5) Refusal to vary the duration or conditions of leave.

(6) Deportation order (except after a recommendation of the court).

(7) Validity of directions for removal.

(8) Removal (on the grounds of objection to destination.)

If there is a decision which is subject to appeal you will be served notice (by hand if at a port of entry or by post at your last known address) informing you of your rights of appeal to the adjudicator and subsequently to the Immigration Appeals Tribunal (◊ p. 114). In the appropriate cases you will be told that you can only appeal after leaving the country. You should also be informed of the services of the United Kingdom Immigration Advisory Service (UKIAS), an organization financed by the government which provides an advisory and representative service for appeals. The Joint Council for the Welfare of Immigrants (JCWI), an independently financed group, also provides help in many cases and the NCCL can help in a limited number of circumstances.

In deciding whether to appeal you should be given the opportunity of contacting any friends, relatives, and lawyers, and your High Commission or Consulate. In cases (7) and (8) above it is possible to obtain bail either before the hearing from a Chief Immigration Officer or police Inspector, or at the hearing from an adjudicator, or at an appeal, from the Tribunal.

If you give notice of appeal, which must usually be within 14 days, a summary of the facts of the case on which the Home Office based its decision will be sent both to you and to the adjudicator. In some cases at ports of entry, an immigration officer will give evidence at the hearing instead of supplying a written statement.

Criminal Offences

Criminal offences under the 1971 Act include:

(1) *Offences which may be committed by non-patrials*, including entering the United Kingdom without leave; exceeding a permitted stay, failing to comply with conditions.

If a person is charged with gaining entry without leave, the burden of proving he had leave to enter lies on him once the prosecution has shown that he entered within 6 months of the proceedings. Anyone who is reasonably suspected of an immigration offence can be arrested without warrant by a policeman or immigration officer. The offences carry a maximum penalty of up to £200 and/or 6 months' imprisonment and must be dealt with in a magistrates' court.

(2) 'Being knowingly concerned in making or carrying out arrangements for securing or facilitating the entry into the United Kingdom of anyone whom the defendant knows or has reasonable cause to believe to be an illegal entrant.' This is punishable by up to £400 and/or 6 months' imprisonment if tried summarily and an unlimited fine or up to 7 years' on indictment.

(3) 'Knowingly harbouring anyone whom the defendant knows or has reasonable cause for believing to be either an illegal entrant or a person in breach of a condition attached to his stay.' This is punishable only in a magistrates' court by a fine of up to £400 and/or 6 months' imprisonment.

These offences are very loosely defined and at this stage the effect of their extent is uncertain. A prosecution in a magistrates' court can be brought up to 3 years after the offence was committed.

Illegal Immigrants

Illegal entrants, including those who have at *any* time in the past entered illegally, can be arrested and then detained and removed

255

without conviction by a court for an offence and without a deportation order. There is no time limit for the removal of an illegal immigrant, although almost all Commonwealth citizens who entered before 1968 are safe, because any person who did not present himself to an immigration officer before that year was not committing an offence and is therefore lawfully here.

Commonwealth Citizens

Special Provisions under the Immigration Act for Those Already Resident Here at the End of July 1971

(1) You will be able to acquire United Kingdom citizenship automatically at the end of 5 years' ordinary residence, provided that you have not been subject to conditions during that period.

(2) You cannot be deported on the 'not conducive to the public good' provision if, at the time of the Home Secretary's decision, you have been ordinarily resident here since July 1971 without conditions.

(3) You cannot be deported on any other ground once you have been ordinarily resident here for 5 years and have continued to live here.

(4) You cannot be recommended for deportation by a court once you have been ordinarily resident here for 5 years and continued to live here.

Rights of All Commonwealth Citizens Resident in the United Kingdom

Unlike aliens, you can vote and be a candidate in both parliamentary and local elections. You can become a J.P. and are liable for jury service.

Patrial Commonwealth Citizens

If you are a Commonwealth citizen and also a patrial (◊ p. 236), you will automatically be allowed to register as a UK citizen once you have completed 5 years' residence here.

Aliens

There are a number of restrictions affecting aliens (but not Commonwealth citizens), including limitations on joining the armed services.

As an alien, if you promote or attempt to promote industrial unrest in any industry where you have not been a *bona fide* employee for at least 2 years, you are liable on summary conviction to up to 3 months' imprisonment (Aliens Restriction (Amendment) Act 1919).

Apart from the restrictions mentioned, aliens in general enjoy the same rights as United Kingdom citizens. In theory, therefore, you may engage in politics, but in practice if your activities in this sphere become too marked, you may find your application for extended stay is met with unsatisfactorily explained refusal. The Commonwealth citizen may also find himself in a similar position under the new Act which has in general 'unified' the law of immigration by reducing most non-citizens to alien status.

Political Asylum

If you do not qualify for admission under the normal terms, you should not be sent away if it would cause you to return to a country in which you would face 'danger to life or liberty, or persecution of such a kind as to render life insufferable, because of race, religion, nationality or political opinion'. If you feel you might be in such a position, you should contact the Home Office. It is essential, whenever possible, to ensure that representations are being made to the Home Office on your behalf. The NCCL will help in many circumstances.

In practice, political asylum is usually very difficult to obtain formally because the Government does not wish to upset publicly the government of any other country, particularly one with whom it shares friendly relations. In a number of cases the Home Office

257

has been prepared to allow people to stay and work, and has eventually lifted the conditions of their stay without giving formal political asylum.

If you are a deserter from an army of a friendly (including NATO) country, you will not be able to claim political asylum, and you may be arrested and removed from the United Kingdom without trial because of the provisions of the Visiting Forces Act 1952.

The position of the 'draft dodger' is different and at the very least an immigration officer should not ask you questions about your status with the army of your home country if you are seeking entry to the United Kingdom. In any event, permission to enter should not be refused solely on this ground, and you should not be arrested or removed from the UK if this is the only offence you have committed in your own country.

Citizenship

Both aliens and Commonwealth immigrants can acquire United Kingdom citizenship.

If you are a Commonwealth citizen and over 21, you can apply for *registration* as a UK citizen provided you have been here for 5 years (whether or not on conditions) up to the date on which you apply to be registered. In exceptional circumstances the Home Secretary may accept a shorter period. Registration is no longer automatic (unless you come within the transitional provisions or are a patrial) (◊ p. 256). You will have to satisfy the Home Secretary that you are of good character, have sufficient knowledge of the English language, and intend to reside in the UK after registration.

If you are an alien you can apply for *naturalization* provided that you have been resident here for at least 4 out of the last 7 years and also for the year prior to the date of the application (i.e. 5 years in all) and provided that there are no conditions attached to your stay. You must also show that you are of good character, have sufficient knowledge of the English language, and intend to reside in the United Kingdom after naturalization. There is no appeal against a refusal to allow you to register or become a naturalized citizen. Your only remedy is to wait for a short period and re-apply. Generally, unless your circumstances change considerably, there is little point in making a new application for at least 12 months.

If you are a woman and you marry a UK citizen, you are entitled to register regardless of residential qualifications, but there is no similar provision for a man marrying a UK woman. (◇ p. 169)

If you have become a citizen by naturalization or registration, you have the same rights and obligations as a native-born citizen.

Further Information and Advice

JCWI (Joint Council for the Welfare of Immigrants)
NCCL
UKIAS (United Kingdom Immigration Advisory Service)

26. Racial Discrimination

Racial discrimination is defined as treating one person less favourably than another on the grounds of colour, race, or ethnic or national origins: it is illegal, in the limited set of circumstances set out in the Race Relations Acts of 1965 and 1968. Illegal discrimination is a civil, not a criminal offence – the only criminal offence in this area is incitement to racial hatred. The Race Relations Board is responsible for enforcing the civil aspects of the Acts, and if you are a victim of discrimination, you should complain to the Board or to one of its regional conciliation committees; in addition there are special procedures available in certain industries for dealing with complaints relating to employment, but you cannot normally sue the discriminator in an ordinary court of law. It is the duty of the Board to try to settle disputes by means of conciliation and it will start court proceedings only if that fails.

Segregation is counted as 'less favourable' treatment and may therefore be illegal, even when it is on 'separate but equal terms', but the segregation must occur in an area covered by the Race Relations Acts.

The Acts are not concerned with discrimination on the grounds of religion, language, sex, political belief, or status: the most unfortunate omission is religious discrimination, as this can be as harmful and as arbitrary as racial discrimination.

Goods, Facilities and Services

It is illegal to discriminate in the provision of any goods, facilities, or services. This includes:

(1) Manufacturers, wholesalers, retailers of goods.

(2) Hotels, boarding houses, restaurants, cafés, snack bars.

(3) Public houses, barbers' shops, cinemas, theatres, amusement arcades, public parks.

(4) Football matches, race meetings, and any other sporting events.

(5) Public transport, taxis, minicabs, travel agents.

(6) Employment agents, estate agents.

(7) Banks, insurance companies, hire purchase firms, building societies.

(8) Schools, colleges, universities, and other places of learning.

(9) Services of all professions; business firms.

(10) The police, local authorities, and government departments, when providing goods, facilities, or services. The Acts do not apply when the police arrest you.

There are several exceptions:

(1) Private clubs are probably exempt unless they are catering for the general public. The position on clubs is still obscure, but may soon be decided by the Court of Appeal.

(2) Small hotels and boarding houses catering for up to 6 guests are exempt where the landlord or his family live on the premises and share toilet and bathroom facilities with guests.

(3) Services and facilities to be provided abroad are generally exempt.

Unlawful discrimination occurs if, on racial grounds, a person refuses or deliberately fails to provide goods, facilities, and services, or if the quality or the way in which the goods are provided is different from that normally available to other members of the public.

261

Employment

Racial discrimination in employment is illegal, whether by employers, employment agencies, or local offices of the Department of Employment. Trade unions and employers' organizations may not discriminate in admitting people to their membership.

It is illegal to discriminate against someone by refusing to employ him on work that is available and for which he is qualified. But it may not be easy to prove that a person is qualified for a job if, for example, he has obtained his qualifications abroad.

It is illegal to employ a person on different terms and conditions, on racial grounds (e.g. lower rates of pay, special canteen facilities); or to dismiss him in circumstances where his fellow employees would not be dismissed (e.g. make him redundant before the others).

An employer may be held liable if one of his employees, acting in the course of his work, or an agent acting on his behalf, commits an act of unlawful discrimination; although it will be a defence if he can prove that he tried to prevent it.

There are certain exemptions, where discrimination on racial grounds is not illegal, including:

(1) Small businesses employing less than 10 people (but this ceases to apply after November 1972).

(2) Employment in private households.

(3) A quota system which involves discrimination 'in good faith for the purpose of securing or preserving a reasonable balance of persons of different racial groups': this has given rise to considerable uncertainty, as there is no way of telling exactly what constitutes a 'reasonable balance'; the proportion of coloured workers in different jobs and similar factors must presumably be taken into consideration; and people can be considered as belonging to the same 'racial group' even if they have been wholly or mainly educated in Britain.

(4) Jobs which require the attributes of a certain nationality, for example, Chinese or Italian waiters.

(5) Other exemptions, including employment on a ship where crew members must share living quarters; employment of aliens in any office or place of trust (Act of Settlement 1700); and discriminatory rules which already exist affecting employment in the service of the Crown.

Property

Racial discrimination in buying and selling or renting housing accommodation, business premises, and other land is illegal. This includes:

(1) Refusing altogether to sell or let property on racial grounds.

(2) Selling or letting on different terms, e.g. charging higher rents to coloured tenants.

(3) Giving separate treatment to people already occupying property, e.g. providing separate bathroom facilities for coloured families in a boarding house.

(4) Treating certain people on a housing list differently from others on the same list – this applies to local authorities and to estate agents.

(5) Preventing assignment or sub-letting to people belonging to particular racial groups.

There are two main exemptions:

(1) Discrimination is legal in 'small premises' if the landlord or a member of his family is living there and intends to go on living there, and shares certain facilities with the tenants (other than the entrance and storage room); premises are considered 'small' where there is room for only 2 families in addition to the landlord's, or where, in hotels and boarding houses, there is accommodation for no more than 6 people apart from the landlord and his family.

(2) The private sale of a house by the freeholder or leaseholder is legal, provided that he occupies the whole house and he does not use an estate agent for selling the house, or advertise the sale in any way.

Advertising

It is illegal to publish or display any racially discriminatory advertisement or notice. This applies to advertisements and notices which indicate (or could reasonably be thought to indicate) an intention to 'do an act of discrimination' – whether or not the act would otherwise be illegal. For example, a notice saying 'Rooms to let: sorry no coloureds' would be illegal, even though it applied to small premises. There are two main exemptions:

(1) Advertising jobs for Commonwealth citizens outside Great Britain: this means that a South African firm can recruit all-white labour and advertise accordingly in this country.

(2) Advertising certain jobs in Great Britain for non-Commonwealth citizens, such as French *au pair* girls or Italian waiters. This has the bizarre result of allowing a Chinese restaurateur to advertise for Chinese waiters, while preventing him from advertising for waiters from Hong Kong or Malaysia.

How to Make a Complaint

You should make a written or oral complaint to the Race Relations Board or to a local conciliation committee within 2 months of the incident. In certain circumstances, the Board will allow a complaint later than that if, for example, the person did not know at the time that he was being discriminated against. Application forms are available from the Race Relations Board's offices, Town Halls, Employment Exchanges, Citizens' Advice Bureaux, and police stations.

Complaints about Employment

There is a separate procedure for complaints concerning employment. Initially, complaints are referred to the Secretary of State

264

for Employment, either directly by the complainant, or by the Race Relations Board, and where possible they are dealt with by voluntary machinery set up in different industries jointly by employers and trade unions for that purpose. If there is no suitable joint machinery or if it fails to settle a dispute, the matter is referred to the Race Relations Board, which then deals with it in the same way as other complaints. However, the existence of this special machinery need not affect the making of a complaint which can be sent to the Race Relations Board or conciliation committee in the usual way.

Procedure

When a complaint is received by the Race Relations Board, it must be investigated, provided it arrives within the required period of time. The Board (which consists of a chairman, 11 paid members and a staff of civil servants) may either make the investigation itself, or refer it to a local conciliation committee. Both bodies may conduct inquiries as they see fit; but they do not have the power to subpoena witnesses (i.e., compel them to attend), or to order documents to be produced – this can be a serious drawback.

As a matter of policy, the Board or committee must do what it can to settle the dispute amicably and obtain a written assurance from the discriminator that he will not discriminate in that way against anyone in the future. If the conciliation process fails, the Race Relations Board may start civil proceedings in a County Court, and it may claim:

(1) An injunction (a court order to restrain the defendant from further discrimination).

(2) Damages for the victim of the discrimination.

(3) A declaration that the discriminatory act is unlawful under the Race Relations Act.

(4) A revision of a contract or term of a contract which contravenes the Act.

Incitement to Racial Hatred

Incitement to racial hatred is a criminal offence. A person commits the offence if he publishes or distributes threatening, abusive, or insulting written matter, or uses such words at a public meeting or in a public place, provided that:

(1) He does so with intent to stir up hatred against any section of the public in Great Britain distinguished by colour, race, or ethnic or national origins, and

(2) The material or the words are likely to stir up hatred against a section of the public on the grounds of colour, race, or ethnic or national origins. Hence, an offence may be committed either because of the words used in a speech or because of placards displayed or leaflets distributed. However, the material must be published or distributed to the public at large before an offence is committed. A member of an organization who distributes racialist literature to other members of the same organization is not breaking the law.

No prosecution may be brought without the consent of the Attorney General. Penalties range from £200 and/or 6 months' imprisonment to 2 years and/or £1,000 fine. In practice, the law has failed to halt the continuous flow of racialist literature and speeches directed against the black community. Banners and speeches calling for repatriation of black people have been tolerated without prosecution. On the other hand the Act has been used on more than one occasion to imprison and fine black 'militants' who have complained of white oppression.

It is also an offence to use threatening, abusive or insulting words or behaviour at any public place or meeting, which is likely or intended to provoke a breach of the peace (Public Order Act 1936 as amended by the Race Relations Act 1965).

Further Information and Advice

Advise
Community Relations Commission
International Personnel
Race Relations Board
I. A. MacDonald, *Race Relations and Immigration Law*,
Butterworth, 1969

27. Customs and Excise

Passing through Customs

When you come back from abroad, you must pass through Customs so that you, your baggage, and any vehicle you have can be examined by the Customs officer. He may ask any relevant questions, require you to open your baggage, and search your car. When he has finished, it is up to you to repack and reload your belongings.

Some busier ports and airports have introduced a process of self-selection for passing through Customs. If you have nothing to declare, you pass through the 'green channel' and go straight to your departure point. If you have something to declare, or are uncertain, you pass through the 'red channel' to the Customs bench. Occasional spot checks are made on people passing through the 'green channel'.

If you arrive in the United Kingdom by private transport, you should arrive only at a port or airport that has the approval of the Commissioners of Customs and Excise (although the rule is relaxed for private yachts), and you must report your arrival to the Customs authorities.

Duty-Free Goods

If you have been abroad for more than 24 hours, you may bring back certain goods duty-free. Notices telling you what these are are displayed in Customs halls, in departure areas if you are travelling by boat or aeroplane, in airport lounges, and on cross-channel boats. A leaflet on *Passing through Customs* is available from travel agents and local Customs and Excise offices. These allowances only apply to the goods you bring back with you, not to anything sent through the post, or to unaccompanied luggage. There are no restrictions on what you can do with your duty-free allowances.

If you take anything valuable abroad which is foreign-made or not easily identifiable as British, but which you bought in the UK, it is advisable to take the receipt with you, as it is up to you to prove that you have paid the necessary duty or tax on it. (It is no use showing the camera, etc. to the Customs officials on the way out.)

Imports

In addition to these duty-free allowances, there is nothing to stop you bringing back as many goods as you like from abroad, provided that you can pay the duty. If you bring them as far as the British Customs and then find that you cannot pay for them, the Customs officer will keep the goods and give you a receipt. If you do not pay the duty within 3 months, the Customs may, after giving you due notice, dispose of them.

If you are importing goods not as passengers' baggage, you must 'enter' them officially, or arrange for an agent to do so. The rates of duty and import prohibitions and restrictions are shown in the *Customs and Excise Tariff*, which can be found in the reference section of a public library or can be bought (price at publication £2·25) from any bookseller; it also tells you how to 'enter' goods.

Postal Imports and Exports

Customs officers are stationed at post offices which receive mail from abroad. They operate the same controls as they do for goods arriving any other way. The only exception is that goods under a certain value need not be officially 'entered': the postman may collect any duties due when he delivers them.

Powers of Customs Officers

Customs officers have wide powers of entry and search, but they are bound by the same Judges' Rules as the police. ($\Diamond$ pp. 9 ff.)

If a Customs officer is not in uniform and you have the slightest doubt as to his identity, ask him to produce his commission, which contains his name and indicates that he has been appointed an officer of Customs and Excise.

Search

A Customs officer may enter any ship, vehicle, or aircraft at any place or time and conduct a thorough search; he does not need a warrant. He may dismantle or break open any part of it and break any lock or container. (If considerable damage is caused and nothing is found it may be possible to claim compensation.)

If the officer finds any goods which appear to be smuggled, he may seize them, as well as the ship, vehicle, aircraft, and any other equipment used for smuggling. He may order a ship or aircraft to go to a certain place for further inquiries; he may demand to see any papers or documents that might be connected with an importation, and make copies of them.

The officer may search anywhere for uncustomed goods if he has a warrant from a magistrate or a writ of assistance from a senior Customs officer; you should always ask to see these documents and read them carefully. During the hours of darkness, the Customs officer must be accompanied by a uniformed policeman.

Do not carry away the officer on your yacht, as it could cost you £100.

Search of Person

If a Customs officer has reasonable grounds to suspect that you have entered or are about to enter or leave the country, and that you are carrying any article on which the necessary duty has not been paid, or which is prohibited, he may search you. You may insist that he first obtains the authority of a J.P. or a senior Customs officer, but you will probably be detained while this is being sought. A woman may only be searched by another woman.

Interception of Literature

Customs officers have the duty of intercepting any obscene or pornographic literature which they find when they are examining cargo or passengers' belongings. They are not given any definition of obscenity, but there is a black list (not available to the public) which contains works thought to be obscene and which is claimed to correspond to the standards applied by British courts (⊳ p. 117). In doubtful cases, the decision is referred to the Commissioners of Customs and Excise.

Exports

The Customs officers also have powers to examine anything leaving the country, particularly currency, and anything that may contravene the Exchange Control Act 1947 or any export prohibitions.

Seizure

Illegally imported or exported goods, including obscene material, may be seized. This may be done with or without written notice, provided that the owner, his employee or agent, or the person whose action led to the seizure, is present. In other circumstances, a written notice of seizure must be delivered to the owner, if known.

The owner has one month from the date of seizure to claim that the goods should not be forfeited. The claim should be addressed to the Customs and Excise department named on the notice of seizure. The Commissioners of Customs and Excise must then take the case to court to prove that the goods were justifiably seized. If no claim is made within one month, the goods may be disposed of.

The owner can also appeal that an article be restored to him on compassionate or similar grounds. If the Commissioners are proved wrong in seizing goods they must restore them to the owner.

Arrest of Offenders

If a person is caught smuggling, he may be detained, taken to a police station, and charged; or proceedings may be started at a later date, by issuing a summons or a warrant. HM Customs and Excise conduct the case. If new evidence comes to light, the Commissioners of Customs and Excise have the power to remit fines or terminate prison sentences already imposed by magistrates and to restore goods that have been seized.

Inspecting Road Fuel

All fuel used by vehicles on public roads must bear the full rate of duty (with certain specific exceptions). Customs and Excise operate Road Fuel Testing Vans which are equipped for detecting specially marked heavy oil (diesel) fuel on which a lower rate of duty has been paid and unusual fuels, such as paraffin.

Customs officers have the power to take a sample of fuel from any vehicle or to enter any premises except a private home in order to take a sample. Any sample taken will be tested by the Road Fuel Testing Unit and if it is found to be suspect, a further formal sample will be taken, divided into three parts and put into marked, sealed containers. One of these must be given to the owner or person in charge of the vehicle.

If a vehicle is found to be running illegally on fuel on which the full rate has not been paid it may be seized.

Purchase Tax

This is paid by the last 'registered' person to handle taxable goods, or on importation. Second-hand goods are not normally liable to purchase tax, except on importation. Customs officers have the power to enter any premises where a wholesale or manufacturing business is believed to be carried on. They may ask for information or take a copy of any relevant document; they cannot take documents away without the owner's permission, or ask to see balance sheets, profit and loss accounts (as distinct from trading accounts), bank statements, etc.

A United Kingdom resident who is going abroad for at least 12 months is, under certain circumstances, allowed to obtain tax-free goods under the personal export scheme. He can also buy a car tax-free and use it here until he leaves, but for no longer than 6 months.

Information on liability to purchase tax, rates of purchase tax, and import licensing can be obtained from your local Customs office (for the address see your Telephone Directory).

Other Powers

A Customs officer also has powers of entry to all premises where an excise trader carries on his business (e.g. where beer, wine, or spirits are being manufactured, stored, or sold), and to places where gaming, betting and bingo are being carried on. (◊ pp. 184 ff.)

Further Information

H M Customs and Excise Department
Press and Information Office, King's Beam House, Mark Lane, London EC 3

28. Northern Ireland

The Government at Westminster is ultimately responsible for 'preserving peace and order' in Northern Ireland, but in theory the Northern Ireland Parliament at Stormont looks after the internal affairs of the province. The law in Northern Ireland differs in many ways from the law in England and Wales, and it would take another book to describe it in any detail. This chapter concentrates on the aspects of the law which affect civil liberties.

The Race Relations Acts of 1965 and 1968 (⟡ p. 260) and the Obscene Publications Act (⟡ p. 117) do not apply to Northern Ireland. Criminal law is governed by Stormont legislation. Many of the rights enjoyed by people in the rest of the United Kingdom do not exist in Northern Ireland, particularly for members of the Catholic minority. A number of emergency laws which used to apply to the whole of the United Kingdom, but were repealed in England, Wales, and Scotland at the end of the Second World War, are still in force in Northern Ireland.

Trade Unions

It is illegal to go on strike for 'any object other than or in addition to the furtherance of trade'. A strike is illegal if it is 'designed or calculated to coerce the Government either directly or indirectly by inflicting hardship on the community' (Trade Disputes and Trade Unions Act (Northern Ireland) 1927).

Civil servants are not allowed to join a trade union.

Special Powers Act

The most serious legislation affecting Northern Ireland is the Civil Authorities (Special Powers) Act, which was passed in 1922. Originally, it was intended to last for one year, but it was renewed until 1933, and then made to last indefinitely. The Act and the regulations made under it give the authorities the following powers:

(1) *To Arrest without Warrant:* 'For the preservation of peace and the maintenance of order' any officer of the Royal Ulster Constabulary may arrest someone without a warrant and detain him for up to 48 hours for the purpose of interrogation; an officer does not have to have reasonable grounds for doing this. In addition, a person may be arrested without a warrant if he is suspected of acting or having acted or being about to act in a way which is 'prejudicial to the preservation of peace or the maintenance of order', or if he is suspected of having committed an offence against the regulations made under the Act. When a person is arrested, he may be detained in prison 'or elsewhere'.

(2) *To Imprison without Trial:* Anyone may be imprisoned without being charged or tried and without recourse to Habeas Corpus.

(3) *To Search without a Warrant:* Any police officer or constable or member of the forces on duty may search any place without a warrant and with force if necessary, at any hour of the day or night, if he suspects that it is being used for a purpose which is 'prejudicial to the preservation of peace or maintenance of order'. He may also seize anything he suspects of being used for such a purpose. There are similar regulations for stopping, searching, and seizing vehicles when travelling along a public road. The person who makes the search does not have to show reasonable grounds for suspicion, as he should do under ordinary criminal law.

(4) To declare a curfew and prohibit meetings, assemblies (including fairs and markets), and processions.

(5) To allow punishment by flogging.

(6) To deny a claim to trial by jury.

(7) To arrest people who are needed as witnesses, to detain them against their will and to force them to answer questions under threat of punishment, even if their answers may incriminate them; these witnesses are guilty of an offence if they refuse to take an oath or to answer a question.

(8) To prevent a person who is imprisoned without trial from seeing his relatives or legal advisers.

(9) To force a person to be finger-printed and photographed without a court order.

(10) To prohibit the holding of an inquest after a prisoner's death.

(11) To arrest a person who 'by word of mouth' spreads false reports or makes false statements.

(12) To prohibit the circulation of any newspaper.

(13) To prohibit the possession of any film or gramophone record.

(14) To arrest a person who does anything 'calculated to be prejudicial to the preservation of peace and maintenance of order in Northern Ireland and not specifically provided for in the regulations'.

Unlawful Associations

It is an offence to be a member of an unlawful association or to do anything with a view to promoting the objects of an unlawful association. It is also an offence to possess documents relating to the affairs of an unlawful association unless the accused person proves that he did not know or had no reason to suspect that such a document was in his possession.

A number of associations are unlawful, including 'Republican Clubs or any like organizations howsoever described'. This regulation is obviously extremely far-reaching.

When a person is tried for an offence under the Special Powers Act, he is assumed guilty until proved innocent – a reversal of the

276

principle applied in all British law courts (that a person is innocent until proved guilty).

The whole of the Special Powers Act is not in operation all the time, but the Government may invoke any section of it at any time. The Act and its regulations are clearly in breach of the European Convention of Human Rights, of which the United Kingdom is a signatory. A number of cases will almost certainly be brought before the European Court at Strasbourg in the early seventies.

Processions

(1) Anyone who intends to organize a public procession must give written notice of the proposed time and route of the procession to a District Inspector, Head Constable, or Sergeant of the Royal Ulster Constabulary, at least 72 hours before it is due to start.

(2) No one should take part in a public procession knowing that the required notice has not been given.

(3) If there are reasonable grounds for suspecting that a procession may cause a breach of the peace or a serious public disorder, an authorized officer of the Royal Ulster Constabulary may impose certain conditions in order to prevent this.

(4) If the Minister for Home Affairs considers it necessary, he may make an order which allows one procession to take place but bans all others in that area for up to one month; or he may make an order which prohibits all public processions for up to one year.

(5) Anyone who takes part in a public procession or meeting, knowing that it contravenes such an order, is guilty of an offence.

(6) It is an offence to use threatening, abusive, or insulting words or behaviour, or to do anything with intent to provoke a breach of the peace at any public place, meeting or procession – and that includes owning or occupying land or premises where such an offence takes place.

(7) It is an offence to break up a public procession; wilfully to

277

obstruct traffic or hinder any lawful activity by sitting, kneeling, or lying down in a public place; to trespass in a public building, or to interfere with any lawful activity in a public building. (A public building means any building which is owned, occupied or used for any purpose by or on behalf of a government department, a local or public authority, or any grant-aided school or institution of further or higher education.)

Public Meetings

It is an offence to act in a disorderly manner in order to disrupt a lawful public meeting. If an authorized officer of the Royal Ulster Constabulary reasonably suspects anyone of committing such an offence, and if the chairman asks him to do so, he may ask that person for his name and address. It is an offence to refuse to give this information, or to give a false name and address (Public Order Act (Northern Ireland) 1951 as amended by the Public Order (Amendments) Act (Northern Ireland) 1970).

Troops

The legal position of troops has been raised on a number of occasions and the following information may be of some assistance:

The Manual of Military Law states:

'When called to the aid of the civil power soldiers in no way differ in the eyes of the law from any other citizens; although, by reason of their organization and equipment, there is always a danger that their employment in aid of the civil power may in itself constitute more force than is necessary.

'The law is clear that a soldier must come to the assistance of the civil authority where it is necessary for him to do so, but not otherwise. No excessive force or display must be used, and a soldier is guilty of an offence if he uses that excess, even under the direction of the civil authority, unless the circumstances are such that he has no opportunity of ascertaining and judging the facts of the case himself and is therefore compelled to accept the opinion and appraisal of the situation of the civil authority concerned.'

In 1911 an opinion was delivered by the Law Officers of the Crown relating to the duty of soldiers called upon to assist the police. The opinion reads:

'A soldier differs from the ordinary citizen in being armed and subject to discipline; but his rights and duties in dealing with crime are precisely the same of those of the ordinary citizen. If the aid of the military has been invoked by the police, and the soldiers find that a situation arises in which prompt action is required, although neither Magistrates nor Police are present or available for consultation, they must act on their own responsibility. They are bound to use such force as is reasonably necessary to protect the premises over which they are watching, and to prevent serious crime or riot. But they must not use lethal weapons to prevent or suppress minor disorders or offences of a less serious character, and in no case should they do so if less extreme measures will suffice. Should it be necessary for them to use extreme measures, they should, whenever possible, give sufficient warning of their intention.'

Recent Legislation

A number of important statutes concerning public order have been passed by Stormont in 1970–71. The most important include:

Prevention of Incitement to Hatred Act (*Northern Ireland*) *1970*, which makes it an offence to publish threatening, abusive or insulting words with intent to stir up hatred or arouse fear of any section of the Northern Ireland public on the grounds of religious belief, colour, race or ethnic origin, or to use in a public place threatening, abusive or insulting words with such intent. It is also an offence under the Act to circulate, with intent to cause a breach of the peace, false statements or reports likely to stir up religious or racial hatred or fear.

Criminal Justice (Temporary Provisions) Act (Northern Ireland) 1970, which requires an automatic minimum sentence of 6 months' imprisonment to be imposed for a wide range of offences covering public order, explosives and firearms. The Act has taken away the power to suspend a sentence in such cases. A conviction for 'disorderly behaviour on a road' in February 1971 caused a man to be imprisoned for 6 months under this Act.

Public Order (Amendment) Act (Northern Ireland) 1970. (▷ p. 278)

Public Order (Amendment) Act (Northern Ireland) 1971, which requires 5 days' notice of certain public processions to be given to the Minister of Home Affairs. The Act gives power to the Minister to prohibit the holding of public processions or open-air meetings for specific periods and also makes it an offence to take part in a procession as a member of an unregistered band.

Further Information and Advice

Association for Legal Justice, 70 Ladybrook Park, Belfast 11

Northern Ireland Civil Rights Association, 2 Marquis Street, Belfast 1

Campaign for Social Justice, Castlefields, Dungannon

Community Relations Commission, Bedford House, 26 Bedford Street, Belfast 2

29. Scotland

Introduction

The law of Scotland differs considerably from that of England and Wales. It is impossible in one chapter to cover adequately the differences – ideally there should be a separate guide. This chapter therefore merely *highlights* these differences in a number of major areas and should not be regarded as comprehensive.

The Scottish Council for Civil Liberties is publishing a number of fact sheets which deal with some of the subjects covered by the Guide: the first fact sheet, on arrest, will be published at the end of 1971. The SCCL is able to take up individual cases involving civil liberty issues and occasionally will be able to refer other cases to appropriate specialist organizations in Scotland. *The address of the SCCL is 1236 Maryhill Road, Glasgow NW.*

Arrest, Bail, and Questioning

Arrest with a Warrant

Arrests with warrants are rare. Warrants are obtained by the Procurator Fiscal (Public Prosecutor) applying to the Sheriff-Substitute following upon information received by him from the police. They are also used in cases of failure to turn up for trial. They are issued without inquiry into the merits of the case.

Arrest without a Warrant

The law relating to arrest without warrant is similar to that in England but the power to arrest is based on the common law and, unlike England, there are very few statutory powers of arrest.

Arrest without warrant almost always requires an explanation by the police officer making the arrest. Whether the explanation justifies the arrest depends on whether the police officer had reasonable grounds for believing that the ends of justice might be defeated if an arrest were not made immediately.

A police officer also has power to arrest without warrant in the following circumstances:

1. If he finds a person in the act of committing, or attempting to commit, a serious crime.
2. If he finds any person under suspicious circumstances with goods in his possession which he knows or believes to be stolen, and the person cannot give a reasonable explanation for having the goods; provided that there is a probability that the person will escape if immediate action is not taken.
3. If he is informed by the injured person, or by a credible eyewitness, that any person has just committed, or attempted to commit, a serious crime, and that there is a similar risk of escape.
4. If he sees a person committing a breach of the peace, or threatening violence, and there is a danger of injury to himself or others.

The police officer is also entitled without warrant to break open doors and enter premises in the course of apprehending the offender. But before doing so he must tell the offender that he is a policeman, and must have demanded and been refused admittance.

Bail

If you are not granted bail by the police, you may apply to the magistrate or Sheriff on your first appearance in court. Bail is more readily granted in Scotland than in England. Police do not have a right to object to bail once the case comes before the court, although the prosecutor may raise objections. There tend to be few unreasonable objections to bail. If bail is refused you have the right to appeal to a High Court judge.

Cash must be handed over before bail is allowed, but the amount required is generally lower than it is in England. For minor offences £10 is normally sufficient, and £20 for slightly more serious ones. Cheques are accepted only from solicitors.

Contacting Your Solicitor

An arrested person has a statutory right to contact a solicitor (Summary Jurisdiction (Scotland) Act 1954). This does not mean that you have the right to telephone him yourself, and the police often insist on doing it for you.

Duty solicitors are normally available to help you if you are pleading guilty the morning after your arrest.

Identification

Police have the power to search, physically examine, photograph and fingerprint any arrested person without seeking authority from a magistrate. They may also make him take part in an identification parade.

283

Questioning

The Judges' Rules do not apply to Scotland, but the courts will not accept as admissible statements which have been improperly obtained by the police.

If a person makes a statement in reply to questions asked by a police officer at a time when he is not under suspicion, the statement will be admissible even if the person has not been cautioned. If he is under suspicion, any statement he makes in reply to questions will be inadmissible unless he has been cautioned. The wording of the caution is similar to that in England.

If a person, whether under suspicion or not, makes a statement which is not in response to questioning, it can be admitted in evidence provided it was made voluntarily. Statements made under duress or in response to an inducement are inadmissible.

Legal Aid and Advice

Application for legal advice and aid should be made to your local Legal Aid office. The address can normally be found in the telephone directory.

Civil Legal Aid

The scheme is administered by the Law Society of Scotland. Civil legal aid is more often available for *claims* than in England. The procedure is more complicated than in England and you will need a solicitor to help you fill in the forms.

Criminal Legal Aid

Criminal legal aid is not available for proceedings in police courts, but is available in the Sheriff Court (◊ p. 286). If you are in custody you will automatically get free legal aid for your first appearance in the Sheriff Court.

If you are eligible for legal aid you will not have to pay any contribution towards the costs of your defence.

Alternative

The Edinburgh Legal Dispensary, Old Quadrangle, The University, Edinburgh, provides free legal advice irrespective of income or the type of legal problem. The Dispensary is open every Wednesday evening.

Court Procedure

Criminal

The types of courts in Scotland which deal with criminal cases are the Police Courts (including Justice of the Peace Court), the Sheriff Courts and the High Court of Justiciary.

Police Courts

Police Courts have a much more limited scope than the English Magistrates' Courts. They have jurisdiction over minor offences and offences under local legislation. The maximum penalty they can impose is usually 60 days' imprisonment or a £50 fine. However, a practice has grown up in some police courts of applying the Prevention of Crimes Act 1871, section 7: this enables a convicted person to be sentenced to 1 year's imprisonment by an unqualified magistrate and without trial by jury.

There is a right of appeal to the High Court on questions of law.

Sheriff Courts

These deal with the vast majority of cases. If a case is tried summarily (by a Sheriff sitting alone) the maximum penalty is generally 6 months' imprisonment with a right of appeal by way of case stated to the High Court. If the case is tried by jury, the maximum penalty is 2 years. The Sheriff has the power to remit a case to the High Court for sentence, which usually means more than 2 years.

A jury is composed of 15 people and reaches its verdict by a simple majority. There is no need to attempt a unanimous verdict. There is an alternative verdict of 'not proven' which has the same consequence as a 'not guilty' verdict.

The decision whether or not to commit a person to a Sheriff Court or the High Court is a matter for the Crown Office who administer prosecutions except in Police Courts.

The High Court of Justiciary

The High Court must always deal with cases of murder and rape. It also tries more serious offences or crimes where the likely sentence is more than 2 years. The judges travel on circuit to try these offences in the major towns. Normally one judge sits with the jury.

Appeals

All appeals are heard by the Court of Criminal Appeal, which consists usually of three Senators of the College of Justice (i.e. High Court judges). There is no appeal beyond this court, unlike England, where it is possible to appeal to the House of Lords. Appeals can really be made only on points of law. The prosecution has an equal right of appeal with the defence, except where the case was tried by jury.

The right of appeal against a jury verdict is severely limited by the Criminal Appeal (Scotland) Act 1926. There is no procedure for ordering a new trial.

Prosecution

In all cases (except those tried before police courts) public prosecution is conducted by the Procurator Fiscal or Advocate Deputy on behalf of the Lord Advocate: the Crown Office in Edinburgh decides in cases of seriousness or importance whether the available evidence justifies prosecution, otherwise the decision is made by the Procurator Fiscal. The police are not involved in the prosecution, though they are responsible for providing the prosecutor with evidence.

In the police courts the prosecution is conducted by the City or Burgh Prosecutor.

Private prosecutions are very rare for common law offences, e.g. theft, homicide. A private person cannot bring a private prosecution for a common law offence or a statutory offence punishable with imprisonment without the leave of the Public Prosecutor.

Procedure for Committal

There is no public investigation by magistrates prior to committal for trial for serious crimes. After he is arrested a person must be brought before the Sheriff as soon as possible. Usually only the accused, his lawyer and the prosecutor are present. No details of evidence may be published before the trial. As a result the examination is usually a formality. After this procedure, the committal proceedings are similar to those in England, but there is a statutory limit of 110 days to the period of detention pending trial. If the accused is not brought to trial within this time he must be freed.

Evidence

Evidence in criminal cases must usually be corroborated – i.e.

there must be credible evidence from two separate sources. Exceptions to this rule include certain motoring offences and cases which involve a series of similar offences.

Civil Proceedings

The Sheriff Court has a similar function to the County Court in England, although there is no financial limit to the type of case it can deal with. Most of the ordinary cases are dealt with by Sheriffs-Substitute but there is a right of appeal to the Sheriff. There is a further appeal to the Inner House of the Court of Sessions if the value of the case exceeds £50. The *Court of Session* itself deals with more complex civil claims and there is a right of appeal from this court to the House of Lords.

Search and Seizure

There is no difference between Scottish and English law relating to search of the person. As to search of premises in Scotland, although in the normal course they can only be searched either with the consent of the occupier or by virtue of a search warrant, there are circumstances when the police in Scotland are entitled to search without a warrant – namely, on the grounds of urgency once a person has been arrested, and if the crime is serious.

The admissibility of evidence obtained by search without a warrant depends on all the circumstances of the case, including the seriousness of the charge. The judge has therefore a discretion whether or not to allow the evidence to be admitted.

Public Order

Breach of the Peace

The offence of breach of the peace has a far wider application in

Scotland than it has in England. It effectively supersedes most other minor offences and provides the authorities with a very powerful weapon. In the past, it has been used to deal with noisy gatherings in private houses which can be heard in the street; peeping toms; schoolmasters making indecent suggestions to pupils; and 'conduct contrary to public order or decorum' which is likely to provoke others to take the law into their own hands or commit reprisals. In fact almost any unorthodox behaviour could technically amount to a breach of the peace. It is left to the discretion of the police and the prosecuting authorities whether to treat a particular act as an offence.

Binding over

There is no 'binding over' procedure in Scotland. In exceptional circumstances (e.g. under a local Act applying to Aberdeen), it may be used as an alternative to a fine or imprisonment.

Obstruction of the Police

This only constitutes an offence under the Police (Scotland) Act if there is a physical act of obstruction.

Insulting Words and Behaviour

This is an offence under the Public Order Act, but it is normally prosecuted as breach of the peace.

Mobbing and Rioting

Anyone who knowingly takes part in a violent or menacing group or demonstration may be guilty of the offence of mobbing and rioting. The essence of the offence is intimidation by numbers or by threats of violence – like the time when 200 people gathered on a highland pier to prevent boats unloading their cargo on a Sunday.

Meetings and Processions

Local legislation gives local authorities the power to restrict the use of public parks, the use of loudspeakers and, in some cases (e.g. Edinburgh), to regulate or ban processions in the streets. Local Acts are often more restrictive than in England.

There is no law of trespass in Scotland as there is in England. Therefore the holding of a meeting in a park or highway cannot be a trespass against the local authority or the owner of the land.

Meetings on Private Premises

Although there is no law of trespass, you do not have the right to hold meetings on other people's property. You would almost certainly be made to leave and you would probably be charged with breach of the peace. Any damage to the property may result in a charge of malicious mischief.

Rights of Police to Attend Meetings on Private Premises

The right of the police to enter meetings held on private premises has never been established in Scottish law. They would probably have to show that there was an urgent threat to public order in order to justify such action.

Complaints Against the Police

Reports of criminal offences by the police should be made to the Procurator Fiscal. Other complaints should be made to the Chief

Constable. The Chief Constable is bound to initiate an investigation when he receives a complaint that an officer has abused his powers, but it is up to the Procurator Fiscal to decide whether or not to prosecute. If it is a purely disciplinary matter, the Chief Constable will deal with it himself under the Police Disciplinary regulations.

In a serious case, the Secretary of State for Scotland has the power to set up a local inquiry. If you think you have strong enough evidence to justify such an inquiry, contact your M.P.

The chief constable is liable for the actions of his officers while they are carrying out their duties (Police (Scotland) Act 1967). In certain circumstances it is possible to sue him, or an individual officer, for damages, but always get legal advice before you take action.

Tribunals

All the administrative tribunals referred to in Chapter 12 apply to Scotland, except for the Mental Health Review Tribunal. (▷ p. 296)

Censorship

The test of obscenity in Scotland is the same as it is under English common law – does the alleged obscene material tend to deprave and corrupt? The Obscene Publications Acts of 1959 and 1964 do not apply in Scotland.

There is therefore no defence of literary merit: expert witnesses cannot be called by the defence to testify to the merits of the publication. There is no legal obligation on the jury or on the court to consider the work as a whole rather than considering the offending sections alone.

In practice, the Lord Advocate or the Crown Office decides

whether to institute prosecutions for obscenity. They tend not to prosecute in cases where the defence of literary merit may succeed in England. Consequently the law has much the same effect in Scotland as it does in England.

Local Legislation

There is, however, one major loophole: local legislation may make provisions for obscene or indecent material to be dealt with summarily by local police courts. This procedure bypasses the Crown Office, which might take a more liberal line, and leaves no effective means of appeal. The position is generally regarded as unsatisfactory.

Local legislation may also apply to film shows which have not been passed by the British Board of Film Censors.

Prosecutions for obscenity in the theatre can only be brought by the Lord Advocate.

Law and the Worker

The position of the worker in Scotland is similar to that in England. The legislation referred to in Chapter 14, including the Industrial Relations Act 1971, applies to Scotland.

Children

Juvenile Offenders

Most juvenile offenders are dealt with by a system of Reporters and Children's Panels, set up under the Social Work (Scotland)

Act 1968. The scheme was first put into practice in April 1971 and varies a great deal in practice from one area to another.

Reporters

Reporters are appointed by the local authorities and can be dismissed only by the Secretary of State for Scotland. There are no prescribed qualifications, but usually they are lawyers or have experience in social work, probation work or criminology. On average there is one Reporter for each local authority.

Children's Panels

Children's Panels are appointed by Children's Panels Advisory Committees which are made up of 3 representatives nominated by the Secretary of State for Scotland and 2 representatives nominated by the local authority. They vary a great deal in size and composition. They are usually quite large and are intended to represent a broad section of the community.

Procedure

If a child under 16 commits an offence he is referred to the Reporter by the police or the Social Work Department. (If the offence is a major one, such as murder, the child is referred directly to the Procurator Fiscal, but the vast majority of cases are dealt with by the Reporters.)

Children up to the age of 18 may also be dealt with in this way if they are already under a Supervision Requirement (⋄ p. 294).

The Reporter considers the case and decides whether any action should be taken. If so, there are four courses open to him:

1. To write directly to the child's parents.
2. To arrange for the police to give the child a formal warning.
3. To refer the case to the Social Work Department for further investigation.

4. To refer the case to a Children's Hearing.

In practice, most cases which come before the Reporter are not referred to a Children's Hearing.

Children's Hearings

If the Reporter decides on this course of action, he sets out his 'Grounds for Referral' and sends a copy to the parents, with 7 days' notice of the date of the hearing.

The hearing consists of a Chairman and 2 members of the Children's Panel – one man and one woman. The child, his parents, a social worker and the Reporter and his deputy attend the hearing. The press, officials from the Social Works Services Group and the Children's Hearings Advisory Committee, and someone to speak on behalf of the child, may also be present.

The Chairman explains the purpose of the hearing, and decides whether people who are not connected with the case should be present. He reads out the Grounds for Referral (which consist of a summary of the case and the Reporter's recommendations) and asks the parents and child whether they agree to them. If the parents or child dispute the Grounds for Referral, the case goes before the Sheriff Court and the parents may claim Legal Aid for this. The court decides whether any further action should be taken: if not, the case is dismissed; if so, the case goes before another Children's Hearing on the assumption that the Grounds for Referral are correct.

The chairman has the casting vote. The hearing may decide:

1. To dismiss the case; or
2. To impose a Supervision Requirement. This means that the child must undergo compulsory supervision, either by a social worker while he remains at home, or in a residential establishment.

If the parents wish to appeal against the decision, they can ask for written reasons for the decision from the Reporter and make their appeal to the Sheriff within 21 days of the hearing.

In any event, the decision must be reviewed frequently by the same hearing that imposed the Supervision Requirement. The child, his parents, the social worker concerned with the case and the local authority all have the right to demand another hearing after 3 months. Parents are given notice of the review system immediately after the hearing.

Sex/Marriage and Divorce

Homosexuals

The Sexual Offences Act 1967 does not apply in Scotland, therefore all homosexual activity is, in theory, illegal. However, the policy of successive Lord Advocates has been *not* to prosecute cases of homosexual behaviour between consenting male adults in private. In practice the law is enforced in much the same way as it is in England.

Of the many minor offences associated with homosexual activities, two are particularly prominent in Scotland:

1. The common law offence of shameless indecency: this covers any public exhibition of homosexual behaviour.
2. Breach of the peace: this offence is so far-reaching that it could be used in almost any case of homosexual behaviour. (◊ p. 288)

Marriage

In limited circumstances a marriage may be constituted in Scotland by two people living together as man and wife and declaring themselves to be married: this is known as marriage by habit and repute.

Divorce

The Divorce Reform Act 1969 does not apply in Scotland. Grounds for divorce are adultery, wilful desertion for 3 years, incurable insanity, cruelty, sodomy and bestiality. Divorce cases can be tried only in the Court of Session (equivalent to the English High Court).

Maintenance

A wife is entitled to maintenance (called aliment) for herself and her children until the rights and wrongs of the case have been established in court. Even if she is found to be the 'guilty' party, she has a right to maintenance for her children if they are in her custody.

Landlord and Tenant

Rent control in Scotland, although not identical to England and Wales, is similar, and the advice given in Chapter 19 is in most cases applicable to Scotland.

The Rent (Scotland) Act 1971 consolidates all previous rent control legislation, although protection against harassment and eviction is still governed by the Rent Act 1965.

Mental Health

There is only one classification for mental patients in Scotland: 'mentally defective' (Mental Health (Scotland) Act 1960).

A mental health patient can appeal against detention to a Sheriff or to the Mental Welfare Commission for Scotland. This is an independent body appointed by the Secretary of State for Scotland. There are 7–9 commissioners. One must be a lawyer who has been in practice for at least 5 years. Two must be full-time medical practitioners trained in psychiatry. The others must represent different sections of society (e.g., present members include an accountant and a trade unionist). The Commission is also responsible for safeguarding the interests and property of mental patients.

Consumer Law

Most of the information contained in Chapter 22 applies to Scotland, although there are differences in the hire purchase laws.

Drugs/Motorist Law/Citizenship and Nationality/Racial Discrimination/Customs and Excise

The law is the same as that of England and Wales.

Appendix A

The European Convention of Human Rights

The European Convention of Human Rights, based on the principles set out in the Declaration, was signed by fifteen nations (including the United Kingdom) on 4 November 1950. Since that date a number of Protocols securing additional rights have been signed, but only the first and fourth Protocols have come into force.

By the Convention, nations have agreed to submit to international control all their actions which concern basic human rights and fundamental freedoms. The Convention provides legal protection for these rights.

The United Kingdom has ratified the Convention although it has not ratified all the Protocols. It is now possible for individuals to complain to the European Commission for Human Rights of alleged violations of the Convention.

As there is no Bill of Rights in this country, there is a strong need for the provisions of the Convention to be incorporated into the ordinary law of the land. Regrettably this has not happened, and an appeal to the Commission can only take place after all remedies have been exhausted in the British courts.

The procedure is lengthy and can involve considerable delay. The Commission will first decide whether the case is within its jurisdiction. If satisfied, it then proceeds to a decision. The functions of the Commission are limited to fact-finding and conciliation. If no friendly settlement can be reached by conciliation then the case is referred to the European Court of Human Rights. Any decision made by the Court can only be enforced by the goodwill of the contracting nations.

Although the direct influence of the Convention is limited (between 1953 and the end of 1969 it declared admissable only 52 out of 3,797 applications), it is nevertheless an important forum for the advancement and protection of civil liberties.

Text

The Governments signatory hereto, being Members of the Council of Europe,

Considering the Universal Declaration of Human Rights proclaimed by the General Assembly of the United Nations on 10 December 1948;

Considering that this Declaration aims at securing the universal and effective recognition and observance of the Rights therein declared;

Considering that the aim of the Council of Europe is the achievement of greater unity between its Members and that one of the methods by which that aim is to be pursued is the maintenance and further realization of Human Rights and Fundamental Freedoms;

Reaffirming their profound belief in those Fundamental Freedoms which are the foundation of justice and peace in the world and are best maintained on the one hand by an effective political democracy and on the other by a common understanding and observance of the Human Rights upon which they depend;

Being resolved, as the Governments of European countries which are likeminded and have a common heritage of political traditions, ideals, freedom and the rule of law to take the first steps for the collective enforcement of certain of the Rights stated in the Universal Declaration;

Have agreed as follows:

Article 1

The High Contracting Parties shall secure to everyone within their jurisdiction the rights and freedoms defined in Section 1 of this Convention.

Section I

Article 2

1. Everyone's right to life shall be protected by law. No one shall be

deprived of his life intentionally save in the execution of a sentence of a court following his conviction of a crime for which this penalty is provided by law.

2. Deprivation of life shall not be regarded as inflicted in contravention of this Article when it results from the use of force which is no more than absolutely necessary:

(a) in defence of any person from unlawful violence;

(b) in order to effect a lawful arrest or to prevent the escape of a person lawfully detained;

(c) in action lawfully taken for the purpose of quelling a riot or insurrection.

Article 3

No one shall be subjected to torture or to inhuman or degrading treatment or punishment.

Article 4

1. No one shall be held in slavery or servitude.

2. No one shall be required to perform forced or compulsory labour.

3. For the purpose of this Article the term 'forced or compulsory labour' shall not include:

(a) any work required to be done in the ordinary course of detention imposed according to the provisions of Article 5 of this Convention or during conditional release from such detention;

(b) any service of a military character or, in case of conscientious objectors in countries where they are recognized, service exacted instead of compulsory military service;

(c) any service exacted in case of an emergency or calamity threatening the life or well-being of the community;

(d) any work or service which forms part of normal civic obligations.

Article 5

1. Everyone has the right to liberty and security of person.

No one shall be deprived of his liberty save in the following cases and in accordance with a procedure prescribed by law;

(a) the lawful detention of a person after conviction by a competent court;

(b) the lawful arrest or detention of a person for non-compliance with the lawful order of a court or in order to secure the fulfilment of any obligation prescribed by law;

(c) the lawful arrest or detention of a person effected for the purpose of bringing him before the competent legal authority on reasonable suspicion of having committed an offence or when it is reasonably considered necessary to prevent his committing an offence or fleeing after having done so;

(d) the detention of a minor by lawful order for the purpose of educational supervision or his lawful detention for the purpose of bringing him before the competent legal authority;

(e) the lawful detention of persons for the prevention of the spreading of infectious diseases, of persons of unsound mind, alcoholics or drug addicts, or vagrants;

(f) the lawful arrest or detention of a person to prevent his effecting an unauthorized entry into the country or of a person against whom action is being taken with a view to deportation or extradition.

2. Everyone who is arrested shall be informed promptly, in a language which he understands, of the reasons for his arrest and of any charge against him.

3. Everyone arrested or detained in accordance with the provisions of paragraph 1 (c) of this Article shall be brought promptly before a judge or other officer authorized by law to exercise judicial power and shall be entitled to trial within a reasonable time or to release pending trial. Release may be conditioned by guarantees to appear for trial.

4. Everyone who is deprived of his liberty by arrest or detention shall be entitled to take proceedings by which the lawfulness of his detention shall be decided speedily by a court and his release ordered if the detention is not lawful.

5. Everyone who has been the victim of arrest or detention in contravention of the provisions of this Article shall have an enforceable right to compensation.

Article 6

1. In the determination of his civil rights and obligations or of any criminal charge against him, everyone is entitled to a fair and public hearing within a reasonable time by an independent and impartial tribunal established by law. Judgment shall be pronounced publicly but the press and public may be excluded from all or part of the trial in

the interest of morals, public order or national security in a democratic society, where the interests of juveniles or the protection of the private life of the parties so require, or to the extent strictly necessary in the opinion of the court in special circumstances where publicity would prejudice the interests of justice.

2. Everyone charged with a criminal offence shall be presumed innocent until proved guilty according to law.

3. Everyone charged with a criminal offence has the following minimum rights:

(a) to be informed promptly, in a language which he understands and in detail, of the nature and cause of the accusation against him;

(b) to have adequate time and facilities for the preparation of his defence;

(c) to defend himself in person or through legal assistance of his own choosing or, if he has not sufficient means to pay for legal assistance, to be given it free when the interests of justice so require;

(d) to examine or have examined witnesses against him and to obtain the attendance and examination of witnesses on his behalf under the same conditions as witnesses against him;

(e) to have the free assistance of an interpreter if he cannot understand or speak the language used in court.

Article 7

1. No one shall be held guilty of any criminal offence on account of any act or omission which did not constitute a criminal offence under national or international law at the time when it was committed. Nor shall a heavier penalty be imposed than the one that was applicable at the time the criminal offence was committed.

2. This Article shall not prejudice the trial and punishment of any person for any act or omission which, at the time when it was committed, was criminal according to the general principles of law recognized by civilized nations.

Article 8

1. Everyone has the right to respect for his private and family life, his home and his correspondence.

2. There shall be no interference by a public authority with the exercise of this right except such as is in accordance with the law and is neces-

sary in a democratic society in the interests of national security, public safety or the economic well-being of the country, for the prevention of disorder or crime, for the protection of health or morals, or for the protection of the rights and freedoms of others.

Article 9

1. Everyone has the right to freedom of thought, conscience and religion; this right includes freedom to change his religion or belief, and freedom, either alone or in community with others and in public or private, to manifest his religion or belief, in worship, teaching, practice and observance.
2. Freedom to manifest one's religion or beliefs shall be subject only to such limitations as are prescribed by law and are necessary in a democratic society in the interests of public safety, for the protection of public order, health or morals, or for the protection of the rights and freedoms of others.

Article 10

1. Everyone has the right to freedom of expression. This right shall include freedom to hold opinions and to receive and impart information and ideas without interference by public authority and regardless of frontiers. This Article shall not prevent States from requiring the licensing of broadcasting, television or cinema enterprises.
2. The exercise of these freedoms, since it carries with it duties and responsibilities, may be subject to such formalities, conditions, restrictions or penalties as are prescribed by law and are necessary in a democratic society, in the interests of national security, territorial integrity or public safety, for the prevention of disorder or crime, for the protection of health or morals, for the protection of the reputation or rights of others, for preventing the disclosure of information received in confidence, or for maintaining the authority and impartiality of the judiciary.

Article 11

1. Everyone has the right to freedom of peaceful assembly and to freedom of association with others, including the right to form and to join trade unions for the protection of his interests.

2. No restrictions shall be placed on the exercise of these rights other than such as are prescribed by law and are necessary in a democratic society in the interests of national security or public safety, for the prevention of disorder or crime, for the protection of health or morals or for the protection of the rights and freedoms of others. This Article shall not prevent the imposition of lawful restrictions on the exercise of these rights by members of the armed forces, of the police or of the administration of the State.

Article 12

Men and women of marriageable age have the right to marry and to found a family, according to the national laws governing the exercise of this right.

Article 13

Everyone whose rights and freedoms as set forth in this Convention are violated shall have an effective remedy before a national authority notwithstanding that the violation has been committed by persons acting in an official capacity.

Article 14

The enjoyment of the rights and freedoms set forth in this Convention shall be secured without discrimination on any ground such as sex, race, colour, language, religion, political or other opinion, national or social origin, association with a national minority, property, birth or other status.

Article 15

1. In time of war or other public emergency threatening the life of the nation any High Contracting Party may take measures derogating from its obligations under this Convention to the extent strictly required by the exigencies of the situation, provided that such measures are not inconsistent with its other obligations under international law.

2. No derogation from Article 2, except in respect of deaths resulting

from lawful acts of war, or from Articles 3, 4 (paragraph 1) and 7 shall be made under this provision.

3. Any High Contracting Party availing itself of this right of derogation shall keep the Secretary-General of the Council of Europe fully informed of the measures which it has taken and the reasons therefor. It shall also inform the Secretary-General of the Council of Europe when such measures have ceased to operate and the provisions of the Convention are again being fully executed.

Article 16

Nothing in Articles 10, 11, and 14 shall be regarded as preventing the High Contracting Parties from imposing restrictions on the political activity of aliens.

Article 17

Nothing in this Convention may be interpreted as implying for any State, group or person any right to engage in any activity or perform any act aimed at the destruction of any of the rights and freedoms set forth herein or at their limitation to a greater extent than is provided for in the Convention.

Article 18

The restrictions permitted under this Convention to the said rights and freedoms shall not be applied for any purpose other than those for which they have been prescribed.

Section II

Article 19

To ensure the observance of the engagements undertaken by the High Contracting Parties in the present Convention, there shall be set up:

1. A European Commission of Human Rights hereinafter referred to as 'the Commission';

2. A European Court of Human Rights, hereinafter referred to as 'the Court'.

Section III

Article 20

The Commission shall consist of a number of members equal to that of the High Contracting Parties. No two members of the Commission may be nationals of the same State.

Article 21

1. The members of the Commission shall be elected by the Committee of Ministers by an absolute majority of votes, from a list of names drawn up by the Bureau of the Consultative Assembly; each group of the Representatives of the High Contracting Parties in the Consultative Assembly shall put forward three candidates, of whom two at least shall be its nationals.
2. As far as applicable, the same procedure shall be followed to complete the Commission in the event of other States subsequently becoming Parties to this Convention, and in filling casual vacancies.

Article 22

1. The members of the Commission shall be elected for a period of six years. They may be re-elected. However, of the members elected at the first election, the terms of seven members shall expire at the end of three years.
2. The members whose terms are to expire at the end of the initial period of three years shall be chosen by lot by the Secretary-General of the Council of Europe immediately after the first election has been completed.
3. A member of the Commission elected to replace a member whose term of office has not expired shall hold office for the remainder of his predecessor's term.
4. The members of the Commission shall hold office until replaced. After having been replaced, they shall continue to deal with such cases as they already have under consideration.

Article 23

The members of the Commission shall sit on the Commission in their individual capacity.

Article 24

Any High Contracting Party may refer to the Commission through the Secretary-General of the Council of Europe, any alleged breach of the provisions of the Convention by another High Contracting Party.

Article 25

1. The Commission may receive petitions addressed to the Secretary-General of the Council of Europe from any person, non-governmental organization or group of individuals claiming to be the victim of a violation by one of the High Contracting Parties of the rights set forth in this Convention, provided that the High Contracting Party against which the complaint has been lodged has declared that it recognizes the competence of the Commission to receive such petitions. Those of the High Contracting Parties who have made such a declaration undertake not to hinder in any way the effective exercise of this right.
2. Such declarations may be made for a specific period.
3. The declarations shall be deposited with the Secretary-General of the Council of Europe who shall transmit copies thereof to the High Contracting Parties and publish them.
4. The Commission shall only exercise the powers provided for in this Article when at least six High Contracting Parties are bound by declarations made in accordance with the preceding paragraphs.

Article 26

The Commission may only deal with the matter after all domestic remedies have been exhausted, according to the generally recognized rules of international law, and within a period of six months from the date on which the final decision was taken.

Article 27

1. The Commission shall not deal with any petition submitted under Article 25 which
    (a) is anonymous, or
    (b) is substantially the same as a matter which has already been

examined by the Commission or has already been submitted to another procedure of international investigation or settlement and if it contains no relevant new information.

2. The Commission shall consider inadmissible any petition submitted under Article 25 which it considers incompatible with the provisions of the present Convention, manifestly illfounded, or an abuse of the right of petition.

3. The Commission shall reject any petition referred to it which it considers inadmissible under Article 26.

Article 28

In the event of the Commission accepting a petition referred to it:

(a) it shall, with a view to ascertaining the facts undertake together with the representatives of the parties an examination of the petition and, if need be, an investigation, for the effective conduct of which the States concerned shall furnish all necessary facilities, after an exchange of views with the Commission;

(b) it shall place itself at the disposal of the parties concerned with a view to securing a friendly settlement of the matter on the basis of respect for Human Rights as defined in this Convention.

Article 29

1. The Commission shall perform the functions set out in Article 28 by means of a Sub-Commission consisting of seven members of the Commission.

2. Each of the parties concerned may appoint as members of this Sub-Commission a person of its choice.

3. The remaining members shall be chosen by lot in accordance with arrangements prescribed in the Rules of Procedure of the Commission.

Article 30

If the Sub-Commission succeeds in effecting a friendly settlement in accordance with Article 28, it shall draw up a Report which shall be sent to the States concerned, to the Committee of Ministers and to the Secretary-General of the Council of Europe for publication. This Report shall be confined to a brief statement of the facts and of the solution reached.

Article 31

1. If a solution is not reached, the Commission shall draw up a Report on the facts and state its opinion as to whether the facts found disclose a breach by the State concerned of its obligations under the Convention. The opinions of all the members of the Commission on this point may be stated in the Report.
2. The Report shall be transmitted to the Committee of Ministers. It shall also be transmitted to the States concerned, who shall not be at liberty to publish it.
3. In transmitting the Report to the Committee of Ministers the Commission may make such proposals as it thinks fit.

Article 32

1. If the question is not referred to the Court in accordance with Article 48 of this Convention within a period of three months from the date of the transmission of the Report to the Committee of Ministers, the Committee of Ministers shall decide by a majority of two-thirds of the members entitled to sit on the Committee whether there has been a violation of the Convention.
2. In the affirmative case the Committee of Ministers shall prescribe a period during which the Contracting Party concerned must take the measures required by the decision of the Committee of Ministers.
3. If the High Contracting Party concerned has not taken satisfactory measures within the prescribed period, the Committee of Ministers shall decide by the majority provided for in paragraph 1 above what effect shall be given to its original decision and shall publish the Report.
4. The High Contracting Parties undertake to regard as binding on them any decision which the Committee of Ministers may take in application of the preceding paragraphs.

Article 33

The Commission shall meet *in camera*.

Article 34

The Commission shall take its decisions by a majority of the Members present and voting; the Sub-Commission shall take its decisions by a majority of its members.

Article 35

The Commission shall meet as the circumstances require. The meetings shall be convened by the Secretary-General of the Council of Europe.

Article 36

The Commission shall draw up its own rules of procedure.

Article 37

The secretariat of the Commission shall be provided by the Secretary-General of the Council of Europe.

Section IV

Article 38

The European Court of Human Rights shall consist of a number of judges equal to that of the Members of the Council of Europe. No two judges may be nationals of the same State.

Article 39

1. The members of the Court shall be elected by the Consultative Assembly by a majority of the votes cast from a list of persons nominated by the Members of the Council of Europe; each Member shall nominate three candidates, of whom two at least shall be its nationals.
2. As far as applicable, the same procedure shall be followed to complete the Court in the event of the admission of new members of the Council of Europe, and in filling casual vacancies.

310

3. The candidates shall be of high moral character and must either possess the qualifications required for appointment to high judicial office or be jurisconsults of recognized competence.

Article 40

1. The members of the Court shall be elected for a period of nine years. They may be re-elected. However, of the members elected at the first election the terms of four members shall expire at the end of three years, and the terms of four more members shall expire at the end of six years.
2. The members whose terms are to expire at the end of the initial periods of three and six years shall be chosen by lot by the Secretary-General immediately after the first election has been completed.
3. A member of the Court elected to replace a member whose term of office has not expired shall hold office for the remainder of his predecessor's term.
4. The members of the Court shall hold office until replaced. After having been replaced, they shall continue to deal with such cases as they already have under consideration.

Article 41

The Court shall elect its President and Vice-President for a period of three years. They may be re-elected.

Article 42

The members of the Court shall receive for each day of duty a compensation to be determined by the Committee of Ministers.

Article 43

For the consideration of each case brought before it the Court shall consist of a Chamber composed of seven judges. There shall sit as an *ex officio* member of the Chamber the judge who is a national of any State party concerned, or, if there is none, a person of its choice who shall sit in the capacity of judge; the names of the other judges shall be chosen by lot by the President before the opening of the case.

311

Article 44

Only the High Contracting Parties and the Commission shall have the right to bring a case before the Court.

Article 45

The jurisdiction of the Court shall extend to all cases concerning the interpretation and application of the present Convention which the High Contracting Parties or the Commission shall refer to it in accordance with Article 48.

Article 46

1. Any of the High Contracting Parties may at any time declare that it recognizes as compulsory *ipso facto* and without special agreement the jurisdiction of the Court in all matters concerning the interpretation and application of the present Convention.
2. The declarations referred to above may be made unconditionally or on condition of reciprocity on the part of several or certain other High Contracting Parties or for a specified period.
3. These declarations shall be deposited with the Secretary-General of the Council of Europe who shall transmit copies thereof to the High Contracting Parties.

Article 47

The Court may only deal with a case after the Commission has acknowledged the failure of efforts for a friendly settlement and within the period of three months provided for in Article 32.

Article 48

The following may bring a case before the Court, provided that the High Contracting Party concerned, if there is only one, or the High Contracting Parties concerned, if there is more than one, are subject to the compulsory jurisdiction of the Court or, failing that, with the consent of the High Contracting Party concerned, if there is only one, or of the High Contracting Parties concerned if there is more than one:

   (a) the Commission;

   (b) a High Contracting Party whose national is alleged to be a victim;

   (c) a High Contracting Party which referred the case to the Commission;

   (d) a High Contracting Party against which the complaint has been lodged.

Article 49

In the event of dispute as to whether the Court has jurisdiction, the matter shall be settled by the decision of the Court.

Article 50

If the Court finds that a decision or a measure taken by a legal authority or any other authority of a High Contracting Party, is completely or partially in conflict with the obligations arising from the present Convention, and if the internal law of the said Party allows only partial reparation to be made for the consequences of this decision or measure, the decision of the Court shall, if necessary, afford just satisfaction to the injured party.

Article 51

1. Reasons shall be given for the judgment of the Court.
2. If the judgment does not represent in whole or in part the unanimous opinion of the judges, any judge shall be entitled to deliver a separate opinion.

Article 52

The judgment of the Court shall be final.

Article 53

The High Contracting Parties undertake to abide by the decision of the Court in any case to which they are parties.

Article 54

The judgment of the Court shall be transmitted to the Committee of Ministers which shall supervise its execution.

Article 55

The Court shall draw up its own rules and shall determine its own procedure.

Article 56

1. The first election of the members of the Court shall take place after the declarations by the High Contracting Parties mentioned in Article 46 have reached a total of eight.
2. No case can be brought before the Court before this election.

Section V

Article 57

On receipt of a request from the Secretary-General of the Council of Europe any High Contracting Party shall furnish an explanation of the manner in which its internal law ensures the effective implementation of any of the provisions of this Convention.

Article 58

The expenses of the Commission and the Court shall be borne by the Council of Europe.

Article 59

The members of the Commission and of the Court shall be entitled, during the discharge of their functions, to the privileges and immunities provided for in Article 40 of the Statute of the Council of Europe and in the agreements made thereunder.

Article 60

Nothing in this Convention shall be construed as limiting or derogating from any of the human rights and fundamental freedoms which may be ensured under the laws of any High Contracting Party or under any other agreement to which it is a Party.

Article 61

Nothing in this Convention shall prejudice the powers conferred on the Committee of Ministers by the Statute of the Council of Europe.

Article 62

The High Contracting Parties agree that, except by special agreement, they will not avail themselves of treaties, conventions or declarations in force between them for the purpose of submitting, by way of petition, a dispute arising out of the interpretation or application of this Convention to a means of settlement other than those provided for in this Convention.

Article 63

1. Any State may at the time of its ratification or at any time thereafter declare by notification addressed to the Secretary-General of the Council of Europe that the present Convention shall extend to all or any of the territories for whose international relations it is responsible.
2. The Convention shall extend to the territory or territories named in the notification as from the thirtieth day after the receipt of this notification by the Secretary-General of the Council of Europe.
3. The provisions of this Convention shall be applied in such territories with due regard, however, to local requirements.
4. Any State which has made a declaration in accordance with paragraph 1 of this Article may at any time thereafter declare on behalf of one or more of the territories to which the declaration relates that it

accepts the competence of the Commission to receive petitions from individuals, non-governmental organizations or groups of individuals in accordance with Article 25 of the present Convention.

Article 64

1. Any State may, when signing this Convention or when depositing its instrument of ratification, make a reservation in respect of any particular provision of the Convention to the extent that any law then in force in its territory is not in conformity with the provision. Reservations of a general character shall not be permitted under this Article.
2. Any reservation made under this Article shall contain a brief statement of the law concerned.

Article 65

1. A High Contracting Party may denounce the present Convention only after the expiry of five years from the date on which it became a Party to it and after six months' notice contained in a notification addressed to the Secretary-General of the Council of Europe, who shall inform the other High Contracting Parties.
2. Such a denunciation shall not have the effect of releasing the High Contracting Party concerned from its obligations under this Convention in respect of any act which, being capable of constituting a violation of such obligations, may have been performed by it before the date at which the denunciation became effective.
3. Any High Contracting Party which shall cease to be a Member of the Council of Europe shall cease to be a Party to this Convention under the same conditions.
4. The Convention may be denounced in accordance with the provisions of the preceding paragraphs in respect of any territory to which it has been declared to extend under the terms of Article 63.

Article 66

1. This Convention shall be open to the signature of the Members of the Council of Europe. It shall be ratified. Ratifications shall be deposited with the Secretary-General of the Council of Europe.
2. The present Convention shall come into force after the deposit of ten instruments of ratification.

3. As regards any signatory ratifying subsequently, the Convention shall come into force at the date of the deposit of its instrument of ratification.

4. The Secretary-General of the Council of Europe shall notify all the Members of the Council of Europe of the entry into force of the Convention, the names of the High Contracting Parties who have ratified it, and the deposit of all instruments of ratification which may be effected subsequently.

Done at Rome this 4th day of November, 1950, in English and French, both texts being equally authentic, in a single copy which shall remain deposited in the archives of the Council of Europe. The Secretary-General shall transmit certified copies to each of the signatories.

Protocols

1. *Enforcement of certain Rights and Freedoms not included in Section I of the Convention*

The Governments signatory hereto, being Members of the Council of Europe,

Being resolved to take steps to ensure the collective enforcement of certain rights and freedoms other than those already included in Section I of the Convention for the Protection of Human Rights and Fundamental Freedoms signed at Rome on 4th November, 1950 (hereinafter referred to as 'the Convention'),

Have agreed as follows:

Article 1

Every natural or legal person is entitled to the peaceful enjoyment of his possessions. No one shall be deprived of his possessions except in the public interest and subject to the conditions provided for by law and by the general principles of international law.

The preceding provisions shall not, however, in any way impair the right of a State to enforce such laws as it deems necessary to control the use of property in accordance with the general interest or to secure the payment of taxes or other contributions or penalties.

Article 2

No person shall be denied the right to education. In the exercise of any

317

functions which it assumes in relation to education and to teaching, the State shall respect the right of parents to ensure such education and teaching in conformity with their own religious and philosophical convictions.

Article 3

The High Contracting Parties undertake to hold free elections at reasonable intervals by secret ballot, under conditions which will ensure the free expression of the opinion of the people in the choice of the legislature.

Article 4

Any High Contracting Party may at the time of signature or ratification or at any time thereafter communicate to the Secretary-General of the Council of Europe a declaration stating the extent to which it undertakes that the provisions of the present Protocol shall apply to such of the territories for the international relations of which it is responsible as are named therein.

Any High Contracting Party which has communicated a declaration in virtue of the preceding paragraph may from time to time communicate a further declaration modifying the terms of any former declaration or terminating the application of the provisions of this Protocol in respect of any territory.

A declaration made in accordance with this Article shall be deemed to have been made in accordance with paragraph 1 of Article 63 of the Convention.

Article 5

As between the High Contracting Parties the provisions of Articles 1, 2, 3 and 4 of this Protocol shall be regarded as additional Articles to the Convention and all the provisions of the Convention shall apply accordingly.

Article 6

This Protocol shall be open for signature by the Members of the Council of Europe, who are the signatories of the Convention; it shall be rati-

318

fied at the same time as or after the ratification of the Convention. It shall enter into force after the deposit of ten instruments of ratification. As regards any signatory ratifying subsequently, the Protocol shall enter into force at the date of the deposit of its instrument of ratification.

The instruments of ratification shall be deposited with the Secretary-General of the Council of Europe, who will notify all Members of the names of those who have ratified.

Done at Paris on the 20th day of March 1952, in English and French, both texts being equally authentic, in a single copy which shall remain deposited in the archives of the Council of Europe. The Secretary-General shall transmit certified copies to each of the signatory Governments.

2. *Conferring upon the European Court of Human Rights Competence to give Advisory Opinions*

The member States of the Council of Europe signatory hereto:

Having regard to the provisions of the Convention for the Protection of Human Rights and Fundamental Freedoms signed at Rome on 4 November 1950 (hereinafter referred to as 'the Convention'), and in particular Article 19 instituting, among other bodies, a European Court of Human Rights (hereinafter referred to as 'the Court');

Considering that it is expedient to confer upon the Court competence to give advisory opinions subject to certain conditions;

Have agreed as follows:

Article 1

1. The Court may, at the request of the Committee of Ministers, give advisory opinions on legal questions concerning the interpretation of the Convention and the Protocols thereto.

2. Such opinions shall not deal with any question relating to the content or scope of the rights or freedoms defined in Section I of the Convention and in the Protocols thereto, or with any other question which the Commission, the Court, or the Committee of Ministers might have to consider in consequence of any such proceedings as could be instituted in accordance with the Convention.

3. Decisions of the Committee of Ministers to request an advisory opinion of the Court shall require a two-thirds majority vote of the representatives entitled to sit on the Committee.

Article 2

The Court shall decide whether a request for an advisory opinion submitted by the Committee of Ministers is within its consultative competence as defined in Article 1 of this Protocol.

Article 3

1. For the consideration of requests for an advisory opinion, the Court shall sit in plenary session.
2. Reasons shall be given for advisory opinions of the Court.
3. If the advisory opinion does not represent in whole or in part the unanimous opinion of the judges, any judge shall be entitled to deliver a separate opinion.
4. Advisory opinions of the Court shall be communicated to the Committee of Ministers.

Article 4

The powers of the Court under Article 55 of the Convention shall extend to the drawing up of such rules and the determination of such procedure as the Court may think necessary for the purposes of this Protocol.

Article 5

1. This Protocol shall be open to signature by Member States of the Council of Europe, signatories to the Convention, who may become Parties to it by:

    (a) signature without reservation in respect of ratification or acceptance;

    (b) signature with reservation in respect of ratification or acceptance, followed by ratification or acceptance. Instruments of ratification or acceptance shall be deposited with the Secretary-General of the Council of Europe.

2. This Protocol shall enter into force as soon as all the States Parties to the Convention shall have become Parties to the Protocol in accordance with the Provisions of paragraph 1 of this Article.

3. From the date of the entry into force of this Protocol, Articles 1 to 4 shall be considered an integral part of the Convention.

4. The Secretary-General of the Council of Europe shall notify the Member States of the Council of:

(a) any signature without reservation in respect of ratification or acceptance;

(b) any signature with reservation in respect of ratification or acceptance;

(c) the deposit of any instrument of ratification or acceptance;

(d) the date of entry into force of this Protocol in accordance with paragraph 2 of this Article.

In witness whereof the undersigned, being duly authorized thereto, have signed this Protocol.

Done at Strasbourg, this 6th day of May 1963, in English and in French, both texts being equally authoritative, in a single copy which shall remain deposited in the archives of the Council of Europe. The Secretary-General shall transmit certified copies to each of the signatory States.

3. *Amending Articles 29, 30, and 94 of the Convention*

The member States of the Council of Europe, signatories to this Protocol,

Considering that it is advisable to amend certain provisions of the Convention for the Protection of Human Rights and Fundamental Freedoms signed at Rome on 4 November 1960 (hereinafter referred to as 'the Convention') concerning the procedure of the European Commission of Human Rights,

Have agreed as follows:

Article 1

1. Article 29 of the Convention is deleted.

2. The following provision shall be inserted in the Convention:
'Article 29

After it has accepted a petition submitted under Article 25, the Commission may nevertheless decide unanimously to reject the petition if, in the course of its examination, it finds that the existence of one of the grounds for non-acceptance provided for in Article 27 has been established.

In such a case, the decision shall be communicated to the parties.'

Article 2

In Article 30 of the Convention, the word 'Sub-Commission' shall be replaced by the word 'Commission'.

Article 3

1. At the beginning of Article 34 of the Convention, the following shall be inserted:

'Subject to the provisions of Article 29. . . .'

2. At the end of the same Article, the sentence 'the Sub-commission shall take its decisions by a majority of its members' shall be deleted.

Article 4

1. The Protocol shall be open to signature by the member States of the Council of Europe, who may become Parties to it either by:

(a) signature without reservation in respect of ratification or acceptance, or

(b) signature with reservation in respect of ratification or acceptance, followed by ratification or acceptance. Instruments of ratification or acceptance shall be deposited with the Secretary-General of the Council of Europe.

2. This Protocol shall enter into force as soon as all States Parties to the Convention shall have become Parties to the Protocol, in accordance with the provisions of paragraph 1 of this Article.

3. The Secretary-General of the Council of Europe shall notify the Member States of the Council of:

(a) any signature without reservation in respect of ratification or acceptance;

(b) any signature with reservation in respect of ratification or acceptance;

(c) the deposit of any instrument of ratification or acceptance;

(d) the date of entry into force of this Protocol in accordance with paragraph 2 of this Article.

In witness whereof the undersigned, being duly authorized thereto, have signed this Protocol.

Done at Strasbourg, this 6th day of May 1963, in English and in French, both texts being equally authoritative, in a single copy which shall remain deposited in the archives of the Council of Europe. The Secretary-General shall transmit certified copies to each of the signatory States.

4. *Protecting certain Additional Rights*

The Governments signatory hereto, being Members of the Council of Europe.

Being resolved to take steps to ensure the collective enforcement of certain rights and freedoms other than those already included in Section I of the Convention for the Protection of Human Rights and Fundamental Freedoms signed at Rome on 4 November 1950 (hereinafter referred to as 'the Convention') and in Articles 1 to 3 of the First Protocol to the Convention, signed at Paris on 20 March 1952,

Have agreed as follows:

Article 1

No one shall be deprived of his liberty merely on the ground of inability to fulfil a contractual obligation.

Article 2

1. Everyone lawfully within the territory of a State shall, within that territory, have the right to liberty of movement and freedom to choose his residence.
2. Everyone shall be free to leave any country, including his own.
3. No restrictions shall be placed on the exercise of these rights other than such as are in accordance with law and are necessary in a democratic society in the interests of national security or public safety for the maintenance of 'ordre public', for the prevention of crime, for the protection of the rights and freedoms of others.
4. The rights set forth in paragraph 1 may also be subject, in particular areas, to restrictions imposed in accordance with law and justified by the public interest in a democratic society.

Article 3

1. No one shall be expelled, by means either of an individual or of a collective measure, from the territory of the State of which he is a national.
2. No one shall be deprived of the right to enter the territory of the State of which he is a national.

Article 4

Collective expulsion of aliens is prohibited.

Article 5

1. Any High Contracting Party may, at the time of signature or ratification of this Protocol, or at any time thereafter, communicate to the Secretary-General of the Council of Europe a declaration stating the extent to which it undertakes that the provisions of this Protocol shall apply to such of the territories for the international relations of which it is responsible as are named therein.
2. Any High Contracting Party which has communicated a declaration in virtue of the preceding paragraph may, from time to time, communicate a further declaration modifying the terms of any former declaration or terminating the application of the provisions of this Protocol in respect of any territory.
3. A declaration made in accordance with this Article shall be deemed to have been made in accordance with paragraph 1 of Article 63 of the Convention.
4. The territory of any State to which this Protocol applies by virtue of ratification or acceptance by that State, and each teritory to which this Protocol is applied by virtue of a declaration by that State under this Article, shall be treated as separate territories for the purpose of the references in Articles 2 and 3 to the territory of a State.

Article 6

1. As between the High Contracting Parties the provisions of Articles 1 to 5 of this Protocol shall be regarded as additional articles to the Con-

vention, and all the provisions of the Convention shall apply accordingly.

2. Nevertheless, the right of individual resource recognized by a declaration made under Article 25 of the Convention, or the acceptance of the compulsory jurisdiction of the Court by a declaration made under Article 46 of the Convention, shall not be effective in relation to this Protocol unless the High Contracting Party concerned has made a statement recognizing such right, or accepting such jurisdiction, in respect of all or any of Articles 1 to 4 of the Protocol.

Article 7

1. This Protocol shall be open for signature by the members of the Council of Europe who are the signatories of the Convention; it shall be ratified at the same time as or after the ratification of the Convention. It shall enter into force after the deposit of five instruments of ratification. As regards any signatory ratifying subsequently, the Protocol shall enter into force at the date of the deposit of its instrument of ratification.

2. The instruments of ratification shall be deposited with the Secretary-General of the Council of Europe, who will notify all members of the names of those who have ratified.

In witness whereof, the undersigned, being duly authorized thereto, have signed this Protocol.

Done at Strasbourg, this 16th day of September 1963, in English and in French, both texts being equally authoritative, in a single copy which shall remain deposited in the archives of the Council of Europe. The Secretary-General shall transmit certified copies to each of the signatory States.

5. *Amending Articles 22 and 40 of the Convention*

The Governments signatory hereto, being Members of the Council of Europe,

Considering that certain inconveniences have arisen in the application of the provisions of Articles 22 and 40 of the Convention for the Protection of Human Rights and Fundamental Freedoms signed at Rome on 4th November 1950 (hereinafter referred to as 'the Convention') relating to the length of the terms of office of the members of the European Commission of Human Rights (hereinafter referred to as 'the Commission') and of the European Court of Human Rights hereinafter referred to as 'the Court');

Considering that it is desirable to ensure as far as possible an election every three years of one half of the members of the Commission and of one third of the members of the Court;

Considering therefore that it is desirable to amend certain provisions of the Convention,

Have agreed as follows:

Article 1

In Article 22 of the Convention, the following two paragraphs shall be inserted after paragraph (2):

'(3) In order to ensure that, as far as possible, one half of the membership of the Commission shall be renewed every three years, the Committee of Ministers may decide, before proceeding to any subsequent election, that the term or terms of office of one or more members to be elected shall be for a period other than six years but no more than nine and not less than three years.

(4) In cases where more than one term of office is involved and the Committee of Ministers applies the preceding paragraph, the allocation of the terms of office shall be effected by the drawing of lots by the Secretary-General, immediately after the election.'

Article 2

In Article 22 of the Convention, the former paragraphs (3) and (4) shall become respectively paragraphs (5) and (6).

Article 3

In Article 40 of the Convention, the following two paragraphs shall be inserted after paragraph (2):

'(3) In order to ensure that, as far as possible, one third of the membership of the Court shall be renewed every three years, the Consultative Assembly may decide, before proceeding to any subsequent election, that the term or terms of office of one or more members to be elected shall be for a period other than nine years but not more than twelve and not less than six years.

(4) In cases where more than one term of office is involved and the

Consultative Assembly applies the preceding paragraph, the allocation of the terms of office shall be effected by the drawing of lots by the Secretary-General immediately after the election.'

Article 4

In Article 40 of the Convention, the former paragraphs (3) and (4) shall become respectively paragraphs (5) and (6)

Article 5

1. This Protocol shall be open to signature by Members of the Council of Europe, signatories to the Convention, who may become Parties to it by:

   (a) signature without reservation in respect of ratification or acceptance;

   (b) signature with reservation in respect of ratification or acceptance, followed by ratification or acceptance.

Instruments of ratification or acceptance shall be deposited with the Secretary-General of the Council of Europe.

2. This Protocol shall enter into force as soon as all Contracting Parties to the Convention shall have become Parties to the Protocol, in accordance with the provisions of paragraph 1 of this Article.

3. The Secretary-General of the Council of Europe shall notify the Members of the Council of:

   (a) any signature without reservation in respect of ratification or acceptance;

   (b) any signature with reservation in respect of ratification or acceptance;

   (c) the deposit of any instrument of ratification or acceptance;

   (d) the date of entry into force of this Protocol in accordance with paragraph 2 of this Article.

In witness whereof the undersigned, being duly authorized thereto, have signed this Protocol.

Done at Strasbourg, this 20th day of January 1966, in English and in French, both texts being equally authoritative, in a single copy which shall remain deposited in the archives of the Council of Europe. The Secretary-General shall transmit certified copies to each of the signatory Governments.

Appendix B

Public Order and Related Offences

Offence	Authority	Penalty
Assaults		
Common	Offences Against Person Act 1861, s.42	Summary: 2 months or £50 Indictment: 1 year
Occasioning actual bodily harm	Offences Against Person Act 1861, s.47	5 years
On police officer in execution of his duty	Police Act 1964, s.51(1)	Summary: £100 and/ or 6–9 months Indictment: 2 years
Wounding or inflicting grievous bodily harm by shooting and other means	Offences Against Person Act 1861, s.20	5 years
ditto, with intent	Offences Against Person Act 1861, s.18	Life
Behaviour		
Threatening or abusive (words or writing)	Metropolitan Police Act 1839, s.54 (13)	£2
	Public Order Act 1936, s.5 amended re: penalties by Public Order Act 1963, s.1 and	Summary: £100 and/ or 3 months Indictment: £500 and/or 12 months
Threatening or abusive with intent to stir up racial hatred	Race Relations Act 1965, s.6	Summary: £200 and/ or 6 months Indictment: £1,000 and/or 2 years
Public nuisance, i.e. an act or omission endangering the life, health, property, morals or	Common law	Fine and/or imprisonment

Offence	Authority	Penalty
comfort of the public		
Being a suspected person loitering with intent to commit a felony	Vagrancy Act 1824, s.4	Summary: £20 or 3 months
Violent or threatening	Local Government Act 1933, s.249 Town Police Clauses Act 1847, s.29 Metropolitan Police Act 1839, s.58	
Public nuisance	Common law	Fine or imprisonment
Blasphemy	Common law	Fine or imprisonment
Conspiracy	Common law	Fine or imprisonment
Obstructions		
Of police	Police Act 1964, s.51(3)	Summary: £20 or 1 month
Of highway without lawful authority or excuse	Town Police Clauses Act 1847, s.28 Metropolitan Police Act 1839, s.54(4) Highways Act 1959, s.121	£20
Of public footpath or thoroughfare in disobedience to police regulations (London)	Metropolitan Police Act 1839, s.54	£20
Breach of orders regulating crowds and preventing obstruction in time of processions, rejoicings or illuminations or when streets are thronged or liable to be obstructed	Town Police Clauses Act 1847, s.21	£20
Meetings		
Infringement of police regulations concerning route, parking, etc.	Metropolitan Police Act 1839, ss.52 and 54	£2
Infringement of police directions re: route, etc. in	Public Order Act 1936, s.3	

Offence	Authority	Penalty
anticipation of serious public disorder		
Infringement of Ministry of Public Buildings and Works regulations re: parks and gardens	Park Regulations Act 1872 and 1926; and Trafalgar Square Act 1844, and Regulations 1952; and London Government Act 1963, s.58	£5
Unlawful assembly, i.e. an assembly of 3 or more persons (a) for purposes forbidden by law, or (b) with intent to carry out any common purpose lawful or unlawful, in such manner as to endanger the public peace or to give firm and courageous persons in that neighbourhood to apprehend a breach of the peace	Common law	£5 Fine or imprisonment
Rout, i.e. an unlawful assembly on the move	Common law	Fine or imprisonment
Riot, i.e. a tumultuous disturbance of the peace by 3 or more persons who assemble together of their own authority with an intent mutually to assist one another against anyone who shall oppose them in the execution of some enterprise of a private nature and afterwards actually execute the enterprise in a violent and turbulent manner to the terror of the people	Common law	Fine or imprisonment
Affray, i.e. the fighting of 2 or more persons to the terror of Her Majesty's subjects	Common law	Fine and/or imprisonment

Offence	Authority	Penalty
Endeavouring to break up public meeting	Public Meeting Act 1908, s.1 as amended	Summary: 3 months or £100 Indictment: 1 year or £500
Prohibition of uniforms in connection with political objects	Public Order Act 1936, ss.1 and 2	3 months and/or £50

Official Secrets

Spying	Official Secrets Act 1911, s.1	14 years
Wrongful communication of information	Official Secrets Act 1911, s.2	2 years

Property (*damage*)

Setting fire to public buildings, dwelling houses, and other buildings	Malicious Damage Act 1861, ss.2,3,5 and 6	14 years to life
Attempting to blow up dwelling houses	Malicious Damage Act 1861, s.9	Life
Putting explosives near buildings, etc.	Malicious Damage Act 1861, s.10	14 years
Attempting to cause explosions or making or keeping explosives with intent to endanger life or property	Explosive Substances Act 1883, s.3	20 years

Property (*damage*)

Demolishing or damaging houses	Malicious Damage Act 1861, ss.11, 12 and 13	Life, 7 years/fine
Destroying telegraphs	Malicious Damage Act 1861, s.37	Summary: £10 or 3 months Indictment: 2 years
Destroying trees, plants, fences, works of art and other property for which no special punishment is provided	Malicious Damage Act 1861, ss.20, 23, 25, 39, 51 and Ancient Monuments Act 1913, s.14	1 month to 5 years
Cutting or injuring electric lines with intent to cut off the supply of electricity	Electric Lighting Act 1882, s.22	5 years

Offence	Authority	Penalty

Property (entering)

| Forcible entry into premises | Forcible Entry Act 1381 | Imprisonment |
| Excessive picketing, i.e. using violence or intimidating by watching or besetting the residence or business premises of another in order to compel that other to do or abstain from doing something he has a legal right to do | Conspiracy and Protection of Property Act 1875, s.7 | |

Sedition

| i.e. exciting discontent or dissatisfaction between sections of the public | Common law | Fine and/or imprisonment |

Weapons

Going armed to terrify the Queen's subjects	Common law	Fine and/or imprisonment
Possessing offensive weapons, i.e. any article adapted for causing injury or intended by the possessor for offensive use	Prevention of Crime Act 1963, s.1 amended re: penalty by Criminal Justice Act 1967	Summary: £200 /and or 3 months Indictment: 2 years and forfeiture of weapon
Having an offensive weapon while at a public meeting or on a public procession	Public Order Act 1936, s.4	Summary: £50 and/or 3 months
Possessing firearms or ammunition with intent to injure or commit a serious offence or resist arrest	Firearms Act 1968, s.16	14 years
Carrying firearms in a public place	Firearms Act 1968, s.19	Summary: £200 and/or 6 months Indictment: 5 years
Trespassing with a firearm in a building or on land	Firearms Act 1968, s.20	Summary: £100 and/or 6 months Indictment: 5 years
Carrying explosives likely to endanger life or property	Explosive Substances Act 1883, s.2	Life

Offence	Authority	Penalty
Possessing explosives under suspicious circumstances	Explosive Substances Act 1883, s.4	14 years
Carrying offensive weapons	Prevention of Crime Act 1953, s.1	Summary: £200 or 3 months Indictment: 2 years/ fine
Possessing air guns, shot guns, and similar weapons	Airguns and Shotguns Act 1962	£20 or 3 months

Appendix C

List of Organizations Which Give Help and Advice

Advise 283 Gray's Inn Road, London w c 1. Comprehensive advisory service, mainly for black people. Advises on wide range of problems: arrest, housing, immigration, employment, and the particular problems of students and ex-prisoners; 24-hour emergency telephone service (01-278-1487).

Advisory Centre for Education 32 Trumpington Street, Cambridge c b 2 1 q y. Valuable source of advice on all problems concerning education. Mainly middle-class, relying on a postal question-and-answer service. Charges small fees for information and advice.

Apex Trust 2 Manchester Square, London w 1. Helps ex-prisoners find jobs.

Association for the Prevention of Addiction 15 King Street, London w c 2. Gives help to parents of young drug addicts. Twenty branches. Day centre in London.

Association of British Adoption Agencies 27 Queen Anne's Gate, London s w 1. Has information on all registered adoption agencies and the area covered by each one.

A A (*Automobile Association*) Fanum House, Leicester Square, London w c 2. Advises members on motoring law, in addition to other services.

Brook Advisory Centre 233 Tottenham Court Road, London w 1. Provides contraceptive advice and supplies to unmarried women. Centres in eight major cities and in London.

Cambridge House 137 Camberwell Road, London s e 5. Legal and family advice centre for London area.

Charity Commission St Alban's House, 57–60 Haymarket, London sw1. Alphabetical, geographical and functional index of charities. Open to public inspection daily.

Child Poverty Action Group 1 Macklin Street, London wc2. Good source of information (and advice by post) on many social problems, especially those concerning welfare benefits.

Citizens' Advice Bureaux Headquarters at National Citizens' Advice Bureaux Council, 26 Bedford Square, London wc1. There are 500 bureaux throughout the country, financed by grants from local authorities and voluntary contributions. Staffed mainly by trained volunteers, they give advice on a wide range of subjects. Especially useful for information about rights to welfare benefits, legal aid and advice.

Citizens' Rights Office 1 Macklin Street, London wc2. New project to help poorer families establish their rights and deal with their business affairs: housing, supplementary benefits, redundancy, matrimonial problems, etc.

Claimants' Unions Community-based organizations to help people claim welfare benefits. New ones are forming regularly, but at the time of going to press the following claimants' unions were established:

Aberdeen: 19 High Street
Barnsley: 120 Stanhill Crescent, New Lodge
Birmingham: 66 Ivor Road, Sparkhill
Brighton: 199 Thorndene Road
Cardiff: Community Centre, Butetown, London Square
Chadderton: 43 Richmond Avenue
Colchester: 20 Fairfax Road
Edinburgh: 6 Dickson Street
Leeds 2: 153 Woodhouse Lane
London: Dame Colet House, Ben Jonson Road, e1
    10 Silchester Road, w10
    17 Duncombe Road, Archway, n19
    Camden Claimants Union, The Hole in the Wall Community
        Centre, 47 Rochester Road, nw1
    The Albany, Creek Road, Deptford, se8

Manchester: 67 Bold Street, Moss Side
Morecambe: 6 Beecham Street
Newcastle-under-Lyme: 102 Newcastle High Street
Newcastle-upon-Tyne: Flat A, Thornton House, 6 Beach Grove
  Road
Oxford: 65 Iffley Road
Plymouth: 48 Stuart Road
Reading: 9 London Road
South Shields: 1 Lowe Road
York: 11a Victor St, Bishop Hill

Community Relations Commission Russell Square House, London wc1. Promotes the welfare of immigrants and advises on local services for them.

Consumers' Association 14 Buckingham Street, London wc2. Carries out research into consumer products and produces the magazine *Which?* Good source of information but caters for members only. The *Which?* Advice Centre, 242 Kentish Town Road, London nw1, is open to all consumer inquiries.

Defence of Literature and the Arts Society 4 Hollywood Mews, London sw10. An association to protect the freedom of the arts and public communications from censorship. Gives moral and other support to authors and producers of work which is censored or under attack on moral, political or other grounds.

Family Planning Association 27 Mortimer Street, London w1a 4qy. Runs over 1,000 clinics throughout the country, giving contraceptive advice and supplies to everyone over 16. Provides regular medical supervision, cervical smear tests, pregnancy tests; runs seven vasectomy clinics.

Howard League for Penal Reform 125 Kennington Park Road, London se11. Pressure group for reforming the prison system.

Independent Adoption Society Red Cross House, 160 Peckham Rye, London se22. Recently-formed non-sectarian adoption agency to help prospective parents who are agnostic or have run into religious difficulties when trying to adopt.

JCWI (Joint Council for the Welfare of Immigrants) Toynbee Hall, Commercial Street, London ec1. Undertakes case work to help Commonwealth and alien immigrants who are having difficulty gaining entry to Britain.

Law Society 113 Chancery Lane, London wc2. Professional organization of solicitors; administers legal aid schemes for civil cases. Inquiries to 29 Red Lion Street, London wc1.

Mary Ward Centre 9 Tavistock Place, London wc1. Legal and general advice centre for London area.

Mental After-Care Association 110 Jermyn Street, London sw1. Runs hostels, homes and holidays for the mentally sick.

Motor Insurers' Bureau Aldermary House, Queen Street, London ec4. Set up by insurance companies to provide compensation for motor accident victims who are not otherwise covered by insurance.

NACRO (National Association for the Care and Resettlement of Offenders) 125 Kennington Park Road, London se11. Informs prisoners, ex-prisoners and their wives and families of their rights and puts them in touch with people who can give further help.

National Association for Mental Health 38 Queen Anne Street, London w1. Trained social workers advise on emotional or psychiatric difficulties; 40 local associations are affiliated.

NCCL (National Council for Civil Liberties) 152 Camden High Street, London nw1.

National Council for the Unmarried Mother and Her Child 255 Kentish Town Road, London nw5. Works to improve the status and conditions of women and girls with illegitimate children.

National Federation of Consumer Groups 22 Buckingham Street, London wc2. Has information on most local consumer groups.

National Marriage Guidance Council 58 Queen Anne Street, London w1. Voluntary organization which helps with marriage difficulties. Nine hundred marriage guidance counsellors operating throughout the country.

NSPCC (National Society for the Prevention of Cruelty to Children) 1 Riding House Street, London w1. Promotes the welfare of children who are in danger of being harmed or neglected; its primary object is to help the child's family to make a better home for it, and to institute legal proceedings only as a last resort.

NUS (National Union of Students) 3 Endsleigh Street, London wc1. Deals with most problems a student is likely to encounter – entrance to college and university, courses, grants, discipline, landladies, legal aid, travel, insurance, etc.

North Kensington Neighbourhood Law Centre 74 Golborne Road, London w10. Free legal advice centre for Notting Hill area.

Pregnancy Advisory Services London: 40 Margaret Street, w1; Birmingham: 109 Gough Road, Edgbaston, Birmingham 15. Advice on where to get an abortion within the terms of the present law.

Race Relations Board Gaywood House, Great Peter Street, London sw1. The official body responsible for looking into complaints of racial discrimination; works with local conciliation committees in different parts of the country.

Release 40 Princedale Road, London w11. Helps people arrested on drugs charges; 24-hour emergency telephone service (01-603-8654), with 100 solicitors on call; two free legal advice evenings a week.

RAC (*Royal Automobile Club*) 89 Pall Mall, London sw1. Advises members on motoring law and on what to do in the case of an accident.

Simon Population Trust West Longsight, Crediton, Devon. Gives advice on male sterilization.

Shelter 86 Strand, London wc2. Its main function is to raise money and distribute it to housing associations to help buy and improve property. Shelter Housing Aid Centre, The Boltons, London sw10, hopes to provide help and advice to families in the London area with any kind of housing problems.

Surveyors' Aid Scheme Provides the professional help of a surveyor to those who really cannot afford it. Operates a severe means test. London area only. Contact through your local Citizens' Advice Bureau.

UKIAS (*UK Immigrants' Advisory Service*) St George's Churchyard, Bloomsbury Way, London wc1. Set up and grant-aided by the Government, but claims to be independent. Helps prospective immigrants appeal against refusal of entry to Britain. Full-time staff in London, Birmingham, Leeds, Manchester, Heathrow, Gatwick, and the Channel ports.

Appendix D

Recent Changes in the Law

Public Order

The Criminal Damage Act 1971 came into force on 14 October 1971. The Act revises the law relating to offences of damage to property and repeals almost all of the Malicious Damage Act 1861 (See Appendix B).

The Act makes it an offence to destroy or damage property without lawful excuse; introduces a new concept of 'threats' to destroy or damage property, which is a separate offence; and also makes it an offence to possess 'anything' with intent to destroy or damage property. Penalties are heavier than under the Malicious Damage Act – up to 10 years and, in the case of arson, life imprisonment is mandatory.

The most sweeping powers concern search (◊ p. 47). A police officer can obtain a warrant for the search and the seizure of *anything* which he has *reasonable cause* to believe has been used or is *intended for use* for committing offences of criminal damage.

Censorship

Although homosexual practices between consenting males in private are no longer criminal (◊ p. 165), publication of advertisements for the purpose of encouraging such activities has been held to be an offence. This decision was upheld by the Court of Appeal although, at the time of writing, leave has been given to appeal to the House of Lords (*International Times* case).

Northern Ireland

Internment without charge or trial was re-introduced in Northern Ireland under the Special Powers Act 1922 and 1933 ($\diamond$ p. 275) on 9 August 1971.

Index of Statutes

341

Index of Statutes

Index of Subjects

Index of Subjects

Index of Subjects

Index of Subjects

The NCCL Protects Civil Liberties in Great Britain

The NCCL is an independent voluntary organization protecting individual civil liberties and the rights of political, religious, racial, and other minorities in Britain. Founded in 1934, the NCCL is financed by membership and affiliation fees, and by donations. It is a pressure group and a case-work organization. It campaigns on issues such as the right to privacy, the treatment of gypsies, immigration and race relations, censorship, police powers, freedom of expression and association. The NCCL provides legal advice, makes representations to central and local authorities, presses for legal reform through the Parliamentary Civil Liberties Group, and undertakes research through its associated charity, the Cobden Trust. The NCCL has Groups in many cities.

The NCCL stands for liberty at a time when unorthodox opinions are suspect, political and social dissent is discouraged, minorities are vulnerable, and liberal values are challenged.

The NCCL stands for justice at a time when the protection of the law is not equally available to all, the application of the law can be arbitrary, and the administration of the law is slow and cumbersome.

The NCCL stands for human rights at a time when most people don't know their rights or how to claim them, and when our rights are being eroded by legislation that often appeals to popular prejudice rather than the demands of justice.

If You Value Liberty
Join the NCCL

To: National Council for Civil Liberties,
    152 Camden High St, London, NW1.

☐ I enclose £   .   p as a gift.

☐ I wish to become a Member and enclose £   in
   payment of my annual subscription (GIRO No.:
   584:0104).

   Subscription Rates:
      Individuals: £2 (£1.75 by Banker's Order)
      Couples: £3 (£2.75 by Banker's Order)
      Students: 75p
      Old Age Pensioners: £1
      Supporting Members: £25

☐ I wish my organization/society to be affiliated. Please
   send me the Rate List. (Rates, generally based on
   membership, range from £2 to £25.)

☐ I wish to make a covenanted gift to the Cobden Trust.
   Please send me a Covenant Form (Reg. No. 228465).

NAME (Mr/Mrs/Miss) ....

ADDRESS ....
                                                    [P]
....
(PLEASE USE CAPITAL LETTERS)

Banker's Order Form

To the .... Bank at

....

....

On the................................next, and on the

.... in subsequent years
until further notice, pay to the account of
THE NATIONAL COUNCIL FOR CIVIL LIBERTIES
(Account Number 50141993), CWS BANKERS,
110 LEMAN STREET, LONDON, E1.

the sum of ....(£ . p)

SIGNATURE ....

ADDRESS ....
                                                    [P]
....
When complete, please return to NCCL, 152 Camden
High St, London, NW1, who will send it to your bank.

More about Penguins and Pelicans

Penguinews, which appears every month, contains details of all the new books issued by Penguins as they are published. From time to time it is supplemented by *Penguins in Print*, which is a complete list of all available books published by Penguins. (There are well over three thousand of these.)

A specimen copy of *Penguinews* will be sent to you free on request, and you can become a subscriber for the price of the postage. For a year's issues (including the complete lists) please send 30p if you live in the United Kingdom, or 60p if you live elsewhere. Just write to Dept EP, Penguin Books Ltd, Harmondsworth, Middlesex, enclosing a cheque or postal order, and your name will be added to the mailing list.

Note: *Penguinews* and *Penguins in Print* are not available in the U.S.A. or Canada

Protest and Discontent

Edited by Bernard Crick and William A. Robson

'Come Mothers and Fathers
Throughout the land
And don't criticize
What you don't understand;
Your sons and your daughters
Are beyond your command . . .' – Bob Dylan

This collection of essays is concerned with the causes
of discontent, the manifestation of discontent and the
methods of protest, dealing mostly with present issues
and the protest of the young.

These themes are considered from various points of
view and Arthur Koestler, Professor David Rapoport
and Douglas Houghton, M.P., are amongst the
contributors. The youth rebellion of America, India,
Japan and France is described, and the discussion on
Britain includes reference to the trade-union movement
and Parliament itself.

The collection has been assembled by the editors of
the *Political Quarterly* and makes a work of immediate
and impressive relevance on a subject that is clearly of
vital importance to the whole structure of society and
to our way of life today.

Freedom, the Individual and the Law

Harry Street

Third Edition

Since this book first appeared over eight years ago,
hardly a day has passed when some case of civil liberty
has not been in the headlines. Many of the criticisms
made by Professor Street in the first and second
editions have resulted in better legislation by Parliament,
but much remains unaltered. In this edition he notes
and comments on many recent incidents, cases and
changes in the law affecting public figures, private
individuals and newspapers. Again and again we
encounter the recurring conflicts between freedom of
speech and the security of the state; freedom of movement
and public order; the right to privacy and the demands
of a vigilant press.

Freedom, the Individual and the Law was the first
comprehensive survey of the way in which English law
deals with the many sides of Civil Liberty. After an
introductory description of the powers of the police,
Professor Street addresses himself in detail to the main
areas of freedom of expression, freedom of association,
and freedom of movement. Protection against private
power, the right to work and other subjects of
contemporary importance make up the citizen's first
guide to the theory and practice of Civil Liberty.